D1131535

Studies in Rhetorics and Feminisms

Series Editors, Cheryl Glenn and Shirley Wilson Logan

CONVERSATIONAL RHETORIC

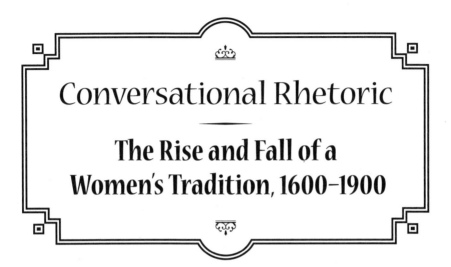

Conversational Rhetoric

The Rise and Fall of a Women's Tradition, 1600–1900

Jane Donawerth

Southern Illinois University Press
Carbondale and Edwardsville

15 14 13 12   4 3 2 1

Library of Congress Cataloging-in-Publication Data
Donawerth, Jane, 1947–
Conversational rhetoric : the rise and fall of a women's
tradition, 1600–1900 / Jane Donawerth.
    p. cm. — (Studies in rhetorics and feminisms)
Includes bibliographical references and index.
    ISBN-13: 978-0-8093-3027-0 (cloth : alk. paper)
    ISBN-10: 0-8093-3027-X (cloth : alk. paper)
    ISBN-13: 978-0-8093-8630-7 (ebook)
    ISBN-10: 0-8093-8630-5 (ebook)
1. Rhetoric—United States—History. 2. Rhetoric—
England—History. 3. English language—Discourse analysis.
4. Women—Education—United States—Language arts.
5. Women—Education—England—Language arts. 6. Oral
communication—United States. 7. Oral communication—
England. I. Title.
P301.D66 2011
808'.042082—dc22   2011006185

Printed on recycled paper. ♻

The paper used in this publication meets the minimum
requirements of American National Standard for Information
Sciences—Permanence of Paper for Printed Library Materials,
ANSI Z39.48-1992. ∞

To my family,
Woody, Kate, and Donnie

Contents

Preface

This book examines rhetorical theory by women in England and the United States (and one widely translated Frenchwoman) from the seventeenth through the nineteenth centuries. It traces the rise and fall of a tradition of women's rhetorical theory that centers on conversation (as opposed to public speaking) as a model for all discourse.

This study is a revisionist and critical, or "constructionist," history of rhetorical theory, like James Berlin's of the nineteenth-century United States, that asks questions and pursues lines of inquiries. This study does not attempt an exhaustive history like those by Gerald Murphy or W. S. Howell or George Kennedy: I doubt that we have yet recovered all the texts by women necessary to attempt such a history.[1] However, this history is less linear even than Berlin's history, for women often remained ignorant of women theorists before them, often reinvented a tradition of women's rhetoric, often developed theories out of similar experiences rather than under the influence of male or female forerunners.

In *The Worlds Olio*, Margaret Cavendish suggests that wit is like "Minerva's loom," for it can "spin out the fine and curious thread of fancy" (sigs. R4^r and E4^r; also in Donawerth, *Anthology*, 54). This book spins out several threads of discourse. If women did not write rhetoric handbooks and composition textbooks, what genres were important to women theorists of rhetoric and communication? If women were denied training and practice in public speaking, how did their theories of communication reflect a different experience with speaking and writing? If men's rhetorics reproduced a politics of privilege, how did women's rhetorics challenge or reproduce such a politics? In this study I look at moments when women cluster around a kind of rhetorical theory—conversation, conduct book advice, defenses of women's preaching, elocution, composition. In order more precisely to place their efforts in social, rhetorical, and gendered historical contexts, I limit myself to women's rhetorical theory from 1600 to 1900, in England and the United States.[2] While the women I treat are quite diverse, one thread runs through most of these texts: for women, because of their relative restriction to domestic roles, conversation rather than oratory becomes the model for all public discourse. Bathsua Makin, for example, in *An Essay to Revive the Ancient Education of Gentlewomen* (1673), her seventeenth-century discussion of women and the history of learning—including rhetoric—praises "wives of excellent parts . . . [who have been] instructed . . . in all kinds of learning, the more to fit them for . . . converse" (in Donawerth, *Rhetorical Theory by Women before 1900* 77). Under the umbrella of "converse," Makin cites women's published writings as well as their oratory and domestic responsibilities, thus employing conversation as a model for all discourse of the educated woman.

This book is aimed at a broad audience of scholars, graduate students, and advanced undergraduates in the disciplines of rhetoric and composition, communication and speech, and women's studies. It began as a teaching experiment. In the early 1980s, when I first designed and taught a graduate course in the history of rhetorical theory before 1900, there were no women theorists in anthologies, and there were no studies of women's rhetorical theory before 1900, although there were a few studies of individual women's rhetoric. In order to help students grasp the intensity of restrictions against women's rhetorical education, I asked my students to do a research assignment—to find the first woman rhetorical theorist before 1900. I expected them not to find anyone, and I planned for the class to have a discussion about the socially imposed limitations on women's rhetoric.

But my students surprised me. If we redefine rhetoric as the art of communicating, then we can make an argument that Sappho, or Margaret Fell, or Aspasia, or Mary Astell, or Pan Chao is writing rhetorical theory. With this encouragement, I began further research and, after more than a dozen years of teaching out of xeroxed packets, published *Rhetorical Theory by Women before 1900: An Anthology*. Research for that anthology did not follow the straightforward path that I had been taught in graduate school. Some women (like Arete) I had to research under a husband's or father's name. Other women, like Sei Shonagon, I found because I asked every humanities colleague I met if they knew of any woman in their field writing advice on communication—conversation, letter writing, composition, or public reading or speaking. Once I had found a woman theorist, I was not always able to gain access to her works. I researched Hallie Quinn Brown by spending one day at Central State University every time I visited my family in Ohio, while my parents took care of my children. For some women, so little is known that I constructed a history for them at the same time as I recovered their work or evidence of their work. And I tried out the usefulness of these women's theories in a senior honors seminar where I asked students to use these theories as a basis for analyzing women's rhetoric. They enthusiastically took up the challenge, trying out nineteenth-century theories of letter writing on Lydia Sigourney's letters, employing Scudéry's theory of conversation to analyze dialogue in novels, and applying Hannah More's restrictions on conversational etiquette to email. My grateful thanks go to my undergraduate and graduate students at the University of Maryland who are, after over thirty years of teaching, too numerous to name; they have been central to the development of this book.

Two professional communities have nurtured this scholarship: feminists, and composition teachers and historians of rhetoric and composition. At the University of Maryland, I was lucky to participate in the Women's Studies Faculty Seminar for many years during the 1980s, alternately led by Evi Beck, Claire Moses, and Deb Rosenfelt. It was mind-changing. I thank Virginia Beauchamp for mentoring me and bringing me to that seminar. At NWSA (National Women's Studies Association) conferences, Rhetoric and Composition conferences, Utopian Studies conferences, and Attending to Early Modern Women symposia, feminist scholars have offered authorization and advice. When other members of the profession have scoffed at the idea of women rhetorical theorists, feminists have simply provided certitude. In a larger sense, my feminist colleagues, especially in Renaissance studies, classics, and Utopian studies, have offered models of recovery: if we found women in these other fields, then my faith in the quest to find women who wrote rhetorical theory was warranted.

I also have been supported by the communities of scholars at CCCC (the Conference on College Composition and Communication), RSA (the Rhetoric Society of America), Penn State Conferences on Rhetoric and Composition, and the Feminism(s) and Rhetoric(s) Conferences, who value the connection of historical scholarship to teaching and assume that an art of rhetoric or advice on composition has a political valence. Within this community, too, I am grateful for those scholars who provided the energy of critical and supportive discussion and faith in this project, especially Patricia Bizzell, Wendy Dasler Johnson, Lucy Schultz, Molly Wertheimer, Andrea Lunsford, Jackie Royster, John Schilb, Catherine Hobbs, Martha Watson, and Jack Selzer, among a host of others. Nan Johnson, my rhetoric guru, generously read a draft and helped me bring focus to my vision. I am grateful to Cheryl Glenn, who gave painstaking and detailed advice. In addition, I have been fortunate to have the best possible colleagues in rhetoric and composition at the University of Maryland. I thank Bob Coogan, Jeanne Fahnestock, Shirley Logan, and Leigh Ryan for the many times I have tried out ideas on them. I am especially grateful to Bob for all the very early versions of these ideas that he read through, and to Shirley for her helpful questions at a crucial moment. I have also been lucky to have the best possible students—for this project, I have especially learned from Jody Lawton, Wendy Hayden, and Lisa Zimmerelli.

My involvement in feminist studies and in rhetoric and composition has encouraged experimental methodologies. Scholarship in this sense is trying out avenues of exploration, adapting methods and theories to the issues at hand, sharing rather than hoarding information and solutions to problems, and being open-minded about what "counts" as scholarship, as a field of inquiry. Especially as a feminist, supported by the community of feminist scholars—all of whom have had this experience—I knew I could transgress the borders of the discipline. I did not have to be held in by the boundaries of the established field, no matter how ardently they were defended.

As a scholar, I have gathered up the needs, energy, and knowledge of a wide community. As a writer of this book, I have been a collaborator and facilitator as often as an author. This discourse grows not out of isolated inspiration but extended conversation.

I would like also to thank the many institutions that made this book possible. I am grateful for a fellowship from the National Endowment of the Humanities; for a sabbatical and a General Research Board Semester Award, as well as a grant for the cover permission, from the University of Maryland; and to the librarians and staff of the Library of Congress, the Folger Shakespeare Library, the Hallie Quinn Brown Memorial Library of Central State University in Ohio, and the University of Maryland system libraries. I especially thank Pat Herron and Susanna Van Sant, UM librarians par excellence, who were always there for me. While the book has merged and revised material in ways that have made it new, I wish to thank the following journals and presses where I published trial versions of some parts of some chapters: I thank the University of South Carolina Press for permission to use material from "Madeleine de Scudéry's Rhetoric of Conversation," *Listening to Their Voices: Essays on the Rhetorical Activities of Historical Women*, edited by Molly Wertheimer (1997), 305–19; the University of Alabama Press for permission to use material from "Authorial Ethos, Collaborative Voice, and Rhetorical Theory by Women," *Rhetorical Women: Roles and Representations*, edited by Hildy Miller and Lillian Bridwell-Bowles (2005), 107–24; and Lawrence Erlbaum Associates, for permission to use material from "Hannah More, Lydia Sigourney, and the Creation of a Women's Tradition of Rhetoric," *Rhetoric, the Polis, and the Global Village: Selected Papers from the 1998 Thirtieth Anniversary Rhetoric Society of America Conference*, edited by C. Jan Swearingen (© 1999 by Lawrence Erlbaum Associates, Inc.), 155–62. I also thank the following journals for permission to include portions of previous essays: "Conversation and the Boundaries of Public Discourse in

Rhetorical Theory by Renaissance Women," *Rhetorica* 16.2 (Spring 1998): 181–99, published by the University of California Press (© The International Society for the History of Rhetoric); "Poaching on Men's Philosophies of Rhetoric: Eighteenth- and Nineteenth-Century Rhetorical Theory by Women," *Philosophy and Rhetoric* 33.3 (2000): 243–58, published by Pennsylvania State University Press; and "Nineteenth-Century United States Conduct Book Rhetoric by Women," *Rhetoric Review* 21.1 (2002): 5–21, published by Taylor & Francis.

Publishing with Southern Illinois University Press has been a great pleasure. I thank Kristine Priddy, the acquisitions editor who also helped considerably in the early editing stages; Wayne Larsen, the project editor, who shepherded the manuscript through copyediting; John Wilson, whose meticulous copyediting saved me much embarrassment; Barb Martin, the editing, design, and production manager, who oversaw the schedule; and the staff who designed the magnificent cover.

In the personal domain, I would like to thank my family—Woody, Kate, and Donnie Scally—my sister Lois Bovard, and my friends, especially Robert Taylor, Adele Seeff, Ana Kothe, Stephane Pillet, Katie Field, Sonja Hansard Weiner, Andy Weiner, and Karen Nelson, for their untiring support.

To the anthology on *Rhetorical Theory by Women before 1900* that I published in 2002, this book adds some new voices (especially in defenses of women's preaching), a critical analysis of the tradition of a women's rhetoric that rose and fell over three centuries, and a more detailed examination of the historical context in which this development of women's rhetoric took place. While there has been a great deal of work done on women's rhetoric, there is relatively little on women's rhetorical or composition theory yet published. While this book joins the conversation on women's role in the history of rhetoric, I hope that soon there will be many others speaking to the issues of women's theory.

CONVERSATIONAL RHETORIC

Introduction: Adding Women's Rhetorical Theory to the Conversation

When Mary Astell, in *A Serious Proposal to the Ladies,* part II, published in 1697, outlines what ladies should study under the rubric of *rhetoric,* she terms the audience of her would-be writers "our neighbors" and the communication these writers would convey a "conversation" (120–22). When Jennie Willing, in the 1887 edition of *The Potential Woman: A Book for Young Ladies* (originally published in 1881) discusses "Talking," she emphasizes public speaking and defends women's preaching, but she begins with conversation: "the sweet and serious words of a sister, the tender counsel of a mother, the whispered confidences of a wife" (113). In his essay on Hugh Blair's use of Quintilian, Michael Halloran suggests that every rhetoric both "situates itself in relation to . . . the rhetorical tradition" and "transforms what tradition offers into symbolic instruments for dealing with the present" (194). Both Mary Astell and Jennie Willing, two centuries apart, are doing just that: they are theorizing rhetoric, the art of communication, for women and are transforming rhetoric by drawing on women's gendered experience in conversation as a model for all discourse.

This book examines the rise and fall of a women's tradition of rhetoric. Between 1600 and 1900, English and American women (and one much-translated Frenchwoman) composed rhetorical theories based on conversation as a model of discourse. Madeleine de Scudéry, Bathsua Makin, Mary Astell, Margaret Fell, Hannah More, Lydia Sigourney, Ellen Stewart, Hallie Quinn Brown, Genevieve Stebbins, Frances Willard, Anna Morgan, Virginia Waddy, Mary Augusta Jordan, and many others theorized rhetoric—conversation, letter writing, testimony and preaching, elocution, and eventually public speaking—for women.

Unlike traditional histories of rhetoric, this one does not tell a story of linear progress and achievement, of contention and influence. The Anglo-American women's tradition of rhetorical theory is a story of moments, not movements, of starts and stops and starting over, not progressive development. Women theorized not in the handbooks of traditional rhetorical education but in whatever places of publication were open to them, and their story concerns the moments when they discover the gendered nature of communication or construct a theory out of the circumstances of women's domestic lives—especially conversation. Until the nineteenth century, then, there is little influence but many discrete moments of discovery, and women are not necessarily influenced by other women before them.

This study enters an ongoing scholarly conversation. Much of the time, historians of rhetoric have defined women's theory in the negative—why there wasn't any. In addition, the scholarly conversation has so far emphasized women's rhetorical practices, not their rhetorical theories. During the 1980s and 1990s, many women orators were recovered, and many studies of women's rhetorical activities were published. Feminist scholars have fully reversed the earlier sense that rhetoric was men's business only and at the same time have thoroughly examined the reasons that so many women were silent and so few women (relatively) attempted public persuasion. We now have a good sense of why women did not write rhetoric textbooks until very late in this period. But there are other forms of rhetoric besides public speaking, and there are places other than rhetoric textbooks where communication may be theorized.

Consequently, it is time to ask new questions and change the course of the conversation. How did women theorize communication, and if they did not do it in rhetoric and composition textbooks, where did they do it? This study shows us how women availed themselves of the genres that women were reading to theorize the communication that women were achieving. Women seized the available means[1] and published theories of communication in a variety of places: in humanist treatises defending women's education, in conduct books for women, in defenses of women's preaching, and in elocution handbooks. In these places, over the course of three centuries, they developed theories of women's rhetoric based on conversation, not on public speaking. But when at last, in the middle of the nineteenth century, they began to write rhetoric and composition textbooks for both male and female students, these theories of conversation-based discourse gradually disappeared, or rather, were absorbed into composition pedagogy.

This study will trace this rise and fall, examining conversation as a model of discourse in women's humanist dialogues and defenses of women's education, the recognition of the gendered nature of communication in women's conduct books, the linking of conversation to women's public speaking and women's rights in defenses of women's preaching, and the incorporation of the female body into communication in women's elocution handbooks. These specialized theories of women's communication rose in a period when there was a particularly rigid distinction between men's and women's cultural roles in England and America, but it was facilitated by a democratization of education, the rise of a modern transatlantic network of print and transportation technologies, and the ingenuity of women who turned restrictions into possibilities. These women's theories of discourse as modeled on conversation faded when women in England and America began to achieve equality in basic education and the right to speak publicly. We can see the vestiges of their theories, however, in the historic and present-day connection of conversation to pedagogy in composition studies.

The Scholarly Conversation: The Cultural Limits on Women's Speech

For the last thirty years, scholars have explored and documented the reasons why women did *not* participate in rhetoric to the same extent as men. As Suzanne W. Hull, in *Chaste, Silent and Obedient* (1982), demonstrated through her carefully selected bibliography of primary materials, men of the European Renaissance insisted that the ideal woman should not speak publicly or try to persuade men concerning their decisions.[2] Joan Gibson, in "Educating for Silence: Renaissance Women and the Language Arts" (1989), further recounted many instances in the early Renaissance when, despite lifting of some restrictions against women's education, the restriction against women's studying rhetoric was reinforced.

As Nan Johnson has shown, in *Gender and Rhetorical Space in American Life, 1866–1910* (2002), these constraints on communication and persuasion of the ideal woman were remarkably long-lasting and still firmly enforced in nineteenth-century America. In her study, Johnson asks why women's rhetorical accomplishments were missing from our histories of rhetoric before 1980, and what cultural interests contributed to their erasure (10–13). She answers by exploring parlor rhetoric, which established women's and men's rhetorical practices as separate and unequal in nineteenth-century postbellum America and typified the typecasting of women's rhetoric during this period (15). Women were thus invited to become educated, but only with those rhetorical skills that allowed them to better perform the roles of wives and mothers, and were discouraged by this same education from intruding on men's "public rhetorical space" (6, 15). The nineteenth-century conduct books and rhetoric textbooks by men, as well as letter-writing handbooks, home encyclopedias, collective biographies, and histories of American oratory, all promoted "a code of rhetorical behavior for women that required the performance of conventional femininity" (2), and women were rhetorically confined to sentimental appeals, domestic space, and social, rather than business, relationships.[3]

Johnson thus reads the rhetoric of the women who forged two of the most important political movements of the nineteenth century (the women's rights movement and the temperance campaign) through the misogyny of cultural limitations on women's speech and the discounting of women's roles that nineteenth-century male historians of oratory and textbook writers put into place. But what if we ask different questions of this same material? What if we had a corpus of theory *by women* that resituated women's roles and feminine rhetoric in conversation? What if we read Frances Willard's speeches through Mary Astell's views on persuasion as conversation, or Susan B. Anthony's and Elizabeth Cady Stanton's publications through Jennie Willing's disparagement of men's views of women's speech?

Thus, as Wendy Sharer has pointed out in her study *Vote and Voice: Women's Organizations and Political Literacy, 1915–1930*, women have been excluded from histories of rhetoric because historians of rhetoric have privileged the individual, not collective, political and rhetorical actions; immediate, not persistent, influence for change; and an understanding of politics based mainly on office-holders (5–8). Hull, Gibson, and Johnson are, of course, right in this respect: many women were restrained from studying rhetoric and from participating in public speaking, publishing, and using their full powers of persuasion. But while this explanation holds for why women did not speak, write, or theorize, scholars have now recovered so many women rhetors that a different approach is needed. Feminist historians have analyzed the misogyny that kept many women in their place but have not fully accounted for the women who stepped out of place. Thus, at this juncture, this line of inquiry, ironically, is more useful for thinking about the gendered nature of men's theory and rhetorical activities than women's.[4] In conduct books, newspapers, and encyclopedias, men told women that they should not speak publicly or try to persuade men out of their superior ideas. What does this say about those masculine theories of women's place in communication?

However, despite many men's and some women's strictures throughout the three centuries we are studying, women did speak out, and they furthermore developed theories specifically addressed to women's communication, building a model of communication based on conversation.

The Scholarly Conversation: Women's Rhetorical Practices

For more than two decades, we have been studying women's rhetorical practices. In a 1992 essay, "Opportunities for Feminist Research in the History of Rhetoric," Patricia Bizzell called for more feminist research, recommending that scholars become "resisting readers" of the classical rhetorical tradition, search for women writers of textbooks, and redefine what counts as rhetoric, to make visible women's accomplishments. Since that time, a substantial body of scholarship on women's composition and rhetoric has accumulated.

Some scholars have offered revisionist rereadings of the classical tradition. For example, in *Rereading the Sophists* (1991), Susan Jarratt argues that both sophists and women are excluded "others" in history, legitimating the classical tradition by their displacement: both groups are associated with opinion instead of truth, the material body instead of rational soul, practical knowledge instead of science, and the temporal instead of the transcendent (65). In addition, in several essays, Cheryl Glenn has recuperated Aspasia and sophistry as a viable strand of the classical rhetorical tradition, erased by later historians. In "sex, lies, and manuscript" (1994), Glenn surveys the contradictory, fragmented sources on Aspasia as a rhetorician in fifth-century Athens, noting the license that Aspasia's status as noncitizen gave her, her partnership with Pericles (perhaps helping to write his speeches), and her influence on Socrates, Plato, and Isocrates. In two follow-up essays, "Rereading Aspasia" (1995), and "Locating Aspasia on the Rhetorical Map" (1997), Glenn elaborates a revisionist method for reading the fragments of history. In these essays, Glenn offers an Aspasia who briefly escaped the limits of her gender to influence the polis through her rhetoric, but who was also reinscribed as an erotic footnote to Pericles's government. Both Jarratt and Glenn provide resistant readings of ancient sophistic rhetoric.

Besides resisting readers of the classical tradition, Bizzell called for redefinitions of what counts as rhetoric in order to recover women's accomplishments. This has been the most fruitful aspect of feminist history of rhetoric to date. Several early studies are especially important. In 1989, Karlyn Kohrs Campbell's two-volume anthology and critical study, *Man Cannot Speak for Her*, introduced nineteenth-century women's rights oratory by women to the rhetorical canon. In her study, Campbell sets out the proscriptions against women's speech that women had to overcome, sketches the parameters of a feminine style based on women's domestic experience (personal, anecdotal, inductive, relying on identification with the audience, treating the audience as peers), and describes the bonds between women's rights and abolition and temperance oratory. In an anthology, *With Pen and Voice: A Critical Anthology of Nineteenth-Century African American Women* (1995), and an analytic study, *"We Are Coming": The Persuasive Discourse of Nineteenth-Century Black Women* (1999), Shirley Wilson Logan explores the contributions of black women to abolitionist and civil rights rhetoric in the nineteenth-century United States.[5] In *Rhetoric Retold: Regendering the Tradition from Antiquity through the Renaissance* (1997), Cheryl Glenn introduces as rhetoricians many women whose rhetoric now seems almost canonical: Aspasia, Sappho, Julian of Norwich, Margery Kempe, Anne Askew, Margaret More Roper, and Elizabeth I.

Several other volumes of essays expanded explorations of women's rhetoric to a global range: Andrea Lunsford's collection, *Reclaiming Rhetorica: Women in the Rhetorical Tradition* (1995); Carole Levin and Patricia Sullivan's *Political Rhetoric, Power, and Renaissance Women* (1995); Christine Sutherland and Rebecca Sutcliffe's *The Changing Tradition: Women in the History of Rhetoric* (1999); and Hildy Miller and Lillian Bridwell-Bowles's *Rhetorical Women: Roles and Representations* (2005). Molly Wertheimer's collection of essays, *Listening to Their Voices* (1997), took a significant new direction in its diversity of coverage of women's rhetorical practice and rhetorical theory, from the early Greek sophist Aspasia to the modern theorist Olbrechts-Tyteca, from early Egyptian to medieval and Renaissance European to nineteenth-century black women's rhetoric. Wertheimer's introduction to the volume, "Roses in the Snow," reviews the misogyny of the history of rhetoric, develops a definition of rhetoric that allow a reconception of what should be included in a history of rhetoric, and explains that some women rhetors adapted themselves to men's traditions, while others developed new forms based on their historical contexts and constraints.

Other studies that offer redefinitions of rhetoric in order to consider women's contributions include many on nineteenth-century American women's writings and oratory. Besides studies of nineteenth-century black women's rhetoric and composition by Carla Peterson (1995), of women's clubs' influence on composition by Anne Ruggles Gere (1997), and of the "feminine" style of delivery by Lindal Buchanan (2005), an anthology edited by Joy Ritchie and Kate Ronald, *Available Means* (2001), further offers an overview and samples of rhetoric that demonstrate a history of women's use of the available means of persuasion (means never as available to women as to men of their times). New studies that aid our understanding of women's rhetoric and women's reading and writing practices are appearing at a rapid pace. In *Traces of a Stream: Literacy and Social Change among African American Women* (2000), Jacqueline Royster has traced the development of a specialized rhetoric in black women's nineteenth- and twentieth-century essays, a rhetoric drawing on multiple, overlapping literacies and emphasizing a participatory audience, pathetic and ethical arguments, incorporation of narrative techniques, and the rhetorical sites of the black press and women's church and club groups. Jacqueline Bacon has compared white and black women's rhetorical strategies in abolitionist rhetoric with that of African American men in *The Humblest May Stand Forth* (2002). In *Their Right to Speak: Women's Activism in the Indian and Slave Debates* (2005), Alisse Portnoy has traced the ways in which the early nineteenth-century debates about Indian removal constituted political agency for women and called forth their rhetorical participation through the petitions of benevolent societies. Vicki Tolar Burton's *Spiritual Literacy in John Wesley's Methodism* (2008) includes a chapter on the rhetoric of Methodist women in testifying, prayer, and spiritual letters. And Shirley Logan's *Sites of Rhetorical Education in Nineteenth-Century Black America* (2008) provides evidence of the many places that offered black women, as well as men, rhetorical education and practice (especially literary clubs, journals, and newspaper advice columns).

This study adds to this scholarship on women's rhetorical practices and artifacts (speeches and writings) a consideration of women's rhetorical theory (writing about the nature and means of communication) and analysis of women's use of conversation as a model for all discourse. While this study would not have been possible without the feminist analysis of women's literacies and rhetorics that has preceded it, we are now at a turning point in the scholarly conversation where we need to consider women's rhetorical theories as a context for their rhetorics.

The Scholarly Conversation: Women Theorizing Communication

What we need now is an examination of the theories of communication that women have offered in order better to understand the rhetorical practices that they produced. Already there are fragments of this examination of the history of women's development of conversation as a model for discourse.

In 1995, in an anthology on women's rhetorics edited by Andrea Lunsford, Christine Mason Sutherland became one of the first scholars to term a woman's writing about rhetoric "rhetorical theory" and the first to announce the importance of conversation to that theory ("Mary Astell" 107). Furthermore, in Mary Astell's *A Serious Proposal*, part II, Sutherland found not only a defense of women's abilities to deploy rhetoric ("Mary Astell" 107, 109) and a plan for women's education, not only a theory of rhetoric influenced by Augustine and the Port Royal French philosophers (112–14), but also a theory modified by Astell's consideration of her audience of women (114–15). In addition, Sutherland suggested that conversation is the touchstone for Astell's modifications of the rhetorical tradition for women: "a sure guide in matters of correctness, . . . essential in the formation of a good writing style," coming "naturally to women," conversation "is extremely important in Astell's theory of rhetoric" because it is the central site of women's experience of eloquence (111).

In *Well-Tempered Women: Nineteenth-Century Temperance Rhetoric* (1998), Carol Mattingly's study of the "tremendous coming to voice" (6) of American women in the political reform movement against alcohol, the author offers glimpses of women teaching women rhetoric and their use of conversation as a model for women's persuasion.[6] Mattingly analyzes the rhetoric of these women but also explores the ways in which the WCTU, in the words of Frances Willard, "educate[d] women out of the silence which has stifled their beautiful gifts so long" (61). The WCTU published pamphlets such as *How to Conduct a Public Meeting*, organized "schools" or workshops on speaking in conjunction with their conventions, set up departments at chautauquas, and eventually established a national department of "Training Schools." Yet, just as their rhetoric began with women's roles of wives and mothers, so their rhetorical theory and training emphasized gendered rhetoric, "conversational or narrative delivery," for example (67). The WCTU, Mattingly observes, "provided extensive rhetorical training for women . . . with a sensitivity to the rhetorical circumstances peculiar to women, as well as an understanding of women's fears [of public display]" (71).

In *Imagining Rhetoric: Composing Women of the Early United States* (2002), Janet Carey Eldred and Peter Mortensen explore the interpenetration of domestic fiction aimed at a female audience and civic rhetoric and offer hints of the development of a women's tradition of rhetorical theory based on conversation. From the beginnings of the United States, republican mothers were encouraged to educate themselves so that they might educate their children. While Eldred and Mortensen do not term the fiction and handbooks they analyze "rhetorical theory," they nonetheless explore the views on composition of early U.S. women writers, including Hannah Foster, Judith Murray, Mrs. A. J. Graves, Louisa Tuthill, Almira Phelps, and Charlotte Forten.[7] Eldred and Mortensen deconstruct the schooling fictions of these women in order to piece together their theories of composition. They hint at a link between women's theories and conversation, pointing out that for early U.S. women, "Letters . . . are not just an exercise or duty, but a crucial, conversational link to others" (58).

In *Regendering Delivery: The Fifth Canon and Antebellum Women Rhetors* (2005), Lindal Buchanan traces the development of a "feminine," conversational style of delivery in the nineteenth century as women moved first into political discussions in the public sphere and then into public speaking. Their manner of delivery, she argues, was meant to reassure audiences who disapproved of women's speaking in public that their performances were merely an extension of women's domestic sphere (77), that they were employing "conversation rather than oratory" (79). According to Buchanan, "correspondence, conversation, and reading . . . became cornerstones of the feminine delivery style" (83) and so enabled women to "subvert dominant gender norms and interject their views into the public milieu" (105).

In addition, in *A Feminist Legacy: The Rhetoric and Pedagogy of Gertrude Buck* (2007), Suzanne Bordelon examines Gertrude Buck's rhetorical and composition theory and her literary and dramatic writings in the context of her feminist pedagogical practices. While many scholars have acknowledged Gertrude Buck's contributions to composition theory (e.g., Allen, "Gertrude Buck," and "Gertrude Buck's Rhetoric"; Rebecca Burke, "Gertrude Buck's Rhetorical

Theory"; and Donawerth, "Textbooks for New Audiences"), only Bordelon has linked that theory and its nature to Buck's career first in public school teaching and then in college teaching. From the tradition of progressive theories of learning in the public schools (where, by the end of the nineteenth century, 90 percent of the teachers were female), Bordelon argues, Buck develops her rhetoric of equality, cooperation, and community building and her view of writing as promoting social transformation. However, Buck's theory, at the turn of the twentieth century, published in textbooks aimed at a mixed male and female audience, demonstrates the influence of the women's tradition of conversation as a model of discourse only in her pedagogy. Thus Bordelon offers us not a study of Buck's rhetorical theory per se, but rather a study of her pedagogy and her whole career as a teacher.

While none of these studies develops a history of women's rhetorical theory based on conversation as a model of discourse, the elements of such a history are beginning, in this recent scholarship, to be visible. In the studies by Sutherland, Mattingly, Eldred and Mortensen, and Buchanan, women are documented as creating rhetorical theory, as using their experience in conversation as a model for their rhetoric, and as employing a gendered rhetoric to assuage audience fears of women's intrusion on the public sphere. At the end of the nineteenth century, we see in Bordelon's work, conversation has become a model not for rhetoric in general but for composition pedagogy. This study will develop in detail the hints from these scholars of the rise and fall of a women's theory of rhetoric.

Historical Method and Definitions

This study offers a revisionist, feminist, critical or "constructionist" history of women's rhetorical theory. As Sharon Crowley wryly observes, "rhetoricians have produced more programs for constructionist historiography than constructionist histories" ("Let Me" 11).[8] There is a need, then, for a revisionist history of rhetorical theory that concentrates on women's conceptions rather than those of the male canon.

Revisionist history does not attempt a chronological, exhaustive narrative. Instead of a chronological lineage, this study examines significant moments in women's contributions to rhetorical theory. Carole Blair reminds us that we must not rehearse "the theme of deterministic progress" (416), and Carole Spitzack and Kathryn Carter, as well as Barbara Biesecker, warn that we should not turn feminist rhetorical history into a story of great women speakers.[9] John Schilb adds that we must not "boil rhetorical history down to a particular set of cherished texts" ("Future Historiographies" 131). Because women did not receive the same education as men, their story is not a particularly coherent one, but rather multiple and fragmented. We have been misled in the past into thinking that the study of rhetorical handbooks and the much more coherent story of the development of masculine rhetorical theory from Aristotle to Campbell constitutes a full history of rhetorical theory. In this study, I challenge that hegemonic history and examine the counterdiscourse of women's rhetorical theory.[10] This study thus answers Berlin's request for "multiple and separate rhetorics, rather than any single, universal and timeless formulation" ("Revisionary History" 135).[11]

Although the narrative of women's rhetorical theory is fragmented and multiple, this study attempts to make sense of it by looking at the details of each woman's life and each moment's era, registering the differences as well as similarities between women. Schilb advises that histories of rhetoric must locate the texts they treat among "a great variety of sociopolitical factors," tracing "discontinuity" as often as "convergence" ("History" 21, 28). Indeed, Crowley defines revisionist history in exactly this manner: "Constructionism prefers difference to identity; it reads the particulars of history rather than its general sweep; and it situates historical events in cultural constructs that may seem exotic and/or foreign to today's readers" ("Let Me" 16).[12] To these considerations, I would add, following Patricia Hill Collins's formulation in "Moving beyond Gender," that a revisionist and feminist history of rhetoric must consider the intersections of class, race, ethnicity, science, and religion, along with gender and historical moment.

Revisionist histories, according to Crowley, must also be "embodied and partial histories." ("Let Me" 11). Under differing historical circumstances, women produced theories different from men's and from each other's. Especially important are the gender constraints that women faced or resisted. I follow Linda Nicholson's analysis of gender: rather than see gender as a social construction placed over an essential body, I treat gender as a social construction of women's possible physical and social roles and activities, and I further assume that sexuality is also constructed. In a crucial essay, Karlyn Kohrs Campbell has pointed out "the significance of gender in rhetorical interactions" because "rhetorical genres are also social constructions" that were initially "gendered masculine" ("Gender" 479). In an early and thoughtful essay, Susan Jarratt argues that "Gender is relational: a history conceived in terms of gender as an analytic differs from 'women's history' in that it investigates. . . . woman's place in human social life not only as a product of things she does but in terms of the meaning her activities acquire through concrete social interaction" ("Speaking to the Past" 193).[13] It is crucial, then, to include elocution in this study, because the most difficult transformation for women rhetors was the transformation of the female body into a publicly speaking and persuading body.

It is also important to clarify the central terms of this study: *rhetoric* and *conversation*. Rhetoric I define in its broad, contemporary sense as *the art of communication through oral, written, or visual discourse.*[14] Like Jackie Royster, I am also interested in the literacies that provide a foundation for "*rhetorical competence*, the process and performance of rhetorical action" (58). Conversation encompasses *small-group communication, from any private, informal verbal communication, to artful verbal dialogue used in informal leisure and social activities.* The first phrase in this definition of conversation indicates the origins of conversation in household and small-group communication, while the second phrase defines the particular social form that most influenced women theorists of the seventeenth to nineteenth centuries.[15]

The history of rhetorical theory is not a matter of listing facts but of interpretation. Consequently, rhetorical history must not simply reflect, but must also analyze, the forms and contexts of the texts it treats, their rhetoric and politics. Carole Blair points out that theories are themselves discourses to be analyzed rhetorically, and histories are also rhetorical (416–17). Berlin reminds us that "rhetorics . . . reflect and, of equal importance, refract the conditions of their creation and functioning" ("Revisionary Histories" 116). Historians are "shapers of texts," not "passive recorders of a naked reality," Schilb explains—they construct plots and tell stories ("History of Rhetoric" 13).[16] Although this history covers three centuries of women's rhetorical theory, it does not simply recount the content of women's dialogues, handbooks, treatises, essays, and textbooks on communication. This study moves beyond such a recounting to analyze the stories that women tell in their theories by situating them historically in their cultures, by examining the authors' biographies, by unraveling the rhetorical means by which theorists chose to insert themselves into a formerly masculine culture, and by examining the politics, especially the gender politics of the resulting discourse.

It is important, then, that the theory on which my framework rests include theories by women. Besides Aristotle and Habermas, I draw on Patricia Bizzell, Linda Flower, Judith Butler, and Andrea Lunsford and Lisa Ede. Habermas allows us to see that women entered the public sphere in their defenses of women's education (especially in rhetoric) in the seventeenth century. If we mine Bizzell's work on discourse communities, we can begin to think of these women theorists not as a line of influence from the seventeenth century, but as establishing a discourse community in their theory (with many false starts), setting up "discourse conventions"—constructing generic conventions and audience expectations within a social context. Thus, because of gender roles—resulting in different educations, different careers, and different professional and civic languages for men and women—most women before 1900 (but importantly, not all) write within different, if somewhat overlapping, discourse communities from men, and their rhetorical theory often outlines these conventions and expectations. I follow Linda Flower in seeing composition not as the simple task of transferring meaning from an expert to a nonexpert, but rather the far more complex task of setting a goal and then negotiating possible meanings with perceptions of their audience. I further draw on Judith Butler on the performance of gender, and Andrea Lunsford and Lisa Ede on hierarchical versus dialogic collaboration. I have chosen these theorists' work as the framework for my analysis not only because of their usefulness to the exploration of cultural history but also because of the values that they bespeak. These theories privilege consensus, collaboration, and collectivity over competition, and so they are especially appropriate for explicating the rise of a women's tradition of rhetoric that offered models for discourse depending on collaboration, conversation, and equality between speaker and audience—models, then, that align with the development of the public sphere and civic conversation. The theories of these historical women anticipated modern developments in composition theory.[17]

The Plan of This Study

This book is divided into an introduction, four chapters analyzing genres where women published rhetorical theory, and a conclusion. At certain historical moments, women turned to particular rhetorical genres in order to theorize communication as conversation from the perspective of women's experience: humanist dialogues and defenses of women's education in the seventeenth century, conduct books in the late eighteenth and early nineteenth centuries, defenses of women's preaching from 1600 to 1900, and elocution handbooks in the nineteenth century. Each of these genres provided a "counterdiscourse," to use Nancy Fraser's term, an alternative to the dominant rhetorical theory of the time. But each of these counterdiscourses drew on women's gendered experience in conversation: this study traces this rise and fall of rhetorical theories and composition advice by women based on conversation as a model for all discourse. When women are finally admitted to college education and start writing textbooks at the end of the nineteenth century, their theory merges with the rhetorical tradition, and gender differences in rhetorical theory are gradually erased, but women's theory remains inculcated in the mainstream in composition pedagogy.

After this introduction surveying historical methodology and the current field of studies of women's rhetoric, chapter 1, "Humanist Dialogues and Defenses of Women's Education: Conversation as a Model for All Discourse," surveys women's theories of communication in the seventeenth century. These women theorists radically revised classical rhetoric by centering their theories on conversation rather than public speech. Madeleine de Scudéry, one of the most prolific and popular of writers, theorizes the discourses of the salon, of conversation and letter writing, offering the rational woman as the ideal speaker and a "natural" writer. Scudéry imagines an ideal woman who speaks only "privately" in conversation and publishes only anonymously, but a world where conversation *is* power. Margaret Cavendish, another prolific writer, draws on humanist rhetorical genres of oration, letter, and encyclopedia to build a feminized theory of empiricist rhetoric, offering a double vision of men as superior orators, but women as natural social communicators. Cavendish feminizes discourse so that it falls within women's sphere and pits class status against gender in order to provide women's speech legitimacy within a "private" circle of social obligation. Bathsua Makin, celebrated throughout Europe for her learning, revises the history of rhetoric to include women by employing the humanist philosophical letter to bring discussion about women's education into the public sphere. Modeling all discourse on conversation, Makin argues that women's education, especially their rhetorical education, benefits their families and the nation. Mary Astell, who made her living as a writer, adapts neo-Platonic and Augustinian rhetoric to English women's written communication; she represents writing as different from public oratory and more like conversation and thus appropriate to women; and she represents conversation as the model of discourse and love as its purpose. Because their experience with education—when they attain it—is so different from that of the educated men of their time who were schooled in Latin, Greek, and classical rhetoric and literature, women construct theories of discourse that are centered on women's experience with domestic communication rather than the masculine experience of public oratory. As their culture moves into a modern world where events are influenced by discussion in the public sphere, they use aristocratic display as a shelter for their forays into what Bathsua Makin calls "public employment" for women's voices. At the same time, their model of discourse based on conversation better serves a world where public discussion assumes greater influence.

In chapter 2, "Conduct Book Rhetoric: Constructing a Theory of Feminine Discourse," I explore the eighteenth- and nineteenth-century conduct books by women that theorized women's cultural roles in writing and speaking, established the social rules for female discourse communities, and taught women conversation skills and letter writing. These women writers of conduct books, chosen because of their popularity or the representative nature of their books, promoted women's education and negotiated the gender constraints of speech and writing with great ingenuity. They established a transatlantic Anglo-American tradition of women's rhetoric, a theory of feminine discourse. While women's communication is narrowly defined by their domestic roles as parlor rhetoric in most of these works, conduct book rhetoric nevertheless promoted the development of complex theories of letter writing and conversation (especially the art of listening and the sophistics of conversation). Hannah More, the conservative progenitor of this feminine tradition, enforces rigid gender roles, especially the feminine trait of good listening, but also defends women's education and their role in the middle-class accumulation of intellectual capital. Lydia Sigourney constructs a separate sphere of women's rhetoric—conversation, reading aloud as parlor entertainment, and letter writing—in the context of republican motherhood; she takes More as a model, but revises More's class-based hierarchy for communication to fit republican values. Eliza Farrar extends Sigourney's theory of maternal republican rhetoric by advising young women on the codified conventions of their class but also revising gendered assumptions about rhetorical behavior, offering women a position of teaching literacy to the lower classes. By the middle of the century, conduct book rhetoric has diverged into a political spectrum: Florence Hartley conservatively revises feminine rhetoric as etiquette strictly regulating conduct, while Jennie Willing radicalizes women's rhetoric by combining her advice on women's speech with a defense of women's preaching.

Chapter 3, "Defenses of Women's Preaching: Dissenting Rhetoric and the Language of Women's Rights," traces the characteristics of this multiform genre and its link to both conversation and to the discourse of women's rights. Defenses of women's preaching by women take many forms, and so I have chosen these texts not for their popularity, but to sample the full range of possibilities: Margaret Fell's Quaker argument from scriptural commonplaces, Jarena Lee's spiritual memoir, Ellen Stewart's conversion narrative, Lucretia Mott's oration, Catherine Booth's pamphlet, and Frances Willard's book-length collage of biblical and contemporary testimony. Although the women before the nineteenth century seem unaware of previous defenses, most defenses center on the same three biblical arguments: they cite scriptures showing men and women as equal in God's eyes; they list biblical women who were preachers, prophets, and ministers; and they refute literalist readings of Paul by placing his commands for women to be silent in church in a specific historical context and identifying them as inconsistent with his praise of women as "laborers in the Gospel" elsewhere. Also, in the early treatises, women often represent their speech as testimony, catechism, or prayer meeting, thus giving up the public space of the pulpit for feminine modesty based on conversation as women's place. Nevertheless, from the mid-nineteenth century onwards, these defenses claim the right for women to speak publicly from the pulpit and to be ordained preachers, often arguing that limitations on women's speech are a corrupt remnant of Roman Catholic practices. Although these authors of defenses of women's preaching approach the problem of gender difference in many ways, they invariably recognize that the church they are part of is a patriarchal institution that denies women's rights. Ironically, then, it is this conservative biblical rhetorical form in which the language of rights first enters the discussion of women's speech. Defenses of women's preaching experiment with rhetorical argument based on collaborative authorship and dialogic authority, searching for a hybrid form that will fit the requirements of their appeals based on scriptural exegesis, emotional religious fervor, and rationalist arguments for human rights.

Chapter 4, "Elocution: Sentimental Culture and Performing Femininity," examines nineteenth-century elocution handbooks by women. Drawing on sentimental culture, beginning with training in reading and conversation, elocution eventually offered women a chance to publicly perform emotion, but emotion viewed aesthetically as both physical act and moral suasion. I have chosen these handbooks to represent the range of women's elocution, from dramatic to gymnastic to terpsichorean to therapeutic. In several handbooks, Anna Morgan developed elocution as a foundation for dramatics; beginning with training in social performance, Morgan rehabilitates acting as a proper career for women, offering physical training as a release for Victorian women from the rigid constrictions of feminine ideology. Genevieve Stebbins combines research in global dance forms, semiotics (the science that decodes the bodily signs of emotions), and Eastern breathing exercises to construct elocution as an art of creative movement, providing women an ideal of femininity as strength and physical expertise. Emily Bishop analyzes movement scientifically, depicting elocution as a correction to "over-nervation," and offering elocution that is a precursor of modern physical education and physical therapy; for her, health is self-expression, and consequently women must *perform* the self through the body so that they free themselves from convention and become "emancipated." African American Hallie Quinn Brown teaches elocution as an avenue toward mastery of the body in order to achieve bodily freedom; her handbook aims to provide its audience training for parlor performance, preparation for public speaking, and a foundation for activist social reform.

The conclusion, "Composition Textbooks by Women and the Decline of a Women's Tradition," traces the combination of these strands of the counter-discourses of women's rhetoric in Mary Augusta Jordan's handbook on composition, the last conversational rhetoric, and the fading of conversation as a model for women's rhetoric as women achieve the right to public speaking. The model of conversation, however, migrates into composition pedagogy as women begin to write composition textbooks for mixed audiences, and women theorize composition as taught through dialogue and debate and conversational collaboration with their students. This study of women's theorizing of their own rhetorical competencies during the sixteenth to nineteenth centuries concludes with an overview of the importance of conversation as a model for all discourse in contemporary composition studies.

Women thus theorized conversational rhetoric well before the twentieth-century interest in conversation as an analogy for effective composition. They put forward conversation as a model for all discourse, urging speaking and writing that is collaborative, not antagonistic in relation to the audience, seeking consensus, not domination as the goal of communication, advising best practices for domestic rhetoric, developing an art of listening. These female theorists acknowledged the gendered nature of rhetorical discourse in their culture and restructured the constraints of gender as means to persuasion. They saw the necessity for defending women's rights to rhetorical performance—to preach, to read aloud, to speak publicly—but they often used the analogy of speech to conversation as a basis of their defenses. They noted the importance for women of claiming their bodies for rhetorical use and developed physiological theories and physical exercises to that end. And they understood the importance of conversational rhetoric as a basis for composition pedagogy. Their theories are thus important because of the many ways they anticipated, under quite different circumstances, our contemporary theories of reading, writing, and teaching.

1

Humanist Dialogues
and Defenses of Women's Education:
Conversation as a Model for All Discourse

At the beginning of her mid-seventeenth-century dialogue, "On Conversation," Madeleine de Scudéry proclaims, "conversation is the bond of society for all humanity, the greatest pleasure of discriminating people, and the most ordinary method to introduce into the world not only civility, but also the purest morals and the love of glory and virtue" (*Selected Letters* 96).[1] In this passage Scudéry is praising the power of speech in the humanist manner derived from the ancient sophists and classical rhetoricians; she is also describing in idealized terms the effects on French society of the salon as an institution. Thus Scudéry is revising the rhetorical tradition by offering conversation as a model for public discourse.

As we shall see in this chapter, the women who devised rhetorical theory in England (and France) during the seventeenth century published their works in the humanist genres of dialogue and defenses of women's education, adapted to conversation the classical vision of speech as civilizing, and theorized discourse as based on conversation, not public speaking.[2] Thus they may be said to contribute to the establishment of the public sphere as Jürgen Habermas defines it: that sphere (birthed in the seventeenth-century institutions of salon, coffee house, reading society, and public library) where civil society met the state and where the reading public engaged in critical discussion of issues of public interest—at first matters of taste and soon politics (ix, 2–3, 23, 29).[3] To represent this group of aristocratic and middle-class educated women theorists, I have chosen Madeleine de Scudéry, Margaret Cavendish (Duchess of Newcastle), Bathsua Makin, and Mary Astell. I include Scudéry in this chapter, in a book that is mainly on English and United States women, because she was one of the most popular writers of the seventeenth century, was immediately translated into English, and is mentioned or alluded to by several of the English rhetors included in this study. The remaining women treated in this chapter were also chosen because of their significance for women's rhetorical history: Cavendish was one of the most prolific English women writers; Makin was famous for her learning; and Astell was influential on later writers.

Because of their gender, it was argued in the Renaissance, women had no need for training in public speaking (Gibson 10–20). Drawing on women's material circumstances, these seventeenth-century theorists offer, instead, defenses of women's need for training in conversation, letter writing, and rhetorical methods in order to help educate their children or to protect themselves from persuasion to heresy. Before we turn to early modern women rhetorical theorists, however, it will be helpful to situate these women historically in Renaissance humanism.

Seventeenth-Century Women and Renaissance Humanism

How is it that, in the seventeenth century, there is a sudden rise of rhetorical theory by women, and why does it appear in humanist dialogues and defenses of women's education rather than textbooks?

The European Renaissance, beginning in the fourteenth century and lasting to the seventeenth century, was a revolution in education, restoring rhetoric and dialectic to a central place in the curriculum. The period begins and ends with rediscoveries of classical rhetorical texts—from the complete corpus of Cicero in the fourteenth and fifteenth centuries to Longinus in the sixteenth and seventeenth centuries (Monfasani 177, 183). Humanism, then, was not so much a philosophy as it was an education program: humanists studied the humanities—classical Latin and Greek, rhetoric, dialectic, literature, moral philosophy, and history (Kristeller 1–10). Humanists, however, only rarely engaged in the republican public speaking exemplified in Cicero's work and theory (see Rebhorn). Humanists did give public Latin speeches in praise of important patrons, but otherwise, they published their ideas in certain humanist genres, which included, besides textbooks for rhetoric and dialectic, the print oration, the dialogue, the letter, and the encyclopedia.[4] Humanist interest in rhetoric encouraged public debate in print (Norbrook) and influenced the rise in aristocratic and court circles of the academy and the salon, and so of handbooks on conversation (Peter Burke 98–108).

Although modeled in classical dialogues by Plato, Cicero, and Augustine and discussed briefly by Cicero in *De Officiis* 1.37.1, conversation did not become an art until the Renaissance. With the decline of aristocratic battle sports and the rise of conduct book literature in the fifteenth to the sixteenth centuries, (male) aristocrats left off jousting and took up academies, collections, and salons as means of display. Women made important contributions to such courtly interaction and display.[5] Humanists not only wrote rhetorical handbooks but also manuals on the art of conversation, delineating politeness codes and the ideal background for a speaker. The most important of these handbooks was Baldassare Castiglione's *The Courtier*, and that work gave rise to a whole set of imitations that both discussed and modeled conversation, including those by Madeleine de Scudéry, as we shall see. By the seventeenth century, conversation had become a major social art and a means of advancement for the middle as well as aristocratic classes in Europe.

But humanist education was for men, not women. Unless they were born into a royal family or had aspirations to marry into one (Warnicke), women were unlikely to acquire humanist education through most of the Renaissance (Gibson 10–20). Conduct and education manuals by men cautioned that women should be chaste, silent, and obedient and that rhetoric was an inappropriate subject for their study (see Hull; and Stallybrass). Consequently, there was no recognized need for rhetoric textbooks for women. However, in this period there were some exceptional women who were given humanist and rhetorical educations. Furthermore, the growth of vernacular humanism in the sixteenth and seventeenth centuries (Boutcher), after most major classical texts had been translated into the vernaculars, gave women easier access to humanist education. Because women were forbidden school education in rhetoric, they did not write rhetoric textbooks. However, because some women received humanist educations and many women were vernacular readers, women did develop theories of communication and did publish in humanist genres—dialogues, epistles, print orations, and encyclopedias.[6]

The women who wrote rhetorical theory during the seventeenth century, then, were exceptions, but they were exceptions enabled by humanism (King and Rabil xx–xxi). Bathsua Makin (1600–c. 1675) and Mary Astell (1666–1731) exemplify the extension of humanist education to women during the seventeenth century. Taught by her father, who ran a school, Makin was a prodigy who published verses in Latin, Greek, Hebrew, Spanish, French, and German, served as tutor to the children of Charles I (especially the princess Elizabeth) and to Lady Elizabeth Hastings, and eventually established a school for gentlewomen. In humanist tradition, Makin corresponded with the notable Dutch scholar Anna Maria van Schurman. Mary Astell was given a humanist education in the languages by her uncle, a curate, and her first publications were theological letters exchanged with an Anglican divine. Although her father was a gentleman, the family was impoverished by his death when Astell was twelve; thus, as a young woman, rather than marrying (which required a dowry), she supported herself through her published writings. Later she established a charity school for poor girls through the patronage of her wealthy aristocratic female friends, who also contributed to her support. Madeleine de Scudéry (1608–1701) of an old but not aristocratic family, and Margaret Cavendish (c. 1623–73), an English aristocrat and eventually the Duchess of Newcastle, are examples, on the other hand, of vernacular humanism: there is no record of an education in the classical languages for either of them, but both are familiar with classical rhetorical concepts, discuss topics characteristic of humanist education, and seem familiar with ancient history. Scudéry, perhaps the most popular novelist of the seventeenth century in Europe, was born in Rouen, came to Paris with her brother, made her way into society through her brilliant conversation in the salons, and supported herself through her writing, eventually winning a prize from the Académie Française for her *Discours de la gloire*. As a teenager, Cavendish, whose family were staunch Royalists, became a lady-in-waiting to Queen Henrietta Maria in exile during the English civil war. While she did not receive a humanist education as a girl, after she had met and married William Cavendish, Marquis (later Duke) of Newcastle, their household was a center for arts and philosophy, and while in exile, they hosted Descartes, Hobbes, and many other men of letters.[7]

Thus these women and the theories of discourse they devised were influenced by the limited women's sphere of activity in early modern aristocratic and middle-class culture, by an enabling humanism, and by the development of the institutions of the salon and the academy and the art of conversation. Experienced in both domestic and salon conversation but not public oratory, finally allowed education in classical or vernacular humanism in the seventeenth century, middle-class and aristocratic women began to devise new theories of rhetoric that centered on conversation as a model for social and written discourse.

Madeleine de Scudéry: Rhetorical Conversation

In works published between 1642 and 1684, Madeleine de Scudéry formulated a new rhetoric of conversation for the French salon, a rhetoric that included women as central participants. In *Le Paradis des Femmes*, Carolyn Lougee has argued that the salon as an institution in seventeenth-century France centered on women and promoted social mobility: the salon brought the educated middle-class and the old aristocracy together for purposes of conversation, entertainment, and appreciation of art; the salon consequently assimilated into the French aristocracy new nobility and some bourgeois through facilitating marriage across class lines and through defining nobility as behavior, not genealogy.[8] While Habermas has argued that the salon was an occasion for monarchical, absolutist display (9–10),[9] the salon was also a site for important discussion of women's equality and the popularization and redeployment of rhetoric. Scudéry was central in formulating these issues in salon culture, and she and her brother quite literally made their livings from their influence in Parisian salons.

Published anonymously in 1641, Madeleine de Scudéry's *Amorous Letters* provides a formulary rhetoric of letter writing, with examples of women's letters between intimate friends and for the business of polite society. Published in 1642 under her brother's name, Scudéry's *Les Femmes illustres; ou, Les haranges heroiques* (Famous Women; or, Heroic Speeches) addresses itself to women as an audience and defends education, rather than beauty and marriage, as a means to social mobility for women, offering to French women a justification for their participation in rhetorical and literary culture and for speaking up in public. Scudéry's later *Conversations* (published anonymously throughout the 1680s), including dialogues "On Conversation," "On Speaking Too Much or Too Little, and How to Speak Well," "On Wit," and "On the Manner of Writing Letters," offer a rhetoric of salon conversation and model scenarios where women take intellectual control of the conversation.[10]

In "On Conversation," Scudéry, whose rhetoric is an adaptation of classical theory to the circumstances of women and the salon, defines conversation as "the bond of society for all humanity" (96). Here she is alluding to the long tradition of rhetoricians who have so celebrated the rhetoric of public speaking: Cicero, for example, declaims, "what other power could have been strong enough either to gather scattered humanity into one place, or to lead it out of its brutish existence in the wilderness up to our present condition of civilization as men and as citizens?"(*De Oratore*, 1.7.33). But Scudéry translates the power of language to conversation and feminizes the rhetor: for example, in "On Speaking Too Much or Too Little" the ideal speaker is one who "speaks as a rational woman should speak—agreeably" (114). Other forms of discourse follow this model of conversation: in "On the Manner of Writing Letters," she calls letters of gallantry, for instance, "a conversation between absent persons" (147). Conversation thus becomes the model for all discourse.

In the preface to *Les Femmes Illustres*,[11] often attributed to Scudéry's brother Georges (even though the body of the work is acknowledged to be Madeleine's), women's rhetoric, spoken and written, is presented as requiring a standard different from men's: "I have not thought that the eloquence of a lady should be the same [as] a Master of Arts" (sig. A2^{r-v}). Arguing that "Exord[ium]s, Narrations, Epilogues . . . and all the beautiful [rhetorical] figures" are reflections of masculine education, the Scudérys favor, instead, "The delicacy of art . . . making believe there is none at all" (sig. A2^r). Playfully borrowing from the *Gorgias*, Socrates's disparaging comparison of rhetoric to cosmetics,[12] the Scudérys compare rhetoric specifically to women's hairdressing, where "it might be judged rather the wind, than your hands, had been helping . . . nature" (sig. A2^v). They rehabilitate Plato's analogy to describe a female art that changes nature but "with such a subtle negligence and agreeable carelessness" that the audience sees only nature, not the art (sig. A2ᵛ). They also use the analogy of arranging flowers to describe the choice of speeches collected in the fictional anthology: the art of rhetoric is like "The skill of these who make nosegays, who mix by a regular confusion roses and jasmine, the flower of the orange [tree] and the pomegranate, the tulip and the jonquil, so that from this so pleasing mixture of colors there appears one agreeable diversity" (sig. A2ᵛ–A3ʳ). The writer's rhetorical goal is like this mixing of flowers: "Just so here I have chosen the finest [historical] matter . . . and the most [diverse] that I could; and I have so orderly mixed, and so fitly concealed them, that it is almost impossible that the reader shall [not] be diverted" (sig. A3ʳ). Women's speech, according to the Scudérys, turns triviality and sophistic rhetoric into art, so that pleasure is unashamedly the end of literary and rhetorical efforts.[13] In the rest of *Les Femmes Illustres*, Madeleine de Scudéry offers the orations of women speakers as models for this female speech, inventing speeches for twenty famous ancient women, including Artemisia of Halicarnassus, Mariam of Judea, Cleopatra of Egypt, Volumnia of Rome, and Sophonisba of Africa. Scudéry thus provides a gendered theory of rhetoric expressed by analogy to female display.

In the final speech of *Les Femmes Illustres*, "Sappho to Erinna," dedicated "to the glory of the fair sex" (Scudéry, *Selected Letters* 86), the older poet Sappho assumes the role of mentor to the younger poet Erinna, urging her to educate herself and to write in order to make herself famous: "Those who say that beauty is women's share and that fine arts, great literature, and all the sublime and exalted sciences fall under the dominion of men, without our having the right to claim any part of them, are far from both justice and truth" (88). "Our sex," Sappho urges, "is capable of anything we would attempt" (92).[14] In *précieuse* salon circles where participants chose classical names for themselves,[15] Scudéry was herself called "Sapho" (the French spelling). In this *essai à clef*, Scudéry is signaling to her readers that this radical claim for women's education and right to a voice is her own.

In this speech by Sappho, Scudéry extends the shocking comparison of female cosmetic arts to rhetoric, arguing that, instead of trusting to men's praises, a woman may paint herself:

> You will ask me, perhaps, if it is not glorious enough to be a beautiful woman to whom all the great minds of the age dedicate verses in order to praise her, without meddling herself in making her own portrait. . . . Believe me, Erinna, it is better to give immortality to others than to receive it from others and to find that same glory in yourself than to wait for it from others. The portraits that others make of you in this way might not ever descend to posterity, except as paintings made for pleasure. People

will admire the imagination of the poets more than your beauty and these copies, indeed, will be taken for the original. But if from your own hand you leave some mark of who you are, you will live always with honor in the memory of all. (93)

Instead of the stereotypical cosmetic painting that was part of the early modern stereotype of the immoral woman, Scudéry playfully recommends a painting with words that will allow women to make their own representations of themselves. Still speaking as Sappho, Scudéry adds, "you only have to speak elegantly and you will be well enough known" (93). Through speech and writing, Scudéry argues, a woman may achieve agency, creating herself. Thus Scudéry's theory of a feminized rhetoric of display generates public discussion of the role of women.

In the later *Conversations*, Scudéry elaborates a rhetoric for conversation, adapting from the classical tradition of Cicero, Aristotle, Quintilian, and the sophists, and describing invention, subjects for speaking, style, wit, and the rules for performing but not dominating talk. Importantly, the dialogue form that Scudéry adapts from humanist Latin literature is also a form that Plato (*Gorgias, Phaedrus*), Cicero (*De Oratore*), and Augustine (*De Magistro*) had used for rhetorical theory.[16] Rather than a Socrates or a Crassus leading the discussion, however, in Scudéry's dialogues, the leader is usually female—a Valeria or a Euridamia. Constructing a nostalgia for a classical past through place names and names of speakers, Scudéry creates a mythical past where women have the right to speak, even to pronounce rules for speech.[17]

Moreover, in the *Conversations*, Scudéry revises classical rhetorical theory to accord with the lives of aristocratic and wealthy middle-class women in seventeenth-century France, who were excluded from the bar, the pulpit, and public political speech, but still might command a great deal of power and influence. Although she draws from the classical rhetorical tradition, Scudéry's revision is so thorough that it constitutes an original contribution. She describes the ideal woman's conversation, for example, by adapting Cicero's influential five divisions of oratory: invention, arrangement, style, memory, and delivery. Plotine is the ideal speaker, says Émile, one of the participants, "For all her expressions are at once noble and natural; she does not hunt around for something to say; there is no hesitation in her words; her discourse is clear and easy; there is a gentle turn in her manner of speaking, no affectation in the sound of her voice, a great deal of freedom in her movement, and a wonderful coherence between her eyes and her words that contributes a great deal to making her speech more agreeable" (114).[18] Plotine's speech shows her adept at invention ("she does not hunt around for something to say"), arrangement ("clear and easy"), style ("expressions . . . noble and natural"), memory ("no hesitation"), and delivery ("voice," "movement," and "eyes").

Elsewhere, Scudéry adapts many other classical rhetorical conceptions to conversation: for example, Aristotle's division of sophistries into tricks with words or with reasoning (108),[19] Quintilian's advice on diction (114),[20] and from Cicero and Quintilian, the debates on art versus imitation and practice, and art versus nature in the ideal speaker (116).[21]

Classical masculine theory is centered on public debate and lecture; Quintilian, for example, claims, "There would be no such thing as eloquence, if we spoke only with one person at a time" (1.2.31). At the beginning of Scudéry's dialogue "On Conversation," Cilénie contemptuously throws out such public speech—"when men speak only about the requirements of their business affairs"—as unworthy of consideration (96). In aristocratic salon society fueled by the favor of an absolute monarch, private conversation might very well garner more power than speech in public forums. Indeed, Scudéry's dialogue form imitates conversation, with each person agreeing on some aspect of the previous person's speech (or apologizing for differing), with each speaker building on the ideas of the speaker before her, and with the option of more than one right answer left open. According to Scudéry, conversation requires of its practitioners mainly the "agreeable": "Of what must the conversation be composed, to make it both rational and pleasing?" asks Cilénie, and Valeria responds,

> what is most necessary to make it sweet and entertaining is that it must have a certain air of civility, which absolutely precludes all bitter retorts, as well as anything that might offend decency. And finally, I want you to know so well the art of conversation that one is able to flirt with the strictest woman in the world; to speak a little foolishness to grave and serious people; to discuss science appropriately with the ignorant (if forced); and, in sum, adapt his or her wit to whatever is discussed and whoever is the company. But besides all I have now said, I would have a certain spirit of joy reign, which . . . inspires in the hearts of all the company a disposition to enjoy everything and to be bored with nothing (*Selected Letters* 105).

Amilcar and the rest of the company immediately assent to this definition and pronounce Valeria's own speech "agreeable" (105). Opting for consensus rather than debate and argument, Scudéry revises the tradition she inherits, adapting it to the circumstances of women's participation and salon culture.[22]

The sophistic conception of timeliness, or *kairos*, which was formulated to explain adaptations to the constraints of public oratory, Scudéry adapts to conversation in "On Conversation," making it a cornerstone of her theory: "there is nothing that cannot be said in conversation, provided it is managed with wit and judgment and one considers well where one is, to whom one speaks, and who one is oneself. . . . yet the conversation must appear [to be] so free as if we rejected not a single one of our thoughts and all is said that comes into the fancy" (104). Appropriate topics of conversation *at times* include what colors of cloth best suit one's complexion and how well one's children are doing, as well as gallantry and science. Although one might argue that shifting the field of rhetoric from public discourse to private conversation is giving up power for women, Scudéry's aim is not conservative: she appropriates rhetoric for women as a means of political power—the right to speak and, so, to influence others. Her society is one in which compliments and graciousness, as well as intelligence and patriotism, move one toward a position of power, in which Georges de Scudéry earned his political post not by military service but through his social skills at Mme. de Rambouillet's salon (Aronson 13).[23] Madeleine de Scudéry's rhetoric of conversation pragmatically acknowledges the importance of these "private" venues for power.

In *Amorous Letters* and in one dialogue, "On the Manner of Writing Letters," Scudéry also explores the "private" art of letter writing, adapting the newly personal humanist form of the letter to women's concerns and constructing the letter as "a conversation between absent persons" (147). *Amorous Letters* is a formulary rhetoric providing model letters for women of the leisured classes. The last third contains letters for private business: letters of consolation to a friend at the death of her friend or family member, a letter of recommendation, and a letter of introduction. The first two thirds, however, model an intimate, passionate friendship between two women: from the humanist tradition, Scudéry borrows philosophical topics and discussion of books; from more recent fictional love letters, Scudéry borrows the anxieties, compliments, and range of moods. In Letter 53, the letter writer praises the style of the recipient's letters, thus theorizing the letters of the volume: "I must learn to write [letters] as good as yours in order to express their excellence. Whatever style you write in, they are always pleasant or useful. If you write on important subjects, there is nothing more enlightening, and if they are written with more ease, there is nothing as amusing. They are serious without being pretentious and easy without being too sloppy. Your style is like those beauties who always appear fashionable and attractive whether they are dressed up or not at all" (52). Notice that here, too, Scudéry employs a comparison between style of letter writing and female cosmetic arts.

Much later, in her second volume of *Conversations*, Scudéry offers a dialogue on the art of letter writing. In "Conversation on the Manner of Writing Letters," Scudéry lists the different genres of letters: business letters, philosophical letters, letters of consolation, letters of congratulation, newsletters, letters of recommendation, letters of gallantry, and love letters. For each form, the participants in the dialogue give advice on length, style, content. For love letters, and for letters in general, art consists of disguise, to imply without direct expression: "But with a woman, who cannot ever admit [to a man] so precisely what she feels and must keep it more a secret, this love that she only shows a glimpse of delights more than that put on display without subtlety" (149). Such advice about writing is far from the medieval *ars dictaminis*, which modeled how to address a patron when suing for a favor, and other such ritual business situations. Instead, Scudéry is providing models and a theory for letters that express the personal and private intimacies of friendship and romance.

Habermas explicitly cites Madeleine de Scudéry as implicated in the salon as a vehicle of monarchical display: court festivities and the salon served not for pleasure or for public discussion but for "the demonstration of grandeur . . . of host and guests" (10). Yet, in "Sappho to Erinna," Scudéry suggests that women's participation in the semipublic world of salon and poetry might provide the freedom of social critique: "if you employ your pen to no other end than to blame the vices of your time, people will never stop praising you" (93).

Through a close examination of "On Wit," a dialogue in Scudéry's first volume of *Conversations* (1680), we can see that, under the guise of display, salon conversation might be adapted to claim some liberty of speech for women and might also be a space for public critique of absolutist power. The dialogue falls into three parts: a description of a reunion and the festivities to celebrate peace between France and Spain; a discussion of wit; and a discussion of the ideal ruler under the guise of drawing a "character" of a famous ancient prince (who is really the contemporary Louis XIV).

In "On Wit," as in other works by Scudéry, conversation is promoted as a model for all discourse. When the participants begin the discussion of wit, they assume that the foundation of this ability is not written but spoken, not oratorical but conversational speech: "In general wit is a type of seasoning that gives a spicier flavor to conversation, and it is rightly a natural result of the human spirit" (121). While the discussants agree that wit is universal, they do not essentialize it but instead demonstrate a sophisticated sense of historical and cultural diversity: "wit . . . is like mineral springs that absorb the qualities of the earth and the mineral veins that they pass through. For according to the temperament of a people and the customs of nations, wit is rude or tactful, nasty or agreeable; it is mocking among some people and among others a simple playfulness that makes society more pleasant" (121–22).

While the consensus of the group discussion in "On Wit" is that women should use wit sparingly and politely or not at all, the dialogue also offers, through the figure of Melinta, an alternative model of wicked wit, a wit that skewers human foibles and allows no friend to escape deserved criticism. Euridamia speaks for the group consensus when she severely limits the targets and forms of wit: one must not make fun of lovers, friends, enemies, social superiors or inferiors, the old, foreigners, those with merit or without it, the other sex, or one's self; one must not tell long stories or use vulgar language or "unload a ton of proverbs" (126). "To make a habit of teasing," Euridamia cautions, "is like walking along a precipice: it is the most difficult thing in the world to do it completely right, without offending friendship" (123).

Melinta provides counterpoint to Euridamia in this conversational fugue. With her sharp retorts, Melinta implies that her host's son and his rescuer, newly returned home from adventures, would be "prodigious liars" (120) were they to tell their tales, and she straightforwardly proclaims to her friends that she prefers travel books to hearing boring recitations from travelers (120). Against Euridamia's remonstrances, Melinta defends laughing at her lover: she protests the idea that she "must listen seriously to his sighs for entire days and . . . not amuse [her]self as a result" (122). Melinta's ideal wit is interactive teasing that depends on "agreeable malice" (122–23).

The company finally agree to accept Euridamia's definition of wit as "a . . . gallant . . . natural . . and . . . bold familiarity, which, without any audacity, has something that pleases and that silences others" (129), a wit, though, that is never turned against one's friends in a spiteful manner (130). But they also agree that Melinta is exempt from these rules, for, she says, "if I were to guide my wit by what she has just said, I would never be able to speak again in my life!" (130). And even Euridamia refuses to call her advice on wit "laws" (128).[24] Thus, in the interaction of Euridamia and Melinta, both the force of society's strictures keeping women silent and also resistance to those strictures are acknowledged, and both sides are supported with reasoned (and witty) argument. The woman question, then, is a subtext of this dialogue, which may be seen as a model for civic discussion that includes critique but remains polite.

The rhetorical effect of this dialogue depends on the charm of its description of aristocratic display in the service of the king's absolutist power: in a chateau overlooking the sea, honnête gens from France and Spain meet on the occasion of peace after a war between the two countries and also the return of a long-lost son captured by pirates; the discussion takes place after a progress through a courtyard garden of orange trees and a multi-course dinner accompanied by a symphony; the conversation occurs in a "magnificent chamber" perfumed by exotic spices from foreign countries; after the discussion, the group is treated to a tour of the estate's formal gardens and, in an arbor, a surprise opera (written by the host) celebrating the king. The display thus publicizes not only the host but also the king: "We drank the health of the King to the sound of trumpets and the roar of the cannon, for this manor was fortified with many [artillery] pieces" (119).

But under the guise of display there is also a discussion of politics, and advice, even critique, is extended to the king. Such advice begins with an anecdote attributed to the king's wisdom, one in which he refuses to mock his courtiers because teasing by a king can only bring terror (131). In response to Clarice's desire for travel stories, Antigene then fabricates a pharaoh, Sesostris the Great, whose character he sketches.[25]

The character explains that this monarch "was the handsomest man in the kingdom" (133), with a deportment that "mixed a kind of civility and a heroic familiarity with . . . grandeur" (134). His accomplishments are listed: he reformed the laws and restored the authority of the royal government; he waged many wars successfully; he inaugurated dozens of important building projects (including the pyramids), and his entertainments and spectacles were magnificent. His court was a continual exhibition of scientific and geographic displays (135). Such praise was part of the environment at court during the reign of Louis XIV and, indeed, was one of his major achievements in modern politics, conscripting the intellectuals of Paris to serve him in public relations. So far, Scudéry's dialogue seems to support Habermas's claim that the salon and its conversation was not political discussion but merely controlled display of a monarch's absolutist powers.

The last paragraph of the praise, however, is quite different. In this paragraph Antigene explains that when the king claimed his government from his counselors after his minority, he changed the corrupt system of rule:

> But as he grew up, civil war died down. The foreign war was ended through new conquests and his marriage. Then he himself began to steer the ship [of state] in which he had been until then a passenger, and contrary to the inveterate practices of rulers during his time, who were nothing but the instruments of their ministers, he made all his ministers his instruments. . . . He listened to all his subjects, who (up to that point) had had hardly any access to their amiable lord. He did not call for diversions except as respite from his work. . . . However impatient he was at his age to extend his reputation in warfare, he applied himself as if [he were] a king of sixty years, to regulate and reform the interior of the state. (136)

When he did go to war, he did not allow long, drawn-out campaigns and usually returned the lands to their original owners in order to establish a lasting peace (136–37). In these passages, Scudéry participates in a critical discussion of midcentury French politics by praising the king for attributes he did not necessarily demonstrate.

Scudéry shows herself quite aware of this Renaissance humanist practice of employing praise as critique in Letter 36 of the *Amorous Letters*: "I take your praise as a modest reprimand and believe that, in attributing such virtuous qualities to me, you [actually] want to inform me of my short-comings and [let me know] what is required in order to deserve such worthy approval as yours (52).

In particular, since La Fronde, the earlier aristocratic rebellion that put Scudéry's brother in exile and her aristocratic friends in danger, was occasioned by the overreliance of the regent, Anne of Austria, mother of Louis XIV, on her counselors, this passage in "On Wit" warns Louis of the consequences of following his mother's practices.[26] Immediately juxtaposed to the display of the opera celebrating the reign and peace of the king, this passage thus suggests that salon conversation is an important transition between the politics of display and the politics of discussion in a public sphere. Moreover, it further suggests that women might participate significantly in such discussions. As Marie Fleming reminds us, in Habermas's model, the new bourgeois publicity is opposed to the older aristocratic secrecy and public display (124).[27] Thus Scudéry's publicity of aristocratic display, her construction of a dialogue about aristocratic display, and her advice to the monarch in the guise of praise—all indicate that she is co-opting print for public discussion and her own, very different ends. In general, then, Scudéry views conversation as a model for all discourse, defends women's right to an education (especially in the private rhetorics of conversation and letter writing), and attempts to incorporate women into public display through these private-public arts.

Margaret Cavendish, Duchess of Newcastle: Domesticating Rhetoric

Margaret Cavendish, Duchess of Newcastle (c. 1623–73), who spent most of the English civil war with the court in exile on the Continent, is the most conservative of the women who wrote rhetorical theory in the seventeenth century. Rather than challenging the inferior status of women, she seems to accept it, yet still manages to establish women's need for rhetorical education. In *The Worlds Olio* (1655), published during the Interregnum, Cavendish appropriates for women the encyclopedia, a form favored by second-generation male humanists a century before her. Like these humanists, Cavendish focuses her book on rhetoric, a central concept recurring in entries such as "Of Eloquence, Art and Speculation," "What Discourses Are Enemies to Society," and "Of Speaking Much or Little." In *Orations of Divers Sorts* (1662) and "The Female Academy" (1662), Cavendish portrays women speaking orations and debating publicly before all-female audiences.[28] In *Sociable Letters* (1664), Cavendish also discusses eloquence in Letters 27, 28, and 30. To be eloquent, she says in Letter 27, is "to Speak Rationally, Movingly, Timely and Properly" (37–38), and declares it to be based, not on words, but on "Sense, Reason, and Wit." She further distinguishes "Premeditated" from "Natural" orators—favoring the latter in Letter 28 (38)—and advances Aspasia as an example of "Vice of . . . Rhetoric" in Letter 30 (43).

But Cavendish's most extensive theorizing of rhetoric occurs in *The Worlds Olio*.[29] She distributes her opinions on rhetorical theory throughout her encyclopedia, covering invention, levels of style, nature versus art in eloquence, discourse as promoting society, and the dangers of privileging words over things. Rather than challenging the distinctions between men's rhetoric and women's silence, she apologetically inserts women into the art of rhetoric, both by drawing analogies for speech and discourse from women's gendered experiences and by assuming the foundation of oratory to be private conversation, not public speech.

Like Scudéry, Cavendish draws on women's arts to form an analogical description of speech and discourse. In the introduction to *The Worlds Olio*, Cavendish addresses a male audience, claiming her femininity as the basis for a counterdiscourse: "and though I do not write the same way you write, yet it is like Nature which works upon eternal matter, mixing, cutting, and carving it out into several forms and figures."[30] This is another of Plato's forbidden analogies to rhetoric: only false rhetoric, according to Plato, is like cookery. But here Cavendish conflates woman's writing with Nature (a common seventeenth-century conflation), and both with cookery, a woman's art.[31] Through her later elevation of nature over imitation in discourse, she has accomplished a reversal of the usual denigration of women's nature, compared to men's reason, into a praise of women's natural discourse, over men's studied and imitative discourse (*Worlds Olio* fol. E1ᵛ; Donawerth, *Rhetorical Theory* 54).[32]

Throughout the encyclopedia, Cavendish likens discourse to women's arts—midwifery and spinning. For example, Cavendish explains that the tongue is the midwife to a witty person's pregnant brain: "their brains are so full of fancy that if their tongue like a midwife should not deliver some of the issue of the brain, it would be overpowered, and lost in painful throes." Cavendish also compares wit to spinning out the thread fancy: "for verses are fine fancies, which are spun in the imagination to a small and even thread, but some are worse spinsters than others" (fols. D1ᵛ and C1ᵛ; Donawerth, *Rhetorical Theory* 52).[33] In these ways, rhetoric is feminized and domesticated so that it becomes appropriate for women to participate in.

Although her encyclopedia includes entries with titles like "Of Orators," "Of Invention," and "Of Gentlewomen That Are Sent to Board Schools"—all topics familiar to classical masculine rhetorical theory (except, of course, men's schools, not women's)—the assumption behind these classical terms is transformed from public to private speech. In fact, like Scudéry, Cavendish discusses oratory in public forums only to disparage it: the disputations of trained logicians dis-rupt social harmony, and the preaching of trained ministers is tedious, self-aggrandizing, and oppressive (fols. C4^r and D2^r; Donawerth, *Rhetorical Theory* 50, 52). Instead, conversation is the center of Cavendish's theory, as it is for the other women in this chapter. When Cavendish analyzes discourse in general, she assumes conversation as the basis of speech: for example, when she discusses facility of speech, she weighs quick and easy speech, "with words on the tongue, as balls with rackets," against thoughtfulness and slow speech, "the tongue apt to falter" (bk. 1, pt. 2, "Epistle," fol. E2^v; Donawerth, *Rhetorical Theory* 54).

Although she did not ever give a speech in public, Cavendish did write a book of speeches—*Orations of Divers Sorts, Accommodated to Divers Places* (1662). One might argue that such a book, written by a woman, undermines the very gendered distinction Cavendish assigns to speech, associating natu-ral rhetoric and conversation with women, and oratory with men. However, in *Orations* Cavendish assigns hundreds of her fictional public speeches to men, devoting only a few pages to speeches by women (225–32). The women's speeches, moreover, are not public debate in the same way as the men's, but a discussion among a group of women only, offering a variety of opinions on the seventeenth-century woman question. One woman tries to use women's abilities at conversation to carry them into the public arena: "let us converse in camps, courts, and cities, in schools, colleges, and courts of judicature, in taverns, brothels, and gaming houses, all which will make our strength and wit known, both to men, and to our own selves" (228). But another woman suggests that women and men have different abilities and that women should rest satis-fied with gendered spheres: "why should we desire to be masculine, since our own sex and condition is far the better? . . . if men are more eloquent in speech, women are more harmonious in voice" (231). According to Cavendish, in her "Preface to the Reader," as "man is made to govern commonwealths, [so] women their private families" (*Worlds Olio*, fol. A4^v; Donawerth, *Rhetorical Theory* 47). Cavendish thus assigns a domestic role to women's rhetoric.

Influenced by Bacon and other seventeenth-century empiricists, Cavendish sketches out a physiology of speech and adopts the empiricist concepts of the mind as a *tabula rasa*, or blank slate, on which experience makes impressions, and of words as marks of things rather than thoughts (fols. D1^v, D2^{r-v}, D4^r–E1^r, E4^r; Donawerth, *Rhetorical Theory* 52–53). She flavors this empiricism with a sophistic concentration on language—both speech and writing—as the bond of human society (fols. C4^r, D2^r, D4^r; Donawerth, *Rhetorical Theory* 49–50, 52–53).[34] Rather than a public end of speech, though, Cavendish uses this social purpose as a standard by which to judge speech in private conversation: ideal discourse is "to speak rationally . . . to clear the understanding," to err with "too much courtesy" rather than too little, to avoid dominating conversation and to know when and how much to speak according to "the manner, time and subject" (fols. D1^r–D2^r; Donawerth, *Rhetorical Theory* 51–52). The ideal is thus a sophistic emphasis on communal private rather than individual public performance: "sociable discourse . . . like music in parts" (fol. D2^v; Donawerth, *Rhetorical Theory* 53).[35]

In *The Worlds Olio*, Cavendish answers objections to women's speech by dividing herself into two voices: her husband, the master, who has taught her what she knows, and her self, the novice, who admires her husband and men's learning. Social duty yet obligates even the novice to speak—"though I do not speak so well as I wish I could, yet it is civility to speak" (fol. E4^r; Donawerth, *Rhetorical Theory* 55). Evelyn Beck and Susan Lanser have argued that such "double-voiced discourse" is characteristic of "women who are struggling to define themselves but have not yet given up a patriarchal frame of reference" (86).[36] Cavendish's is such a "double-voiced discourse," and she even names the voices: her husband the duke and herself. Cavendish struggles even with women's right to conversation because of her double voices, both condemning and justifying women's speech. Echoing patriarchal restrictions, she explains that "the reason . . . women . . . talk too much, is an overweening opinion of themselves, in thinking they speak well, and striving to take off that blemish from their sex of knowing little, by speaking much." But when struggling to define herself, silence is *not* a virtue, according to Cavendish, for "it is a melancholy conversation that hath no sound, and . . . it is better to speak too much than too little, as in hospitality, . . . for civility is the life to society" (fols. D1^v–D2^r; Donawerth, *Rhetorical Theory* 52). While Cavendish contributes to the radical instability of woman as subject that Catherine Belsey has identified as characteristic of seventeenth-century discourses (*Subject of Tragedy*, ch. 6, "Silence and Speech" 149–91), Cavendish also condemns silence for women as opposite to the social purpose of speech.

Cavendish is not as successful in freeing herself from other biases. One strategy she uses to legitimate women's speech is to erase gender as the primary line between those who speak and those who remain silent and to substitute, instead, class: "vulgar discourse" is a serious fault of speech for Cavendish, at least partly because emphasizing the faults of lower-class speakers distracts from the societal injunctions against women's speech (fol. D1^{r-v}; Donawerth, *Rhetorical Theory* 51). By insisting on the aristocratic prerogative of speech used as display, Cavendish counters her society's restrictions on women's speech: class trumps gender. Cavendish thus deploys the screen of aristocratic display to cover her participation in a public discussion of the role of women in society and also of the role of communication. And indeed, Cavendish does enter into public political debate in her writings, defending her Royalist husband, William Cavendish, Duke of Newcastle (who was the commanding officer for one of the spectacular defeats of Royalists at the Battle of York) in her biography of him, in her narrative utopia (*Blazing World*), and in sections of her *Orations*—in particular, citing his lack of funds and troops against accusations of military mismanagement (Kathleen Jones 32–41).

Thus Cavendish, like Scudéry, employs the humanist genres: letters, orations, dialogues (which she terms plays), and the encyclopedia. Moreover, both women defend women's education, especially in rhetoric, and view conversation as a model for all discourse. Furthermore, both deploy aristocratic display to legitimate women's right to speak and both domesticate rhetoric to private arenas in order to secure women's power of influence.

Bathsua Makin: Marketing Women's Conversational Rhetoric

In *An Essay to Revive the Ancient Education of Gentlewomen* (1673), Bathsua Makin (1600–c. 1675) revises the history of rhetoric to include women speakers, making an argument for women's rhetorical education and resituating rhetoric as necessary to the private as well as the public realm. Like Scudéry and Cavendish, Makin promotes a model of discourse based on conversation, not public speaking. Like Cavendish, she poses as a conservative, representing women's place as helpmeet to a husband, but she also offers instances of women's public employment and public speaking. Makin reserves rhetorical education for an elite class of wealthy, leisured women but builds her defense of women's education on a bourgeois ideal of the centrality of profit and usefulness to society. Indeed, *An Essay* is a marketing brochure for Makin's school for girls and for such bourgeois use of women's education.

The essay is constructed as an epistolary argument—an epistolary dialogue, if you will—between two gentlemen, the first letter addressed to a general reader and proposing women's education, the second raising objections, and the third (making up the bulk of the pamphlet) answering objections with detailed arguments for the use and necessity of women's education. The argument proceeds as many Renaissance arguments do, listing reasons to support women's education with suitable examples from biblical and classical reading (in the fashion of commonplace books). It offers a new kind of argument, however, in the turn from women's nature as inherently good (as in Margaret Cavendish's works) to women's nature as damaged by the custom of neglecting women's education.[37] Indeed, Makin opens her initial dedication "To all ingenious and virtuous ladies" with this argument: "The barbarous custom to breed women low is grown general among us, and has prevailed so far that it is verily believed . . . that women are not endued with such reason as men, nor capable of improvement by education, as they are" (3).[38] This argument based on custom also moves the pamphlet controversy about women securely into the realm of discussion in the public sphere: Makin gives her argument a political slant when she equates women's ignorance with slavery (5, 34, 41).

Like Scudéry and Cavendish, Makin assumes conversation as a model for all discourse and so also of rhetoric. One purpose of women's education is to allow husbands to consult with and seek advice from their wives (4). Since "God intended woman as a help-meet to man, in his constant conversation," if we do not provide education for her, then "we renounce God's blessing" (23). Indeed, families are ruined if "the men find no satisfactory converse or entertainment at home" and so "seek abroad" for that intimacy. For that reason, wise men may themselves instruct their wives, "the more to fit them for their converse" (27). The major roles of the middle-class housewife that Makin envisions depend on this facility in conversation and communication: tutor, husband's adviser, children's teacher, shopkeeper's aid (26–27).

Having defined discourse as private, based on conversation, Makin is able to revise the history of rhetoric to include women as speakers. Miriam, Priscilla, Eunice, and Lois from the Bible are advanced as examples of "women [who] have . . . been educated in arts and tongues" (8). Besides Queen Elizabeth I, a truly public figure, Makin further cites Cornelia, Sulpicia, Portia, Valeria, and Zenobia from classical times, and Lady Jane Grey and the Princess Elizabeth, daughter of Charles I, as having "been eminent" in learning languages (9–10). Indeed, Makin offers Margaret Cavendish as an example of the well-educated woman (10). Ruefully, she admits, "Many say one tongue is enough for a woman." But, she responds, "The tongue is the only weapon women have to defend themselves with, and they had need to use it dexterously" (11 [75]). In the category of "good linguists," Makin supplies Tecla, whose copy of the Septuagint was used by the authors of a polyglot Bible, and Anna Maria van Schurman, with whom Makin had corresponded in Latin (11–12 [75]). Under "orators," Makin places Androgine, who earned her name of "Androgine," or "Man-Woman," in pleading her own case in a Roman law court, and Hortensia, whose oration convinced the Roman Triumvirate to reduce a tax on women's property (12 [75]). In this revised history of rhetoric, the best women are well educated in the classical languages and the humanist arts and sciences, and they use their resulting knowledge in public as well as private discussion. Indeed, Makin's own pamphlet is a public contribution to the controversy about women, and it is modeled on Schurman's similar Latin pamphlet, *Whether a Christian Woman Should Be Educated.*

While Makin advances a conservative argument that only women of a certain class should be educated, and only for the role of helpmeet, she sophistically provides numerous examples of women's public employment. Education, Makin argues, will "persuade women to scorn those toys and trifles they now spend their time about. . . . This will either reclaim the men, or make them ashamed to claim the sovereignty over such as are more wise and virtuous than themselves." Nevertheless, "your husbands have the casting voice in whose determinations you will acquiesce" (4). To attach conservative status to her proposition, Makin advances women's education as a cure of their frivolity (22, 30) and a prevention against heresy, associating it with the Reformation, since all good Christians need to read the Bible (23, 25, 28). In response to the objection that "The end of learning is public," she explicitly claims that "it is private instruction I plead for, not public employment" (33). However, Makin gives many examples of women who used their education for public ends: in biblical times, she reminds us, "women extraordinarily enabled were publically employed" (9), and in classical Rome, "Cornelia read public philosophy lectures" (10). In an interesting section on the range of women's learning, Makin violates both gender and class restrictions. While "public employment in the field and courts are usually denied to women," Makin argues, "yet some have not been inferior to many men even in these things also" (24). As examples of women publicly employed, Makin cites the Babylonian queen Semiramis, the biblical Miriam and Deborah, Catherine de Medicis of France, and Queen Elizabeth of England. Descending from prophets and rulers to ordinary women in wartime, Makin reminds her readers, "In these late times there are several instances of women, when their husbands were serving their King and country, defended their houses, and did all things as soldiers, with prudence and valor, like men" (25).

Another signal that we have moved from aristocratic display (despite Makin's Royalism) to the political discussion of the bourgeois public sphere is the centrality of the argument of profit or usefulness to husband and society in women's education. "Married persons, by virtue of this education, may be very useful to their husbands in their trades, as the women are in Holland, and to their children, by timely instructing them before they are fit to be sent to school," Makin asserts, appealing to the need for household and business help that might be met with no cost to the husband. To women, she points out that educated "widows will be able to understand and manage their own affairs" (27). Appealing to the general good, Makin argues that well-educated English women "will be beneficial to the Nation" (28); they will then be like "well-bred, ingenious, industrious Dutch women," for they would use their knowledge in natural philosophy "To buy wool and flax," and in arithmetic to "merchandize" (35). Indeed, Makin argues, education will be better than a dowry: "You cark and care to get great portions for them, which sometimes occasions their ruin. Here is a sure portion, an easy way to make them excellent" (41).

With historical allusion and rhetorical wit, Makin puts her learning on display in the manner of humanist rhetoric celebrating aristocratic display. She wittily argues for reversing the fall through women's education: "Because evil seems to be begun here, as in Eve, and to be propagated by her daughters," then women are in greater need of an education, "to season them with piety and virtue" (7). She imagines that Huldah, the biblical leader, "dwelt in a college . . . where women were trained up in good literature" (8). Besides the many instances of biblical and classical learning in women that we have already reviewed, Makin further adduces "The two orations delivered at the universities by Queen Elizabeth's own mouth" (20). Finally, she cites Erasmus's dialogue between an abbot and a learned woman in favor of women's education (23). Thus, while her rhetorical wit and her historical learning may seem part of courtly display, since Makin was tutor to a princess, nevertheless they are employed in support of public discussion of an issue important to both household and public responsibilities: they bring the issue of women's status in the private domain into the realm of public discussion. Makin makes a clear political argument for women's rights to a rhetorical education and a public voice.

Thus we may see that Makin's rhetorical theory carries the arguments for women's education and the conceptions of communication a step further. Like Scudéry and Cavendish, Makin adopts a humanist genre, the letter, in order to legitimate in a public arena women's private role of speaker. Like Scudéry and Cavendish, Makin defends women's right to education (especially rhetorical education) and views conversation as a model for all discourse. Even more than Scudéry and Cavendish, Makin defends women's right to the public employment of her speech, to a rhetorical voice.

Mary Astell: Conversational Composition

In 1694, Mary Astell published *A Serious Proposal to the Ladies*, arguing that women, like men, should receive a humanist education; she followed this with *Part II* in 1697, detailing a curriculum that included an art of rhetoric for women. Like Makin, she moves the argument concerning women's education from essentialism to social construction, arguing that women are mentally inferior to men neither through God nor through nature but only through "the mistakes of our education."[39] As a corrective to women's condition, she offers a retreat from the world that would also prepare women to serve in the world: a "monastery" or a "religious retirement" for women that is really a women's college (14, 30).[40] A member of the lower gentry, an Anglican, Astell reassures her audience that she does not mean that women should preach (20). But she follows this denial with the biblical example of Priscilla, who "catechized" Apollos. Her reference to the catechism, a dialogic rather than sermonic form, thus signals Astell's reliance on conversation as a basis for her rhetorical theory.

Mary Astell's conception of rhetoric as conversation grows naturally out of her idea of a women's college as holy orders. In this place women "will quit the chat of insignificant people" for a "holy conversation" with God (15, 29). Adapting the emphasis on the good life as persuasion from Augustine's rhetorical theory, Astell pictures the women's life together as "an exemplary conversation, the continual and most powerful sermon of an holy life" (25).[41] Such a life will prepare women for marriage, since "An ingenious conversation will make [the husband's] life comfortable," and "A good and prudent wife would wonderfully work on an ill man . . . [through] those gentle persuasives . . . she would use to reclaim him" (38). Still, Astell enlarges the importance of women's province by comparing women's traditionally private to men's traditionally public discourse: "catechizing," or private religious instruction through conversation, is more useful than "discourses of the pulpit," for one cannot understand sermons without first achieving "clear ideas" of religion (26). While women could not preach, they could catechize each other and their children and did lead evening prayers for the family servants. According to Astell, then, men's or women's private conversation may work better than men's public lecturing to move a soul to God.

In *Part II* of *A Serious Proposal*, Astell offers the study of rhetoric to women, an art previously forbidden them (Gibson 10–20). Like Quintilian, who argues that only the good man can be the good orator, and Augustine, who argues that rhetoric is appropriate to Christianity when it is used to good ends, Astell hedges the kind of rhetoric that will be taught in her school for women: "I shall not therefore recommend under the name of Rhetoric an Art of speaking floridly on all Subjects, and of dressing up Error and Impertinence in a quaint and taking garb; . . . [it is] a mistake to think that any Argument can be rightly made, or any Discourse truly Eloquent that does not illustrate and inforce Truth" (117 [102]).

Astell also remodels classical rhetoric into an art of rhetoric for women who write, building a theory of the relation between writer and reader by analogy to conversation. In Astell's theory, the writer as "friend" converses with the readers as "neighbors": "They write best perhaps who do it with the gentle and easy air of conversation" (121–24 [104–6]). Astell treats method, arrangement, imitation, style, self-criticism, ornament, and sophistry, creating an entire rhetorical curriculum for women. In her long section on logic, she criticizes the system of syllogistic reasoning as causing obscurity, and outlines her own method. Despite the discarding of the technical details of the syllogism, Astell discusses deduction and analogy as important modes of reasoning. She follows Augustine and Plato in her belief in a verifiable truth and adapts Cartesian empiricism, from Descartes, Pascal, and Antoine Arnauld, to emphasize clear and evident principles as the basis of reasoning. Astell's method, however, is original: the steps of this method include thoroughly defining the question and terms used, avoiding irrelevant issues, ordering concepts from simple to complex, dividing the subject into parts for analysis, distinguishing between evident truth and the probability one must sometimes settle for. Since invention is treated under logic, Astell turns to arrangement and style under rhetoric: she outlines six levels of style appropriate to different situations and discusses the excesses of each that can ruin discourse; she discusses the importance of self-criticism, putting oneself in the place of the audience; and she treats figurative language as a means to clarity rather than to excite emotions. Astell's greatest contribution to theory, however, is her treatment of audience.[42]

The development of empiricism in the eighteenth century will steer men's rhetorical theory away from the audience as equal partner into a mechanistic conception of operating on the audience's wills through language—a modern alienated theory.[43] Astell, on the other hand, grants the audience respect, equality with the speaker, and freedom: "For the design of rhetoric is to remove those prejudices that lie in the way of truth, to reduce the passions to the government of reason; to place our subject in a right light, and excite our hearers to a due consideration of it" (117 [102]). The purpose of the writer, imagines Astell, is "not to dictate to [the audience's] ignorance, but only to explain . . . what they . . . might have known before if they had considered it" (120 [104]). Thus the audience may be viewed as "neighbors," and we writers "permit them to fancy . . . that we believe them as wise and good as we endeavor to make them" (121 [104]). Astell's model of conversation encourages speakers to construct an implied audience in the image of an ideal audience, and invite their real audience to live up to it: "By this we gain their affections which is the hardest part of our work, excite their industry and infuse a new life into all generous tempers" (121 [104–5]).

Since the speaker's end is "the gaining of our neighbor," not the gaining of applause (121 [105]), she must generally use the "mode of inquiry" rather than the mode of lecture, so that her audience will not "imagine their liberty is imposed on" (121 [105]). Here again Astell prefers conversation over public lecture as a model, now to liberate the audience from a dictatorship by the speaker. At bottom of Astell's description of the audience is an Augustinian-Platonic faith in the attractiveness of truth: "Truth being always amiable, cannot fail of attracting when she's placed in a right light" (121 [105]).[44] It is no accident that truth is presented here as an amiable female friend. Persuasion thus results from love. Rather than the power over the audience that rhetoric gives the speaker emphasized in Renaissance and empiricist men's rhetorics, Astell emphasizes the freedom that rhetoric provides women: "without such knowledge it is by chance that we are good. . . . We are their property into whose hands we fall, and are led by those who with greatest confidence impose their opinions on us" (127). The image of the seducer against whom women with rhetorical training may protect themselves thus answers the charge that teaching women to speak will teach them to be unchaste.[45] But Astell's rhetoric modeled on conversation is not a constraint: her aim is to free women by teaching them rhetoric, a goal of feminists for the next two centuries.

While Astell does not claim the public oratory of bar, podium, and pulpit for women, she does move them into the public sphere through her theory of a rhetoric of composition for women. She does not imagine women speaking to mass audiences, but she does imagine women writing persuasive letters and discussing spiritual issues with each other in a way that constructs a more than domestic community of discourse. Astell herself, of course, published her findings and thus participated in the fully developed public sphere of the early Enlightenment. She makes women's education a public issue through her writing.

Conclusion

In the late Renaissance in England and France, women appropriated classical rhetorical theory for their own purposes, presenting discourse as modeled on conversation rather than public speaking. Madeleine de Scudéry treats the forms of discourse of the salon, arguing that women must be educated in order to construct identities for themselves in their writings, developing a theory of communication centered on the rational woman as the ideal communicator, and setting out a theory of letter writing that takes advantage of the seventeenth-century stereotype of woman as "natural" writer. In the humanist rhetorical genres—oration, letter, encyclopedia—Margaret Cavendish appropriates empiricist rhetoric for women, acknowledging men as better public speakers but reserving conversation as a natural feminine talent. Bathsua Makin employs the humanist epistolary form to enter the debate in the public sphere about women's education; she supports her position with arguments that women's rhetorical education benefits her family and nation. Because Makin uses conversation as a model for all discourse, she is able to revise the history of rhetoric to include women. In addition, Mary Astell considers women's written communication, borrowing the French appropriation of neo-Platonic and Augustinian rhetoric, and urging love as the basis of persuasion. All these women consider the gendering of discourse in their culture, questioning "private" and "public" as defining terms for communication.

These women theorists radically revised classical rhetoric by centering their theories on conversation rather than public speech. They seize on conversation as permitted to women in order to challenge the construction of categories of private and public that confine them to a certain sphere (although in the seventeenth century there is nothing like so stable a conception of women's sphere as obtains by the nineteenth century). If the ideal woman in Renaissance culture inhabits a sphere in which she is silent (does not speak or write publically), chaste (private), and obedient (listens to the speech of the men who own her), then each of these women uses the category of "ideal woman" to challenge the nature of restrictions on women. Scudéry's ideal woman speaks only in private conversations and publishes only as an anonymous writer but achieves power through influence. In this woman's world, everyone knows who the anonymous writer is. Scudéry calls into question the line between private and public with regards to power. Cavendish's metaphors for speech suggest a feminized discourse, and she offers a set of class categories in place of gendered spheres: lower class forbidden to speak versus upper class required to speak.[46] Makin's ideal woman is a wife who steps beyond women's roles in the interests of her family; but, inconsistently, Makin offers historical examples of women who successfully used their voices in public employment. Finally, Astell argues that writing is like conversation and thus appropriate to women. The categories in which their culture divides discourse are gendered: these women use other aspects of the categories of gender or of discourse to challenge the particular limits that gendered discourse allows them by custom.

Habermas linked the growth of the public sphere to the development of the patriarchal single-family household, for that intimate domesticity fostered a new sense of humanity that was carried into discussions in the public sphere. Although he did not explicitly develop this idea, clearly the concept of conversation as a model for all discourse enabled this development of public discussion. The women discussed in this chapter theorized this novel concept of conversation rather than oratory as the basis for speech, developing a counterdiscourse of conversational rhetoric that they envisioned as equally powerful to men's public speaking. Their success—Scudéry and Astell supported themselves through writing, while Astell ran a school for girls—calls into question the confinement of power to the public sphere in the use of classical rhetorical theory in the seventeenth century. While there is little indication that any of these women knew the theories of the others, nevertheless, these several women, drawing on their humanist heritage and the domestic experience of women, have disparately constructed a counterdiscourse of women's rhetorical theory based on conversation as a model of discourse.

2

Conduct Book Rhetoric: Constructing a Theory of Feminine Discourse

In Jane Austen's *Lady Susan* (1793–94?), the wicked Lady Susan declares to her friend, "If I am vain of anything, it is of my eloquence. Consideration and esteem as surely follow command of language, as admiration waits on beauty. And here I have opportunity enough for the exercise of my talent, as the chief of my time is spent in conversation" (64). While Lady Susan would have been viewed in her time as inappropriately masculine in her claim to excellence, she nevertheless is in keeping with her society's understanding of women's roles when she cites conversation as the arena in which a woman exercises her eloquence. This chapter examines the ways that women constructed a transatlantic women's tradition of conversational rhetoric, a theory of feminine discourse, in the works of Hannah More, Lydia Sigourney, Eliza Farrar, Florence Hartley, and Jennie Willing.

The history of the teaching of rhetoric and development of theory to serve new cultural contexts in the eighteenth and nineteenth centuries has emphasized men's education and men's theory. The trends and categories advanced by the canonical histories of eighteenth- and nineteenth-century British and American rhetoric do not adequately account for the genres and strategies emphasized in women's rhetorical theory. Conduct book rhetoric grew out of and contributed to this culture of continuing education and women's clubs. Since the mid-1990s, feminists have recovered some of the history of the practice of women's speech making and composition.[1] But there has been relatively little consideration of conduct book rhetoric.

This chapter remedies that lack, surveying the Anglo-American women's tradition of conduct rhetoric that was established in the late eighteenth and early nineteenth centuries. I have chosen to treat conduct books by Hannah

More and Lydia Sigourney because they were the most popular British and American conduct book writers and because they demonstrate the origins of a women's transatlantic network and tradition. I have chosen the conduct books by Eliza Farrar, Florence Hartley, and Jennie Willing because they demonstrate the development of a self-consciously feminine rhetoric and because these texts mark the limits of the range of politics for the genre. Beginning with More in Britain, and Sigourney in the United States (who was strongly influenced by More), conduct books by women theorized women's cultural roles in writing and speaking and taught women conversation skills and letter writing. Women's conduct book rhetoric developed a gendered theory of feminine rhetoric, constructed a women's tradition by citing other women's handbooks, offered advice on domestic uses of rhetoric and composition, elaborated a theory of conversation as a foundation of all discourse, and imagined discourses as collaborative and consensual even if deferring to masculine superiority.

These women writers of conduct books promoted women's education and theorized the gender constraints of speech and writing as means to persuasion, while not challenging these constraints outright until after 1850. Although women's rhetorical role in this literature is, as Nan Johnson has pointed out, narrowly defined by their household roles as domestic or parlor rhetoric (*Gender* 15), conduct book rhetoric is nevertheless important for its development of detailed theories of letter writing and conversation (especially the art of listening and the sophistics of conversation). Moreover, the conservative role allotted to women in conduct rhetoric is not uncontested, as we shall see in analyses of the moderating influence of Lydia Sigourney and the radicalizing theory of Jennie Willing.

Conduct Literature and Its Relationship to Rhetoric

Late medieval and early modern courtesy literature, advice to princes and aristocrats on how to behave at court (such as Christine de Pizan's *The Book of the Body Politic* or Baldassare Castiglione's *The Courtier*) eventually migrated down the social ladder because of increasing social mobility during the sixteenth through nineteenth centuries in Europe and America, and from mainly male to also female readership. Madeleine de Scudéry's *Conversations*, for example, is courtesy literature on its way to conduct book. From the late sixteenth century to the present, conduct books have advised the middle classes on how to behave: how to be good wives or husbands, how to educate oneself, how to converse and compose convincing letters, how to impress people with one's knowledge, how to behave socially, how to succeed and appear to be a member of a superior class.

In the seventeenth and eighteenth centuries, conduct books by men warned women against speaking too much, being witty, or gaining too much education.[2] At the end of the eighteenth century, however, women began writing conduct books for women.[3] Since communication is fundamental to courtesy and good conduct, English and American women's conduct books generally include rhetorical advice—social guidelines for conversation, letter writing, and sometimes education in rhetoric or composition.

Most significant as a foundation for this chapter are the modern studies of gender and nineteenth-century rhetoric by Nan Johnson and by Janet Cary Eldred and Peter Mortensen. In *Gender and the Rhetorical Space in American Life, 1866–1910*, Johnson analyzed the conduct literature, letter-writing manuals, encyclopedias, biographical sketches of female orators, and histories of American oratory to demonstrate that separate spheres of rhetoric for men and women were maintained throughout the nineteenth century, indeed, that the domestic scene of women's rhetoric was itself a means of constructing and enforcing gender ideology.[4] In *Imagining Rhetoric: Composing Women of the Early United States*, Eldred and Mortensen examined nineteenth-century United States women's theory and practice of civic rhetoric and the "schooling fictions" in which they promote these values, arguing that domestic fiction relies on civic rhetoric to promote a new ideology of republican mothers.[5] My study builds on Johnson's identification of misogynist stereotypes of women's speech in conduct literature by men and Eldred and Mortensen's analysis of women's civic rhetoric. To this base, this chapter adds an exploration of women's theories of communication as developed in conduct book rhetoric.

Conduct book rhetoric is preoccupied with the linguistic and rhetorical signs of class and gender. Its goal is to teach the reader how to behave as a middle-class citizen and member of society and how to act like a man or a woman. As such, it is related to what Dorothy Broaddus defines as "genteel rhetoric" in her study of the rhetoric of nineteenth-century Harvard-educated Bostonian men.[6] It is helpful, then, to think of conduct book rhetoric as initiating the reader into a discourse community, and such an approach helps to explain why conduct books almost always include sections on reading, writing, and speaking. Patricia Bizzell defines a discourse community as "a group of people who share certain language-using practices," consisting of "stylistic conventions [that] regulate social interactions both within the group and in its dealings with outsiders," and "canonical knowledge [that] regulates the world views of group members [and] how they interpret experience" (*Academic Discourse* 222). To Bizzell, writing depends on "discourse conventions," a combination of audience expectations, generic conventions, and social context (91). In written forms, initiation into a discourse community is demonstrated by the ability to employ the conventions of the genres of that community to generative rather than merely mechanical ends (91–92).

If we apply Bizzell's ideas to the subject of this chapter, we see that conduct book rhetoric by women teaches both the *stylistic conventions* and language etiquette that signals class status (for women who do not necessarily have the same education as men of their class), and also the *canonical knowledge* or ideology leading to shared assumptions for interpreting rhetorical behavior, including, very importantly, gender roles.[7] In the eighteenth and nineteenth centuries, women adapted the limits of women's gendered sphere to construct a women's theory of rhetoric that emphasized communication between women, listening as a communicative skill, and the domestic genres of conversation, letter writing, and reading aloud. At the same time, they forged a women's tradition of rhetoric, citing each other's works and centering their theory on conversation as a model for all discourse.

Hannah More: Conversation as Women's Work

In a mock-heroic poem on conversation, and in numerous conduct books for women, Hannah More (1745–1833) offered young girls of the middle and upper classes initiation into feminine roles, good breeding, and the discourse community of the British salon, thus constructing a theory of conversation as women's work. At the end of the eighteenth and beginning of the nineteenth century, she parlayed her success in London salon culture into a career in women's education, founding a school, writing textbooks, and pioneering in the British Sunday School and working-class literacy movements. One of four sisters, More was instructed in household crafts by her mother and in Latin and mathematics by her father, a schoolmaster. Later, she and her sisters attended a boarding school, studying Latin, Italian, Spanish, French, and hearing lectures in literature, astronomy, elocution, religion, philosophy, and science. Together the sisters established their own school for girls in Bristol in 1758, teaching French, reading, writing, arithmetic, and needlework. Never married, More participated, from 1774 on, in the London Bluestocking Circle centered on Elizabeth Montague and her "conversation parties" and including such luminaries as Samuel Johnson, Joshua Reynolds, Fanny Burney, and David Garrick. In the 1790s, the More sisters established Anglican Sunday Schools in impoverished districts to counter the spread of Methodism.[8] More also wrote plays, a novel, abolitionist poems and pamphlets, and a whole series of moral tracts meant to promote literacy among the working class.

Most important for our purposes, More also published many conduct books: *Essays on Various Subjects, Principally Designed for Young Ladies* (1777), *Thoughts on the Importance of the Manners of the Great* (1788), *Strictures on the Modern System of Female Education* (1799), and *Hints for Forming the Character of a Young Princess* (1808). In addition, she wrote a mock-heroic poem, "The

Bas-Bleu, or, Conversation" (1783–86), which outlines the qualities of ideal conversation and suggests the Bluestocking conversation parties as a model. While More is an important pioneer in women's education and women's use of their intelligence in public life, hers are conservative texts emphasizing women's roles as good listeners, as facilitators of men's conversation, and as household managers of communication.

In "The Bas-Bleu, or, Conversation" More presents conversation as a model for all discourse and as a social activity that best displays women's intellectual talents. She advises her readers that the stylistic conventions and language etiquette of a higher social class may be achieved by accumulating the intellectual capital of education, and she enforces appropriate gender roles by demonizing the unfeminine behavior of the *précieuses* in French salon culture of the previous century.

As the title, "The Bas-Bleu, or, Conversation," suggests, More's mock-heroic poem poses conversation as a model for all discourse for the Bluestocking. In the climactic middle of the poem, More addresses Conversation as a goddess: "Hail, Conversation, soothing power, / Sweet goddess of the social hour!" (367). To this personified social force, More attributes idealized qualities; functioning as the "balm of care," originating in "taste with wit and science," conversation is forged in "Education's moral mint." Conversation thus unifies a person's inner faculties. More further claims for conversation the power to create social harmony: bringing even "Whigs and Tories in alliance" (366), conversation is the "Soft polisher of rugged man!/ Refiner of the social plan!" (368).

In addition, More constructs her idealized portrait of British salon society at the end of the eighteenth century as managed by women. Elizabeth Vesey, to whom the poem is addressed, is celebrated as the hostess who broke the large British circle for evening parties (a circle we are all familiar with from numerous films of Jane Austen's novels) into smaller conversational groups that allow free exchange of ideas (365). Likewise, More praises "bright Montagu," Elizabeth Robinson Montagu, who "Proved that the brightest are the best," and Elizabeth Carter, who "taught the female train, / The deeply wise are never vain" (362). While More emphasizes the British women of her generation who, to her mind, rescued the salon from French dissipation, she also cites a female forerunner, Aspasia, giving classical authority to her construction of a female tradition.

More champions the British middle class as setting the standard for this ideal of conversation through education and depicts the process of acquiring such knowledge in mercantile imagery: taste is the gold standard of conversation, and conversation is "That noblest commerce of mankind." Wit, taste, and science circulate; education is the "moral mint" that stamps a person with status; and conversation is "commerce" of the mind (368). These metaphors taken from trade expose one goal of the salon and of More: the inclusion into society of the middle class, the class defined by trade. Implicitly, these metaphors indicate conversation as women's trade, equivalent to men's oversight of financial exchanges.

Thus More suggests that the stylistic conventions and language etiquette of a higher social class may be achieved by accumulating the intellectual capital of education. Class status is signaled, according to More, by allusion: those with the intellectual capital of a broad classical and modern literary education may "trace the image to its source" and use "ancient wit [to] elicit new" (370). In terms of reception, those with the intellectual capital of a broad humanist education understand the coded language of upper-class status:

> The language to th'elect alone
> Is, like the mason's mystery, known;
> In vain, th' unerring sign is made
> To him who is not of the *trade*.
>
> (370)

In contrast to this legitimate currency among the elite, More mocks "ton," the pretence of taste and wit celebrated in French salons, mere imitation of the true wit that is a sign of class status in Britain:

> Her fancy of no limits dreams
> . . . A circumnavigator she
> On Ton's illimitable sea.
>
> (365)

More enforces the requirements of femininity, as well, in her condemnation of inappropriate rhetorical behaviors for conversation. She cites "*Good sense, of faculties the best*," as the regulator of proper British conversation (362). In contrast, she attacks the seventeenth-century French salon made famous by Mme. Rambouillet (whom she names) and Madeleine de Scudéry (whom she does not name):

> O! how unlike [was British wit to] the wit that fell,
> Rambouillet! at thy quaint hotel;
> Where point, and turn, and equivoque
> Distorted every word they spoke!
> All so intolerably bright,
> Plain common sense was put to flight;
> Each speaker, so ingenious ever.
> 'Twas tiresome to be quite so clever;
> There twisted wit forgot to please,
> And mood and figure banished ease;
>
> . . . .

But forced conceit, which ever fails,
And stiff antithesis prevails;
Uneasy rivalry destroys
Society's unlabored joys:
Nature, of stilts and fetters tired,
Impatient from the wits retired.

(362–63)

Following Moliére, More mocks *précieuses ridicules* (362), blaming French salons for unwarranted attention to grammatical precision, and demonizes the French salon of Scudéry's era in order to defuse potential anxieties about women's role in the current salon in England. In place of the French ideal of play with language and easy familiarity among speakers, More proposes a British feminine ideal of "kindling sympathies" that "impart / Communion sweet from heart to heart" (369). As we shall see in our examination of More's prose conduct books for women, through this means More is helping to construct and enforce separate spheres of conversational duties for men and women as a basis for quite rigid gender roles.

Indeed, in the essay "Thoughts on Conversation" from *Essays on Various Subjects, Principally Designed for Young Ladies* (1777), More focuses her remarks on the rhetorical behaviors that define the class-gender category of "lady," while also indicating that she sees conversation as the model for all communication. More begins by condemning the idea that women are obliged to hide their intelligence and knowledge but soon qualifies that defense of women's display of education by cautioning that it is wrong for a woman to take the lead in conversation, interrupting others and introducing her own subjects (343–44). In fact, for More, women's best contribution to conversation is silence, "the silence of sparkling intelligence" that prompts witty and sensible speech in men (344).[9] In further cautioning young women to be sparing in their use of wit in society, avoiding ridicule and offense to others, More advises a young speaker to beware of "false applause, which is given, not to her merit, but to her sex"; balancing this negative view of women's weaknesses with a positive view of their strengths, More suggests "That species of knowledge, which appears to be the result of reflection rather than of science, sits peculiarly well on women" (349). Thus More offers a list of rhetorical behaviors that signal femininity and class, acknowledging the separate spheres of communication in her society, but theorizing women's communication as a means of revising those limits to gain persuasion and influence.

More develops these ideas about conversation at greater length in *Strictures on the Modern System of Female Education* (1799), a conduct book that justifies its negative admonishments by presenting itself as a critique of current educational and social practices. *Strictures* begins with a glance back at humanist defenses of women's education, arguing that one cannot deny women education yet expect appropriate behavior from them (1:ix). As in her other works, More represents conversation as the model for all discourse for women, arguing that "That kind of knowledge which is rather fitted for home consumption than foreign exportation, is peculiarly adapted to women" (2:3). Women's knowledge, in contrast to men's public performances, "come[s] out in conduct" (2:1), and especially in conversation. Thus conversation, for women, "must not be considered as a stage for the display of our talents, so much as a field for the exercise and improvement of our virtues; as a means for promoting the glory of our Creator, and the good and happiness of our fellow creatures" (2:68). Thus the gendered role for women must be facilitating what is valuable to society in general, rather than obtaining personal acclaim (2:69).

More constructs a tradition of women's rhetoric, not by citing other women as rhetoricians, but by essentializing certain powers of communication as inherently feminine. For example, More claims that, "In the faculty of speaking well, ladies have such a happy promptitude of turning their slender advantages to account, that there are many who, though they have never been taught a rule of syntax, yet, by a quick facility in profiting from the best books and the best company, hardly ever violate one; and who often exhibit an elegant and perspicuous arrangement of style, without having studied any of the laws of composition" (2:56–57). Granting women an inherent, essential knowledge of grammar and style, More nevertheless circumscribes their role by reminding women of their place—"their slender advantages." Unlike Cavendish, who uses imagery relating to feminine occupations to signify women's strength in communication, More uses such imagery to indicate women's inherent weaknesses: "[Women's] acquirements have not been worked into their minds by early instruction; what knowledge they have gotten stands out as it were above the very surface of their minds, like the *appliquée*, of the embroiderer, instead of having been interwoven with the growth of the piece, so as to have become a part of the stuff" (2:57–58). "Every kind of knowledge which appears to be the result of observation, reflection, and natural taste, sits gracefully on women" (2:57), More explains, but that which is acquired by reading and study, talents natural to men, never will be integral to women's role as speaker.

As in her poem, in this conduct book More uses the *précieuses* of Scudéry's generation as a negative example, this time to enforce the necessity of gendered behavior in conversation and social life generally: women must not become "*precieuses ridicules*, who, assuming a superiority to the sober cares which ought to occupy their sex . . . have acted as if knowledge were to confer on woman a kind of fantastic sovereignty, which should exonerate her from female duties;

whereas it is only meant the more eminently to qualify her for the performance of them" (2:3–4).[10] While More here seems to recognize gender as performance, she does so only by setting aside those unnatural and irresponsible women who fail to perform femininity. Nevertheless, More is also claiming conversation, that form of communication that in eighteenth-century society operated at the intersection of the public and private, as one of the "female duties." Conversation thus becomes, for women, "a wholesome exercise to our humility and self-denial" (2:71), for they must "bring forward to notice any talent in others, which their own modesty, or conscious inferiority, would lead them to keep back"—even if the speaker herself is superior in conversational talent in most areas (2:70). In this way, More outlines a separate spheres theory of communication for men and women, but also, through women's essential gifts, sets up a standard for the eighteenth-century British salon quite different from that of the seventeenth-century French salon, one that emphasizes knowledge and high moral purpose, rather than play.

More's rhetorical advice, however, is not directed to all women, but to women of a certain class: to "fashionable women" and "Ladies" (2:44–45). Only the "ill-educated" love to astonish (2:79), we are told, and profanity is outlawed because "It offends against *delicacy* and *good breeding*"—words surely coded for class-based behavior (2:60). More's strategy is then to correct inherent gender faults with a class-appropriate education, and she carefully delineates the stylistic conventions that regulate class behavior in the salon. The upwardly mobile female speaker in salon society must be careful to cultivate "truth, sobriety, and correctness of language" (1:222) through clear, simple, and well-defined word choice (1:216–22).[11] More further warns against "unappropriate quotations or strained analogy" that tastelessly display the young woman's reading (2:61), a natural "facility of style" that leads to exaggeration (1:222), and the use of too many epithets (1:223–24). More is not only advising women on behavior appropriate to gender and class, but is also trying to reform British society on a model combining the progressive London salon with conservative Anglican, evangelical religion, a model where women do not assume an "artificial quality" when they enter society, but maintain "true Christian good-nature . . . the soul, of which politeness is only the garb" (2:96).[12] Consequently, according to More, "fashionable women" must solicit "instructive conversation," avoid "frivolous" expression, and discourage "loose" talk (2:44–45); and "well bred women" should rescue conversation from "vapid common places, from uninteresting tattle, . . . from false sensibility, . . . and from all the factitious manners of artificial intercourse" (2:48). Indeed, part of the language etiquette of the upper classes is restraint: according to More, "true judgment will detect the infusion [of one's reading] which true modesty will not display; and even common subjects passing through a cultivated understanding, borrow a flavour of its richness" (2:62). The trick of acting as part of the upper classes for women is to signal knowledge that one does not display outright.

More's conduct book further initiates women of a certain class into the canonical knowledge necessary for performing the rhetorical behaviors of femininity. "A lady studies," More explains "not that she may qualify herself to become an orator or a pleader; not that she may learn to debate, but to act" (2:1–2). Indeed, it becomes clear that in More's system of rhetorical education, a lady studies in order to act like a lady. More denounces claims for women's rights (2:21–22) and is adamant that women need to be trained for their professions as wives, mothers, and mistresses of families (1:70). The kind of knowledge that women require is that for "home consumption" (2:3); the kind of communication allotted to women is "the common intercourse of domestic society" (2.98). While More defends education for women, she does so for conservative reasons: "The more a woman's understanding is improved, the more obviously she will discern that there can be no happiness in any society where there is a perpetual struggle for power; and the more her judgment is rectified, the more accurate views will she take of the station she herself was born to fill, and the more readily will she accommodate herself to it" (2:15).

For More, a woman's education serves its purpose when it enables her to accept her place, enacting her roles as private conversant or approving and disapproving public audience. Indeed, More's sermon on domestic happiness uses the analogy to the larger society that was traditional in English political theory, and women are relegated to the position of subordinate classes in More's description, but a class that nevertheless has social influence. In More's rhetorical advice, we can see how influential women were in the construction of a "separate spheres" theory of gender: women's right to education is underwritten by her contract "cheerfully to fulfil those humbler duties which make up the business of common life" (2:75) and to make "continual sacrifices of [her] own taste, humours, and self-love" (2:97–98).

More enthusiastically catalogues women's faults of conversation: inappropriate allusion, assertion rather than proof, competitive display, girls' hiding their intelligence, vanity. But in the process of attacking falsehood in speech, More offers a brilliant analysis of the sophistics of conversation,[13] including taking words out of context, relating half the truth, and changing the meaning of the original words by a new tone or look. Even this catalogue of conversational sophistries, however, is coded female. According to More, women must learn to avoid "absurd affectation" and "the unfounded pretensions of literary vanity" because they have only had the small amount of learning that "furnishes them with a false and low standard of intellectual excellence" (2:3). By their nature, reinforced by a shallow education, women are more liable to "arm themselves with a metaphor" than a deduction:

> Those also who do not aim so high as eloquence, are often surprised that you refuse to accept of a prejudice instead of a reason; they are apt to take up with a probability in place of a demonstration, and cheaply put you off with an assertion when you are requiring a proof. The same mode of education renders them also impatient of opposition; and if they happen to possess beauty, and to be vain of it, they may be tempted to consider that as an additional proof of their always being in the right. In this case, they will not ask you to submit your judgment to the force of their argument, so much as to the authority of their charms. (2:63–64)

Other sophistries and sins of conversation that women are prone to include "Vanity, . . . misrepresentation, resentment, disdain, levity, impatience, insincerity" (2:69), "affected humility" (2:77), "the betraying of confidence" (2:81), and a "shallow sprightliness" that manifests itself in jumping to conclusions (2:66). Misrepresentation is so important a fault that it is catalogued through a list of subcategories several pages long: "withholding part of a truth," taking details or quotations out of context (2:86–87), "ambiguity and equivocation," (2:88), "deviations from strict veracity . . . from mere levity" (2:89), and exaggerated commendation (2:90).

Still, what is bargained for in More's conservative strategy of agreeing to women's subordination is education for women, respect for women's intellect, and appreciation of the domestic realm of rhetoric. More denounces the feminine pretence of ignorance as flattering to men (2:44) and requires women to "converse up to their understandings" (2:53). She attacks the habit of teaching women from abridgements and collections of short pieces (2:58–59) and proposes "Serious study" and reading that is a "severer exercise" to correct the "spirit of trifling" and "the frivolous turn of female conversation" (1:184). More imagines a conversation between the sexes in which "the mind which is active expands and raises itself, grows larger by exercise, abler by diffusion, and richer by communication" (2:54).

At the same time, More sets careful limits to women's education, although they are the limits of self-control, not external discipline. She advises young women that no modest lady ever shows her entire intelligence (2:47) and suggests that the proper young woman contents herself with bringing "good sense, simplicity, and precision, into those common subjects, of which, after all, both the business and the conversation of mankind is in great measure made up" (2:49). To More, wit is dangerous for women (2:72), and for the proper young woman, the silence that facilitates others' conversation should suffice: "An inviolable and marked attention may shew, that a woman is pleased with a subject, and an illuminated countenance may prove that she understands it, almost as unequivocally as language itself could do; and this, with a modest question, is in many cases as large a share of the conversation as it is decorous for feminine delicacy to take" (2:67).

In *Strictures on the Modern System of Female Education*, More thus describes the qualities of the ideal Christian female speaker of the upper classes—simplicity, truth, restrained wit, and a sound education providing knowledge that is never concealed under the guise of feminine innocence, but may very well be concealed under the guise of charitable self-effacement for others' pleasure.

James Berlin has reminded us that

> Rhetorics provide a set of rules about the dispositions of discourse at a particular moment. They codify who can and cannot speak (the wealthy but not the poor, men but not women, the certified expert but not the ordinary citizen); what can and cannot be said (the wealthy must be protected from the poor, the expert always knows best); who can and cannot listen and act (men only, the propertied classes only, the certified experts only); and the very nature of the language to be used (the register of the ruling class, the parlance of technocracy, the narratives of patriarchy) ("Revisionary Histories" 116–17).

Hannah More's conduct books are just such codifications for women of the middle and upper classes in eighteenth-century England. They enable women to participate in social conversations, but they also enforce strict class and gender codes of behavior, thereby certifying the women who may speak (middle and upper classes) and under what conditions (deferring to men).[14] Still, More also theorizes an art of communication for women that is passed along through female teachers, a gendered art that theorizes the constraints of femininity as means to persuasion, and a domestic rhetoric that assumes conversation as a model for all discourse.

Lydia Sigourney: A Women's Tradition of Rhetoric

Lydia Sigourney (1791–1865) was self-educated under the supervision of the woman for whom her father worked as gardener. Sigourney opened a school in 1811 with a friend, later moving to Hartford, Connecticut, to open a school for girls. She published her first book in 1815, married a widower with three children and a hardware business in 1819, and when the business went downhill, supported her family with her writing—a historical epic about the destruction of Native Americans, novels, and over fifty volumes of verse, becoming the best-known woman poet in the United States. She was an activist—involved in abolition, schools for the deaf, and protests in support of Indians. Maria Edgeworth read and praised Sigourney's works, and Sigourney read and praised Hannah More's, establishing a transatlantic conduit of women's conduct rhetoric.[15]

Sigourney's *Letters to Young Ladies* (1833) is a conduct book of reflections in essay form on the education of girls and women: what they need to know in a very particular discourse community: middle-class United States females. Both this book and also her later *Letters to My Pupils* (1851) are designed to be used either in a school for girls or in homeschooling, for these handbooks set out a curriculum for girls, as well as encouraging them to continuously improve themselves. Sigourney is thus translating the "self-help" ideology of American masculine culture into feminine terms. In the chapter on "Manners and Accomplishments" in *Letters to Young Ladies,* for example, Sigourney not only discusses etiquette, music, dancing, and the crafts of traditional feminine education, but also reading aloud. Women must have training in reading, she argues, because it provides entertainment and pleasure for those in the family she serves—and Sigourney pushes this claim fully into the realm of formal training in elocution, with the goal to be *"clearly understood"* (114–15). A discussion of handwriting (a traditional part of women's education by the nineteenth century) leads to a discussion of letter writing as an art worthy of Cicero, but also a claim that women have a "natural" gift of "epistolary composition": "It is an appropriate attainment, for it admits the language of the heart which we understand, and rejects the elaborate and profound sciences in which we are usually deficient" (116). The chapter on "Books" in *Letters to Young Ladies* includes discussion of the value of logic and the importance of systematic training of the memory (154–60). These are considered not as valuable in themselves, or only for the character of the reader, but as part of a larger view of the rhetorical obligations on women: they need something sensible to say. Sigourney suggests grounding such study in all-women reading societies (160), where "partnership in knowledge" will lead to "great increase of intellectual wealth" (161).[16] Here the adaptation of republican ideals to women's concerns is especially clear: knowledge is quite literally capital in this nineteenth-century American system, and women may indeed own such capital and draw interest from its circulation.

As More brought a new detail and perspective to women's conduct literature in Britain, so Sigourney did in the United States. Her *Letters to Young Ladies,* first published in 1833, went through many editions. In this volume, she constructs a transatlantic women's tradition of rhetoric and, through her citations of Hannah More, the beginnings of a women's tradition of rhetorical theory. In her conduct rhetoric, Sigourney redirects More's advice on communication to young women to fit United States republican values. The volume is addressed to and concerns "The daughters of our country," the young women who will "nurture future rulers" (10). Sigourney represents them as heroic, offering "noble service to the government in the home" (14). As models for the next generation of young women, she praises the mother of the Gracchi (13), the mother of George Washington (108), Lady Jane Grey (119), and Elizabeth Rowe (191). She thus establishes an ideal of feminine, republican, Protestant, domestic rhetoric as exhibiting plain speech, simplicity, and extensive learning, but also as public service. Referring specifically to mothers who are also domestic teachers, Sigourney urges that teachers must be honored in a republic (12). She places her own work, as well, in a transatlantic women's lineage, citing Hannah More on morals and conversation (115, 192, 150), and in later editions, Mrs. Farrar on letter writing (116). She buttresses this feminine tradition by essentialism—the "natural vocation of females is to teach" in the domestic sphere (10–11), she explains, and further claims that women have "a natural" ability in letter writing (116). Thus Sigourney's theory constructs a gendered domestic rhetoric founded on an essentialist view of women's roles, but supporting a full rhetorical education for women to fit them for service to the Republic in their home duties.

Like Hannah More and other theorists before her, Sigourney views conversation as a model for all discourse. But Sigourney also sees the exchange of conversation as a model for the Republic. Women, for example, by their respect for elders and their concern to bring outsiders into the discussion, help to build a union rather than a hierarchy. Sigourney cites the example of a lady who was praised because, "when in company, she always selected the oldest persons for her first and highest attentions, afterwards, children, or those who, from humble fortune or plain appearance, were liable to be neglected, shared that regard from her, which made them happy and at ease" (107). In this republican society, rhetorical training for women allows their husbands and fathers to enjoy "daily intercourse with a cultivated mind" (159). Consequently, conversation assumes a vast importance: "So great a part of our time is devoted to conversation, and so much has it the power to influence the social feelings and relative duties, that it is important to consider how it may be rendered both agreeable and useful" (186). Women, as well as men, need a serious education in order to qualify themselves for this life-long republican responsibility: conversation "requires good talents, good education, and a good heart" (201).

Sigourney adapts the dignity that earlier conduct books assigned to the higher classes to the republican ideal of dignity for all (107). She cites Washington's mother as example, a woman "without . . . elevation," but with "courteous and dignified deportment" (109). Offering the position of "lady" to all her readers, she defines class status by behavior, not blood, suggesting, for example, that in letter writing, class is demonstrated in the details: "The lesser niceties of folding, sealing, and superscription, are not beneath the notice of a lady" (116).

While for Hannah More the cultivated memory that might create and recognize allusion to canonical texts signals class status, for Sigourney such literate memory signals adult participation in the business of the Republic: "To form a written memory," rather than to build a cultivated internal memory, "is like 'making to ourselves a graven image,'" and "it is keeping her in leading-strings, when she should walk erect, like a labourer to the field" (157). Leading strings, the ties sewn on toddlers' clothing that parents might hold to help them stand and take their first steps, were cut off when the children were able to walk on their own. Thus Sigourney depicts women not as permanently inferior, but as growing into partnership with men in society. Sigourney employs a language of codifying or regulating society to describe communication, but it is not hierarchical: interrupting someone else's speech in a conversation, for example, "is an infraction of the principle of mutual exchange, on which this department of social intercourse depends," but no speaker has the right to talk too long, for all "condemn the injustice of the monopoly" (187).

While Sigourney modifies More's hierarchy for a republican model, she certainly promotes gendered spheres, although I would argue she does so in order to garner support for women's right to education and to take an authoritative stand for women's inclusion in public-sphere discussions. Still, gendered assumptions about rhetorical behavior are omnipresent in Sigourney's *Letters to Young Ladies*: women are natural teachers, but in the domestic sphere (12); in mixed company, "the dignity of the sex" must be upheld (200). Because of their role as moral repository for society, women must use their influence on young men to good ends (198). Like More, Sigourney details a sophistics of conversation: women must avoid exaggeration, flattery (192), frivolity (199), and insincerity (193), which their sex is often accused of. Because women's focus is on a narrower world than men's, they are more likely to magnify faults of character and fall prey to character assassination (193), and the dangers of evil-speaking, slander, and gossip (193–95, 197). But, Sigourney scolds, "The wide circle of the sciences, the whole range of literature, the boundless world of books open for you sources of conversation, as innumerable as they are sublime. Subjects to which your mothers were strangers. . . . You have no need to dissect character. You have no excuse for confining your attention to the frailties of your associates" (195).

As this plea to use women's education demonstrates, Sigourney deploys this separate-spheres ideology to gain the ground of equal partner with specialized responsibilities: "In our own republic, man, invested by his Maker with the right to reign, has conceded to her, who was for ages in vassalage, equality of intercourse, participation in knowledge, dominion over his dearest and fondest hopes" (13–14). In this schema, man is public worker, but woman is his partner overseeing the heart of his domain, the home and family, his "fondest hopes." Thus, while Sigourney, like More, cautions women that they must not interrupt, it is not because women should know their place and keep silent (as in More), but because, in a republic, society requires mutual exchange and partnership (187).

Letters to My Pupils, twenty years later, is a condensed version of much of the material of Sigourney's earlier conduct book, but it is also more conservative. It seems simplified, as well, as if addressed to younger pupils, so perhaps Sigourney's ideas have not changed, but have been solidified into regulations for less sophisticated girls. In this later work, however, conversation remains the model for all discourse and the basis of social intercourse: "So much of our time is devoted to oral intercourse, that it is no slight object of education to regulate, and render it effective. It is expected of a well-trained lady, that she should converse both agreeably and usefully" (44).

As in the earlier work, the stylistic conventions that determine class status are redefined as the characteristics of the republican citizen: young ladies must observe the courtesies of refined society, but are cautioned to let such manners sit easy on them (32); good breeding does not entail subservience to those of higher class, but respect for superiors and elders (33). While one does not interrupt in "well-bred" society (46)—the discourse community Sigourney's readers are being invited to enter—conversation is built on "reciprocity" (47).

In this later volume, gendered assumptions about rhetorical behavior are accepted with less resistance by Sigourney: young women must study to be articulate, because clear enunciation is a gift to others (45); they must learn to listen, must avoid gossip, and must cultivate the "sweet tones" of social "harmony" (48). Women's conversation is a service to society: their words should "give pleasure" through "kindness and affection" (49), establishing "the sweetness of domestic intercourse" (50); their words may convey instruction because knowledge grows by imparting it and because women are natural teachers of their family (50–52). In addition, women's words soothe sorrow (52), and their silence gives energy and harmony to intercourse: "well-timed silence . . . heightens the succeeding harmony. Like shades in a picture, it illustrates the design. Like repose to the toil-worn, it gives energy for future action. (55)

But Sigourney yet employs this separate-spheres theory of communication to strategic ends: because women's conversation is important to society, they must be well educated and respected as teachers, and they must take an active part in establishing a society based on equal roles for all citizens. Nor are women always expected to be silent while men talk: Sigourney's example of the virtue of silence is a man, Ulysses (56). Thus, more than Hannah More, Sigourney advocates a mixture of compliance and resistance to separate-spheres ideology, and she markedly expanded the communication roles of the ideal young woman.

In chapters on "Conversation" in *Letters to Young Ladies*, and on "Fitly-Spoken Words" in *Letters to My Pupils*, Sigourney develops a rhetoric for the spoken discourse of domestic relations that lies outside "public" discourse, but not outside the realm of public influence. She borrows from the tradition of women's treatments of conversation the precept that women's conversation should be "agreeable" (*Ladies* 187).[17] She borrows from Hannah More the conception of women's role in conversation as the good listener (192). As in traditional conduct book literature, much of the advice on feminine conversation is couched negatively: women should not talk too much (187); women should not talk simply to display themselves (191); women should not interrupt others (*Pupils* 46); women should not flatter (*Ladies* 192); women should not dissect the characters of other women (*Ladies* 193–95; *Pupils* 48); women should avoid frivolous speech (*Ladies* 198–99). Sigourney extends these strictures, through her mainly male examples, however, to men as well as women: men, too, should not talk too much; men, too, should listen well. In sentimalizing and moralizing the art of conversation, Sigourney also universalizes the "feminine" qualities of good conversation and opens room to further extend women's social power.

Sigourney adds to previous discussions of conversation an analysis of conversations between men and women as moral uplift, a move that suggests the benefit of sentimental culture to nineteenth-century women. "The degree of influence," she warns young women, that "you possess over young men. . . . is exceedingly great." What Sigourney wants women to do with this influence is to improve everyone's character: steer men to "useful" rather than frivolous conversation and knowledge; encourage "habits of industry" and "just economy" (*Ladies* 198–99). The good conversationalist thus seems very like the good speaker of traditional rhetoric, although she is female: she possesses "disciplined intellect, to think clearly, and to clothe thought with propriety and elegance; knowledge of human nature, to suit subject to character; true politeness, to prevent giving pain; a deep sense of morality, to preserve the dignity of speech; and a spirit of benevolence to neutralize its asperities and sanctify its powers" (200–201). Cicero and Quintilian would applaud such a speaker. To these qualities, in the later *Letters to My Pupils*, Sigourney adds the republican virtues of simplicity and respect for others: a lady should lay aside "any claim to distinction" (32) and "enforce respect . . . especially to those who wear the crown of honorable age" (33). Indeed, the aim of conversation for Sigourney is very close to the aim of Ciceronian rhetoric and Horatian poetry: as speakers in the Roman tradition aim at *utile et dulce*, Sigourney's speakers "converse both agreeably and usefully" (44).

That these qualities of good conversation amount to a sentimental adaptation of traditional rhetoric to new purposes in United States and feminine society may be most clearly seen in *Letters to My Pupils*. In her summary of the nature of "fitly spoken words," Sigourney requires her pupils to use "words that give pleasure" (49), "words that convey instruction" (50), and "words that soothe sorrow" (52). "Sympathy" is the virtue of a good speaker that is most characteristic of the nineteenth century in Sigourney's canon of speakerly virtues (52–53). Sigourney thus paradoxically ends her section on "fitly spoken words" with several pages on silence: silence in the presence of the sublime, silence as comfort to the ill and the grief-stricken, silence for devotion (53–55).[18]

Sigourney thus takes the first step in establishing conduct book rhetoric as a transatlantic women's tradition that theorizes a feminine rhetoric. Her theory emphasizes women's roles in communication and offers conversation as a model for republican discourse.

Eliza Farrar: Conversational Letters

By the time Eliza Farrar (1791–1870) published *The Young Lady's Friend* (1836) and *The Youth's Letter-Writer; or, The Epistolary Art* (1840), she was writing in a transatlantic women's tradition of conduct rhetoric, offering rhetoric to women who tutored children at home or had left school for family responsibilities. Farrar borrows the outlines of her theory of feminine discourse from Hannah More and Lydia Sigourney. In her work on letter writing, Farrar also borrows the narrative textbook form from the Edgeworth family experiments with educational textbooks: *The Youth's Letter-Writer* is a didactic novel, as well as a handbook on epistolary rhetoric.[19] Even *The Young Lady's Friend* includes long passages of interpolated dialogue on points Farrar wishes to emphasize. Like More and Sigourney before her, Farrar's aim is to initiate young women (and in her work on letter writing, children of both sexes) into the codified behaviors that constituted nineteenth-century middle-class social rhetoric.

Eliza Farrar was born in Dunkirk, France to Elizabeth Barker and Benjamin Rotch, a New England Quaker family in the whaling business, who had been burned out by the British in the Revolutionary War even though, as Quakers, they did not take sides in the hostilities. In 1819, Eliza was sent to the United States to live with her grandparents in Boston; there she met and married John Farrar in 1828. Her husband, an instructor at Harvard, wrote textbooks on astronomy, electricity, optics, and mathematics. Mrs. Farrar was part of a transatlantic intellectual community that included poets Helen Maria Williams and Anna Letitia Barbauld, painter Benjamin West, Admiral Lord Nelson, Maria Edgeworth, founder of the Red Cross Florence Nightingale, astronomer and mathematician Mrs. Sommerville, Shakespeare scholar Mrs. Cowden Clark, factory reformer Harriet Martineau, asylum reformers Sir William Ellis and his wife, and orators Daniel Webster and Jacob Barker. In Boston, she socialized with transcendentalist Margaret Fuller, and several years before Margaret Fuller's Conversations (lecture-discussions with a circle of Boston women in Elizabeth Peabody's bookstore), Eliza Farrar helped Delia Bacon set up for women courses of lectures on history, first in Brattle House and then in Farrar's own parlor in Cambridge.[20] Farrar authored children's books, memoirs, and the conduct book and letter-writing textbook discussed here.[21]

In *The Young Lady's Friend*, Farrar treats the existence of a women's tradition of conduct rhetoric as a given: she cites Maria Edgeworth's "Practical Education," and her writings in general as guides to manners and morals (289, 310, 367); she further references Mrs. Hamilton's "Letters on the Elementary Principles of Education," and "L'Education progressive" by Mme. Necker de Saussure (230), as well as Anna Barbauld's "Female Studies" (422). While Farrar explicitly cites both Lydia Sigourney's *Letters to Young Ladies* (254) and *Letters to My Pupils* (300), elsewhere Farrar borrows from Hannah More (or perhaps from the general tradition founded by More) without comment. Her participation in this transatlantic women's tradition is reinforced by her references to her audience: she is even more specific about her republican female audience than is Sigourney, directly addressing "the daughters of our republic" (40). Both Sigourney and Farrar stress the moral role of women in families and society, and Farrar, like Sigourney, sentimentalizes that role, founding it on the sympathy that binds all society together (208–10, and 364). Also like Sigourney, Farrar represents women as natural teachers who form the character of their children (3). Moreover, Farrar gives explicit directions for the role of daughters in the family, who are expected to teach younger children (228–29), and provides for the continuing education of women through reading societies (259).

Near the end of *The Young Lady's Friend*, under the topic of "Mental Culture," Farrar gives advice on the desirability of continuing practice in writing and reading after leaving school. For beginners, she recommends studying essays on women's education and the classics in English and other languages (422–23). But for older students, Farrar advocates a "course of reading," suggesting that she sees such reading as an alternative to college for women: "A course of reading, undertaken for the purpose of ascertaining some particular points in history, or by way of testing some theory in morals, or for any specific object, will fructify the mind more than years of aimless reading" (423). Such reading will then substitute for the courses that the men of the family will take in college.

Writing is central to this kind of continuing education for women in Farrar's plan: "However irksome may have been the writing of themes at school," Farrar comments, "you cannot relinquish the frequent exercise of the mind in composition, without neglecting one of the most important means of mental culture" (425). Women should note words they do not know in a notebook so that they can inquire concerning their meaning later (423–24). They should take notes on sermons, lectures, conversations, and passages from books that might serve as a topic for a practice theme (the classic rhetorical exercise of the paraphrase). Farrar hopes that young women may pursue a course of reading on philosophy of language, grammar, and rhetoric: "Rhetoric may next claim your attention; and if your mind is properly awakened to the subject, you will find great entertainment, as well as instruction, in the following works: 'Blair's Lectures on Rhetoric,' 'Kames's Elements of Criticism,' and 'Campbell's Philosophy of Rhetoric' (429). Farrar encourages women to read the standard nineteenth-century texts for men's college composition and rhetoric. Thus, in her conduct book for women she is interweaving many of the same subjects and skills that are taught in the early nineteenth-century to men in college textbooks.

Like Sigourney, Farrar attaches her advice on the stylistic conventions of class-coded behavior to republican values. In this country, Farrar reminds her readers, "refinement of manners and cultivation of mind," not wealth or inherited degree, are the marks of class status (215), and she admonishes her fellow Americans to rid themselves of all "taint of aristocracy" (217), urging respect for parents and elders as the first sign of manners (203). Farrar's book demystifies this republican code of conventions signifying class status: although republican women must be adept at domestic duties, it is not polite to talk about such duties in general society (41); no lady assumes that wealth equals privilege (as in demanding the front seats at a lecture when she arrives late, 319). Republican class status is paradoxically signaled by recognizing that those who serve you are servants only in role, but fellow citizens in status. Teachers and tutors are the equals of those who hire them and require respect (213–15), Farrar explains, and "Politeness is as necessary to a happy intercourse with the inhabitants of the kitchen, as with those of the parlour," lessening "the pains of service," and checking "unbecoming familiarity."[22] In republican society, the lady must "always ask rather than command . . . service" (244). This recognition of the citizen status of servants extends to a family's obligation to offer education to the domestics who work for them (247).

While Farrar's conduct book is meant to initiate young women into the codified conventions of their class, it is also meant to reinforce, but also revise, gendered assumptions about rhetorical behavior. The ideal woman for Farrar is the nineteenth-century version of the superwoman: she is an avid reader for moral and educational purposes (and always willing to teach others what she knows); she is a skilled manager of domestic affairs; she is a scientifically trained nurse who also dispenses pastoral care to the sick; she is a talented seamstress and needlewoman; and she is an agreeable and knowledgeable partner in conversation (esp. 39–40). As a result, Farrar defends women's need for education.[23] In the opening to *The Young Lady's Friend*, Farrar observes, "the influence of mothers is greater than that of fathers in forming the characters of their children" (3), and then sketches the traditional humanist, rhetorical education that lasts a lifetime—but for women, so that they can properly influence their children.

Farrar advises that women's education is put to use in constructing family community as an intellectual circle: the ideal woman offers conversation about a range of authors in several languages while sewing (40); in the ideal family circle, the father or brother reads aloud while the women sew (122–23); and the conversational duties of the daughter include offering knowledgeable interest in politics and business to her father, sympathetic attention to her mother, and affectionate and intimate conversation to her brothers that will keep them at home and out of trouble (223). In her role as nurse, a young woman must furthermore provide spiritual communion (87). Even in her commerce in the marriage market, young women must take the high road, not the low road, using their education to represent themselves as intellectual companions, not flirts: "The less your mind dwells upon lovers and matrimony, the more agreeable and profitable will be your intercourse with gentlemen. If you regard men as intellectual beings, . . . if you talk to them, as one rational being should with another, . . . you will enjoy far more than you can by regarding them under that one aspect of possible future admirers and lovers" (287).

While Farrar generally approaches the communicative roles of young women positively, she repeats and elaborates the strictures on communication with young men that is part of the feminine tradition of conduct rhetoric. Young women must avoid vulgar familiarity with young men (293) and any kind of familiarity with male schoolmasters or music teachers (214); they must not trust flatterers (307); and they must avoid the near occasion of familiarity by eschewing sentimental talk (300). Young women must never speak loudly in public assembly because ladies are never conspicuous (323).

Under "Evening Parties," Farrar adds to previous conduct book rhetoric a discussion of women's "self-possession" (*Young Lady's Friend* 363)—a telling term signaling American individualism. In Farrar's discussion, "self-possession" turns out to be a feminine equivalent of delivery. She instructs women in the curtsy of greeting, posture and graceful movement, holding still, and advises, "Your whole deportment should give the idea that your person, your voice, and your mind are entirely under your own control" (362–63). Here one sees how mainstream rhetorical advice for men becomes radical reform when applied to women: teaching graceful posture has led Farrar to advocate control over themselves to women.

Like the other women discussed in this chapter, Farrar views conversation as the model for all discourse. She further represents conversation as the cornerstone of family harmony: in discussing conversation between siblings, for example, she comments that "Genuine politeness is a great fosterer of family love; it allays accidental irritation, by preventing harsh retorts and rude contradictions; it softens the boisterous . . . and harmonizes the whole" (225–26). Farrar devotes a whole chapter to conversation. The purposes of conversation, Farrar suggests, should be "innocent recreation" and "intellectual growth" (374). But more revealing is her comment that conversation "is the readiest way in which gifted minds exert their influence" (385). Like many female rhetorical theorists before her, Farrar realizes that power operates in private, domestic speech, as well as in public speaking.

Like her precursors in conduct book rhetoric, Farrar warns young women against "the faults of conversation" (273): telling family secrets (257); gossiping (258); meddling (261); theatrical displays of offense at minor irritations (267); "traffic in flattery" (270); using ridicule and wit at others' expense (272, 375–76); exaggeration (377–81); inappropriate irony and joking (381–83); and speaking only to display one's knowledge (421). Farrar, like More and Sigourney before her, raises listening to an art: "Great are the advantages to be reaped from listening attentively to the conversation of intelligent and cultivated people, and you should be earnest to improve every such opportunity. . . . Some persons seem to forget that mere talking is not conversing; that it requires two to make a conversation, and that each must be, in turn, a listener; but no one can be an agreeable companion who is not as willing to listen as to talk (384–86). Farrar requires both partners (not just the female partner) to listen in turn.

According to Farrar, the good conversationalist employs method, clarity, and force in speech just as the orator does. "The art of conversation" is, however, a collaborative art, enabling "a company, when a good topic was once started, to keep it up, till it had elicited the powers of the best speakers, and . . . [to] prevent its being cut short in the midst, by the introduction of something entirely foreign" (386). Farrar further adds a discussion of delivery in conversation, treating the signals of countenance and body that maintain connection between listener and speaker (387–88). Throughout her text, Farrar is at pains to detail the sources and purposes of conversation. For example, it is the hostess's duty to unobtrusively lead the conversation into intellectual pathways, so she should leave out an art album in the parlor when expecting company (260). Reading and Lyceum lectures are useful for young women because they provide topics for conversation other than gossip (258, 317–18). Farrar's examples imply that the purpose of conversation, for women as well as for men, is cultural exchange.

While Farrar briefly covers letter writing in *The Young Lady's Friend* under "Female Companionship" (279–83), she devotes a whole book to teaching this art, as well. In *The Youth's Letter-Writer; or, The Epistolary Art*, Farrar offers a manual of letter writing for use in school or home. In the fashion of reformed education championed by the British Edgeworth family and others at the end of the eighteenth century, Farrar turns her textbook into a story with morals as well as instruction: a young boy, Henry, spends several months visiting his uncle's family and so learns the value of letter writing, since it maintains the bonds and affection between him and his family while he is away. Thus education in this volume is given a motivation very much in keeping with sentimental culture. "Young men who leave their pleasant homes" the volume tells us, "consider a letter [from a family member] one of the greatest blessings" (4). In sentimental terms, a letter is a gift to loved ones (9). This moralizing of the art of writing also pushes this manual over into the category of conduct literature. The virtues that writing letters inculcate include exactness in expression (telling the truth) (142), civility and kindness (66–67), simplicity and economy (156–58), and sympathy.

In her narrative textbook, Farrar thus sentimentalizes the letter as basis for building the family as a republican institution. That Mr. Price, the instructor in letter writing, is widowed and so plays the roles of both father and mother (10) is a means of attaching sentiment to the role of family patriarch. The textbook furthermore details the familial feelings of letter writers: "The consciousness of having gratified those he best loved, and the novel pleasure of exchanging thoughts and feelings with his absent family," the textbook avers, "made Henry feel the importance of letter-writing more than he had ever done before" (30).[24] Family entertainment includes Anna's reading aloud from published letters (71–72). Letter writing is represented as reinforcing American individualism: as in conversation, letter writers develop individual styles (123, 131) and adapt their content to each different audience (158).

In *The Youth's Letter-Writer*, Henry receives lessons from his uncle on writing concisely (to get all the events on a page and not waste precious paper); punctuation and paragraphing; spelling; beginnings and endings; folding, sealing, addressing; and making pens and penmanship. The models for letter writing recommended include Cicero, Benjamin Franklin, and the poet Cowper. Still, the bulk of instruction in this story of children learning how to write letters is conducted through the children's own writing (10–11). Mr. Price, the uncle, is assisted in these lessons by his eldest daughter, Anna, and when he goes on business, she continues the lessons. Anna helps Henry with openings, finding and developing subjects, and the best way to prepare an audience for bad news.

Both Mr. Price and Anna, however, view conversation as the model for all discourse. Frequently, they remark that "The best letters are the most like the best conversation; and if you will only fancy yourself talking to your father and mother, in a limited portion of time, and therefore consider what they must most wish to hear, you may venture to write exactly what you would say to them" (6).[25] They quote Cicero's observation to that effect, as well (70). They furthermore see conversation as a method of teaching children (10) and forbid reading another's letters because it is like eavesdropping (105).

Learning to write letters is consequently a means of achieving class status in republican society: it is a social duty (vii) and expresses civility (179). Mr. Price's instructions emphasize judgment and taste as the basis of letter writing (74), the careful selection of facts and the employment of a natural order (21), the proper formality of language to someone of higher rank and elder years (110–14), appropriate topics for a school boy (85–86), and even tasteful (rather than showy) imprint designs for sealing wax (113–14). Anna tells a long tale about French and American wives waiting for news about their husbands after the Battle of Dunkirk and contrasts the French style of exaggeration or falsifying with the American virtue of always speaking the truth (141–42). Mr. Price recommends the simple title of "Mr." for most correspondence on the basis of republican customs (115).

In the book's second to last chapter, Farrar democratizes her lessons by having Anna teach the working-class boy who helps with chores on their farm how to answer a letter from his parents. At the same time that education is democratized, the class system is firmly reinforced, not only by the separation of the farm boy from the other students, but also by an increased emphasis on correctness compared to the instruction in letter writing given to the middle-class children (10–11). Farrar marks the middling professional class status of the Prices by their difference from Jem the farm hand. Fourteen-year-old Jem, who has been working on the Prices' farm since he was thirteen, could read and write, but feared writing a letter. The details of Jem's literacy suggest that he must have had the standard two-year, lower-class education consisting of one year of reading and one year of accounts and writing. Because of his background, the narrator observes, Jem has to be taught differently (153–54). Anna designs a curriculum in composition that Jem can fit into the evenings after he has finished his farm chores: he first copies manuscript samples from the other boys and book passages; then he begins keeping a daily diary about the farm; then he moves to letter writing. Once he becomes a competent writer, he needs to correct his bombastic style (154–53). Indeed, like comic servants in eighteenth- and nineteenth-century drama, Jem couldn't be convinced that simple words are best (a stylistic convention that is peculiarly an American class marker) (158). In the chapter on Jem's education, then, Farrar is unique in picturing conflicts between discourse communities as natural.[26]

Farrar's *The Youth's Letter-Writer* also replicates gendered assumptions about rhetorical behavior: the women of the two families, Anna and Maria, serve as family correspondents (3, 28). Anna practiced letter writing when she played with her dolls, we are told (19), and is now the model letter writer whom all imitate (18). Girls are neater and more painstaking in letter folding and addressing (56–57), the textbook explains, and "girls always had a knack at writing" (62). Girls furthermore incline to gender-specific faults in letter writing: Jane's letters are "scatter-witted" or disorganized (77), and Louisa's are extravagant in emotional response and theatricality (137).

Girls also excel at letter writing because of the sentimental attributes Farrar attaches to the act: girls exhibit help and sympathy in deciphering letters (149); they recognize the agreeable, ordinary behaviors that make the best topics for letters (119). Anna naturally moves into the role of teacher (23) because she is an "obliging girl" (86), but always defers to her father as authority (23–24, 92). She is a peacemaker, allaying her brother's passions so that he may write when he is calm what he will not then later regret (146–47). Moreover, Anna advises Jem simply to tell his heart if he has difficulty finding subject matter to write: "She contrived to make him speak out some of the affectionate things he had in his heart" (150).

Thus Farrar's texts exemplify the nineteenth-century development of a transatlantic women's tradition of rhetoric: she draws on More and cites Edgeworth, Sigourney, and other women; she theorizes a gendered, domestic rhetoric for women that yet is based on republican values; and, in her work on letter writing, she models a composition pedagogy based on conversation.

After the Civil War, this transatlantic women's tradition of conduct book rhetoric disintegrates into culture wars, as we can see in the quite different purposes of Florence Hartley's and Jennie Willing's contributions to conduct book rhetoric. Hartley merges the conduct book with the etiquette manual, formulating a regimented theory of women's communication; Willing radicalizes conduct book rhetoric by combining it with a defense of women's preaching.

Florence Hartley: Listening Like a Lady

Florence Hartley's *The Ladies' Book of Etiquette and Manual of Politeness: A Complete Hand Book for the Use of the Lady in Polite Society* (1870) is a much more conservative view of women's roles, education, and responsibilities than the volumes discussed in this chapter by Sigourney and Farrar, or even by More.[27] The purpose of Hartley's volume is clearly to regulate social life, and her advice to young women on communication is much more regimented and conservative than that in other conduct books by women. Almost nothing is known about Florence Hartley. Her first book, *The Ladies Handbook of Fancy and Ornamental Work*, was published in Philadelphia in 1859, and her conduct book was published in Boston eleven years later. She never married.

The content of Hartley's *The Ladies' Book* derives from the women's tradition of conduct book rhetoric, although Hartley never cites or acknowledges her predecessors. Indeed, in several places she lifts passages from Farrar without citing her source: for example, when Hartley urges, "Politeness is as necessary to a happy intercourse with the inhabitants of the kitchen, as with those of the parlour; it lessens the pains of service, promotes kind feelings on both sides, and checks unbecoming familiarity" (298), she is quoting Farrar's *The Young Ladies' Friend* word for word,[28] and Hartley is furthermore contradicting the much more hierarchical advice she gave in her chapter on managing servants. "True Christian politeness" (3) had become a cant phrase from the women's tradition by the time of Hartley, although invoked in a more purposeful way by More, Sigourney, and Farrar earlier. Like Farrar, Hartley sentimentalizes letter writing as the basis of family community (117, 139), but is actually more interested in regulating letter writing, through formal models, as a basis for an orderly society (140). While More, Sigourney, and Farrar used the requirements of women's domestic roles as a reason for claiming women's rights to education, education for Hartley is an afterthought, and she invokes the deeply conservative argument that women need education in order to be proper companions to husbands (295)—an argument that was radical when Makin used it in the seventeenth century, but by the last third of the nineteenth century, when many women were entering careers, had become quite conservative.

Hartley's view of an orderly society also enforces class distinctions, and she has no illusion that the Republic is a class-free society. While Hartley states in one section that class status is based on education (18), throughout the text, especially in the sections instructing on protocols and display for hosting dinners and balls, we can see that she actually views wealth as the basis for the capitalist republic she celebrates. While Hartley voices the opinion that education is within reach of all (178), suggesting a classless society, she frequently represents the United States as a firmly classed system: she comments that in America "the mania for traveling extends through all classes, from the highest to the lowest" (40); and she admonishes that there is "no station, high or low, where the necessity for correspondence is not felt. . . . From the President . . . to the Irish laborer, who, unable to guide a pen, writes, . . . by proxy" (116).

Elsewhere Hartley readily and approvingly cites class distinctions, especially with regard to recent Irish immigrants: she cautions that, even in dramatics, a true lady may act an Irish maid but will always remain a lady (210); she advises that one must never indulge servants, who will only feel contempt in return, since servants are "rarely grateful" and "generally incapable of appreciating those advantages which, . . . you know to be the most conducive to [their] welfare" (232–33). While she quotes "an English writer" on treating servants as "fellow-laborers," she immediately cautions, "Some attention is absolutely necessary, in this country, to the training of servants, as they come here from the lowest ranks of English and Irish peasantry, with as much idea of politeness as the pig domesticated in the cabin of the latter" (242).

Hartley offers her readers a list of regulations to follow in order to achieve middle-class status. One must never interrupt, for it is "ill-bred" (13); it is the "height of ill-breeding" to finish another's sentence (14); and only the "ill-bred" discuss disease and other unpleasant things (17). A lady will never question the veracity of a guest (11), never disparage an absent friend (15), never denigrate foreign customs while defending America (16), never take religion as a topic (17), and never insist in a matter of taste (18). Among the "well-bred," every conversation is confidential (18), and slang is never used (291). Republican customs may intrude on Hartley's class-based system, but she has an answer: while American manners require that a lady converse with fellow passengers on a boat or train, one doesn't have to recognize them as acquaintances after getting off (37). Thus Hartley is not promoting the conventions of the women's tradition of rhetoric she has inherited, but rather revising it in a decidedly conservative direction.

As with class codes, Hartley enforces the rhetorical codes that certify a gendered social system. In conversation, she instructs, professional gentlemen wish to discuss miscellaneous subjects, not business, with ladies, and ladies should never question men about their work (15). In contrast, More is also deeply conservative on gender roles, yet she questions the social system that places intellectual and business topics off-limits for women. According to Hartley, young ladies must listen politely, showing interest (16), may repeat compliments but never criticisms (18), and should facilitate the conversation of others (50, 93). "Remember," Hartley advises, "from the moment your first guest enters the parlor, you must forget yourself entirely to make the evening pleasant for others. . . . It requires much skill and tact to make a party for conversation only, go off pleasantly. . . . Where you see a couple conversing slowly and wearily, stir them up with a few sprightly words, and introduce a new person. . . . Never interrupt an earnest or apparently interesting conversation" (49–50). Young ladies must be careful, Hartley warns, never to use or indicate understanding of sentences with double meanings, for that is "indelicate" (17). According to Hartley, young ladies should never attract attention through loud talking or laughter (41, 56, 100, 168–70), should never ridicule a suitor (248), and should never use sarcasm (150). For Hartley, young women who show "self-sufficiency and confidence" are not to be endured (182). How different are Hartley's cautions from Farrar's instructions on poise and self-control! Hartley advises that ladies should employ only elevated sentiments and cultivated intellect when conversing with a gentleman (20) and should never correspond with one (124). Outspokenness is rude behavior on the part of young women, Hartley pronounces (143).

For the lady, rather than an education, Hartley emphasizes "accomplishments," built on a firm foundation of schooled education. The accomplishments expected of a lady include piano, drawing, French, German, Italian (or at least one language), dancing, needlework (178–79), and reading aloud (206–7). Hartley discusses reading in general, but as a "course of reading" essential to the role of lady (181)—reading is not fundamental, but a labor to be achieved in order to gain status as lady. Thus the purpose of education in feminine accomplishments is not to make republican citizens or mothers of these girls, but rather to allow the wealthy to exhibit class status through their well-polished women. In contrast to the love of education and the dream of freeing women's intellect in the handbooks by More, Sigourney, and Farrar, in Hartley's tome we see only an ambition for social status and a view of education as restriction. When Hartley finally lists some specific authors under specific languages, she spends as much or more time on what *not* to read as what to read (196–98), intent on protecting "ladies" from dangerous worldly knowledge. While Hartley, like Sigourney and Farrar, recommends that someone read while women sew, she indicates her view of the relative importance of sewing and reading for women when she encourages young ladies to form sewing circles rather than reading societies (216).

In Hartley's text, the most important accomplishment for a lady is conversation, for it "enlivens society" (179); conversely, conversation is also improved by society (181). Conversation is a model for all discourse, but rather than a basis of the republican family, it is a foundation for hierarchical order. Much of Hartley's advice constitutes regulating conversation in the interest of the orderly working of society: "It is a very different thing to shine and to please," Hartley cautions, and young women should aim to please, which "is in the power of all" (181). Ladies should not talk first, and their replies should be neither too short nor too long (182–83). While Hartley repeats the dicta now part of the women's tradition of conduct book rhetoric, that listening is an "art" (184), and that the basis of conversation is observation, reading, and studying (185), she reinterprets this advice on constructing community as means of regulating social intercourse: one must allow the other person to speak but one must also respond (12)—conversation is part of the social dance.

Jennie Willing: Speaking Up

In sharp contrast to Hartley's use of the etiquette manual to regulate conduct rhetoric, Jennie Willing (1834–1916) uses the defense of women's preaching to radicalize it. Born to Horatio and Harriet Ryan Fowler on January 22, 1834, in

Burford, Ontario, she left there with her family when they fled to the United States after participating in the failed rebellion of 1837. Jennie and her brother Charles grew up in Illinois, where Jennie Fowler began teaching at the age of fifteen. In 1853 she married William C. Willing, a Methodist preacher, and she became a licensed preacher herself in 1877 (but the church revoked all women's licenses in 1880). An activist throughout her life, Willing helped to organize the suffrage movement, the WCTU (Woman's Christian Temperance Union), and the Women's Home Missionary Society of the Methodist Church. She further worked in abolition and settlement causes. After receiving an honorary degree in 1872 from Evanston College for Ladies (where Frances Willard was then president), Willing was appointed a professor of English at Illinois Wesleyan University in 1874. In 1889, the Willings moved to New York, where Jennie Willing began reform work with immigrant and working-class women, the main audiences for *The Potential Woman*.[29]

In *The Potential Woman* (1881) Willing appropriates the conduct book as a genre in order to reform rather than maintain social values. The title, *The Potential Woman: A Book for Young Ladies*, places the volume squarely in the conduct genre. As a consequence, her manual includes chapters on the traditional subjects of conduct books (such as homemaking and nursing), but it expands some subjects, such as conversation (to preaching) and nursing (to scientific health and hygiene practices) and includes new topics (such as "breadwinning" and "economy"). Her volume radically argues that women should aim for college-level education (70–75), should be trained to earn their own living (109), and should build their home around books, music, religion, and familial conversation (197–99).

In *The Potential Woman*, Willing adapts the tradition of conduct book rhetoric to a broader audience and to a more radical purpose—social reform. Willing's accessible, conversational style is aimed at a broader audience than many nineteenth-century conduct books, as the chapter on "Bread-Winning" implies: this audience includes not only middle-class but also working women (although perhaps only those women who work before marriage).[30] Addressing the women who are in "the market" (25), Willing argues that even women who do not expect to may very well need to earn their livings: their men may be in prison, on the frontier, or at war (23). "Probably the majority of the young ladies who read this book, earn their own living" (88), Willing observes at the beginning of her chapter on "Bread-Winning," and later she argues that every woman *should* be able to earn her own living (109). Willing's conception of the United States as a classed society, then, is radically different from Hartley's, since Willing is addressing the class that Hartley condescendingly dismisses in her chapter on "Servants."

In Willing's *The Potential Woman*, gendered assumptions about rhetorical behavior reinforce conversation as a model for all discourse. In the chapter on "Talking," Willing begins with the radical proposition that men and women are equal, and that education in speech needs to be reformed to reflect women's status. "God respects the mental capability of women" (11), Willing reassures her audience. Willing appends to these claims an analysis of the linguistic roles of men and women that result from unjust social discrimination against women. "Women," she observes, "like all who have not had a fair field, have fallen into diplomacy, carrying by favor points that they are not permitted to win by direct argument" (112). With a perceptive, parodic analogy, she critiques the expected role of woman as good listener: "[women] say 'Yes,' and 'No,' and keep up a gentle jingle of the small bells of assent and applause, hoping to gain by pleasing what they are not allowed honorably to claim; their hearts, meanwhile, hungering for the mental food of excellent, ennobling speech" (112). This passage also calls into question the advice on conversation of the preceding fifty years of conduct book rhetoric for women. Women should *not* be sympathetic, agreeable, mainly good listeners, according to Willing, for it cramps their souls. Instead, women need to have proper vocal training so that they can speak up for themselves (40–41). In contrast to More, Willing even represents the French salon positively, as the heyday of women's conversation (114).

Willing acerbically critiques the finishing school education for elite women that depends on accomplishments, the education that Hartley had offered to young women who read her conduct book. Rejecting the role that Hartley assigns women of elite class, never to stand out, Willing complains that it is not women who have their voices heard at dinner parties (113–14). Drawing on anti-Catholic biases in the nineteenth-century United States, Willing represents continental finishing school education for young women as a Roman Catholic conspiracy to keep them ignorant and so supporting the church (55). Willing offers a list of exemplary educated women as models for her readers: Elizabeth Barrett Browning, Harriet Beecher Stowe, Mme. de Staël, and Susannah Wesley (63). Because women do nine-tenths of the public school teaching, Willing argues, they need solid education (64). Moreover, Willing ridicules the attainment of "accomplishments" (71–72), such as "the making of slippers, cushions, and the like, in a pretty tasteful fashion" as mere "knick-knacks" (84).

In her chapter on talking, then, Willing begins with the role of woman as conversationalist from the tradition of conduct book rhetoric (113), but expands that role considerably. Like Mary Astell and Hannah More before her, she argues that because they converse, women must be educated (113–14). Following Sigourney and others in the women's tradition of conduct book rhetoric, Willing argues that women must read the classics so that they have something to talk about: "Few and the best [books], wasting no time on that which is shallow and trashy,—only so can she gather material for intelligent conversation" (116). She adds to this tradition the insistence that they must be well educated (if only by self-help texts) in grammar. Reading for Willing also means writing: in the classical and renaissance tradition, Willing wants her pupils to write down their summaries, selected quotations, and comments in a commonplace book: "Going through a good book is like walking in a garden of flowers. . . . But in that garden of spices,—a noble volume,—you must use pencil and commonplace book, so as to enrich your own thought with that which was planted for that very purpose" (116).

This rhetorical program, a traditional program used to radical ends in women's education, is also Christianized: "to talk well, it is necessary that the motive prompting our speech be right and pure; and we can be sure of that only as it is cleansed by the blood of Christ" (117). "To talk well" is a translation of Quintilian's rhetorical dictum that only the good speaker speaks well. But the words are translated not only from another language, but also to another forum—conversation. In addition, Willing's Christian interpretation has roots in Augustine's famous transformation of rhetoric in *De Doctrina Christiana*: for Willing, as well as for Augustine, only the good Christian can be a good speaker. And finally, this program is also feminized: Willing combines these principles from the masculine tradition with the instructions from conduct book rhetoric for women not to gossip, but instead to speak so no one is caused pain (117–18).

Willing reminds us that "Christianity could not at once overturn social customs" (120), a rhetorical move that allows her to imply that the main purpose of Christianity was, in fact, to overturn and reform social customs, although not all at once. Willing is thus placing herself and her women who talk in an honored tradition, and she moves on to claim further privileges. Women must not only be educated, but must also teach (121). And women who are called should also preach (118–27). The last third of her chapter, in fact, merges the defense of women's preaching into her chapter on women's conversation in a conduct book. Like the women who will be discussed in chapter 3, Willing offers a reading of St. Paul's regulations against women's preaching that lifts its restrictions from most women (119–21), argues that men and women are equal, and provides a list of contemporary women preachers (122–23). Thus Willing seizes the conservative form of the conduct book and separates it from the separate-spheres theory of women's rhetoric that had been promoted in that genre. Instead, Willing fully claims for women a private and a public voice.

Conclusion

During the nineteenth century, women appropriate the conduct book for women as a means of teaching each other how to speak and write, since they are excluded in most cases from colleges.[31] Because of the separate spheres of men's and women's activities in the nineteenth century, the forms these women concentrate on at first are "feminine": reading aloud, conversation, letter writing. But they also situate rhetoric for women in the context of nineteenth-century culture, especially in their republican, sentimental, self-help rationale for women's education in rhetoric and composition. Indeed, they use this ideology to claim a larger and larger portion of the arts of rhetoric and composition, so that by midcentury, they offer advice about continuing education in reading and composition, and by the end of the century, much of the men's rhetoric, as well.

What seems most different from men's rhetoric, other than the genres treated, is the consideration of reading and writing as social activities rather than individual activities. If we compare the treatment of conversation by Sigourney or Farrar or Mary Augusta Jordan to that by the nineteenth century's Thomas De Quincey (*Selected Essays* 269–79) for example, we can see that the American women emphasize the art of collaboration (listening, acknowledging the audience, selecting topics to please the audience), while the Englishman emphasizes individual performance (competitive conflict, wit, displaying one's intellect). Women's rhetorical theory, then, is an important and neglected precursor for one motif of modern rhetoric and composition studies: the dialogic nature of even written communication.

By the mid-nineteenth century, women have established a transatlantic women's tradition of rhetoric, theorizing communication as gendered and domestic, but wielding powerful influence. They have developed an elaborate analysis of the rhetoric of conversation that includes the art of listening and the faults and fallacies of domestic interchange. Finally, they have elaborated a view of speaking and writing that sets up the collaborative nature of conversation as a model for all discourse and have suggested a composition pedagogy also based on domestic conversation. Thus, from now on when we consider the rhetoric of the nineteenth-century United States, we need to consider not just academic textbooks, but also other venues for education, especially conduct book rhetoric by women. We need to see, as nineteenth-century writers and speakers did, that conversation and letter writing are rhetorical activities just as much as public speaking and essay writing. Conduct book rhetoric by women is clearly one important step in the gradual democratization of rhetorical education that continues to the present.

3

Defenses of Women's Preaching: Dissenting Rhetoric and the Language of Women's Rights

Chapter 1, on women's humanist treatises and dialogues on women's education, traced the development of a women's theory of rhetoric based on conversation as a model of discourse. Chapter 2 examined the continuance of this model in Anglo-American conduct books by women for women that further acknowledged the gendered circumstances of communication. This chapter introduces a parallel strand of women's rhetorical theory—women's defenses of women's preaching.

From the seventeenth to the twentieth centuries, Christian women published defenses of women's preaching—until they successfully gained the right to preach. In these defenses, even though women are arguing for women's right to public speaking, they yet assume conversation as a model for preaching. Furthermore, they enter this public realm by means of arguments about their domestic roles as mother, caretaker, healer, and helper. This chapter considers works by Margaret Fell, Jarena Lee, Lucretia Mott, Ellen Stewart, Catherine Booth, and Frances Willard. Some of these women were famous and their works saw multiple editions (Fell, Mott, Booth, and Willard), and the others, while not famous, recorded, like their more famous sisters, industrious traveling preaching careers (Lee and Stewart). These six have been chosen out of the dozens of defenses of women's preaching because they span the seventeenth to nineteenth centuries and the transatlantic Protestant religious network. Moreover, they are representative of the full range of genres of defenses of preaching and epitomize a vvariety of argumentative strategies.

Through conservative strategies of biblical close reading, women's defenses of women's preaching argue for a radical goal: women's public speaking in church or religious assembly. The women who composed these treatises joined a public debate about scripture, claiming that Paul's restrictions on speaking in church applied only to some women and constructing lists of biblical women who were prophets or preachers. Moreover, these defenses experiment with forms of rhetorical argument based on collaborative authorship and dialogic authority. Interestingly, however, women's defenses of women's preaching often modified definitions of the sermon in the direction of catechism or conversation, giving up the site of the public sermon to male authority only to seize witnessing and moral persuasion as distinctly appropriate to women.[1] Still, the goal of these defenses was to confront women's differences from men as speakers in order to claim some space for women's public speaking. By the nineteenth century, English and American women who preached increasingly saw themselves as a transatlantic community, sharing arguments and defending each other across the ocean.

Why should defenses of women's preaching be included under the category of rhetorical theory? From Plato, Cicero, and Quintilian on, a central question of rhetorical theory has been "who is the ideal orator?" In Plato's *Gorgias*, for example, Socrates argues that it is not the man who uses rhetoric for power over others who is the ideal, but rather the man who controls himself for the good of the state and his own soul. In Cicero's *De Oratore*, the rhetoricians seated in a garden debate whether the orator should be a specialist in the law or an eclectic philosopher who has a broad range of knowledge. In his massive *Institutes*, Quintilian offers a lifetime program of education and requirements for the orator and counters Plato's skepticism by a definition of eloquence as the good man speaking well. Augustine carries this question into sermon rhetoric when, in the last book of *De Doctrina Christiana* [*On Christian Doctrine*], he explores the virtue required of the preacher who persuades with his life as example. The unspoken assumption throughout these debates about rhetoric, though, is that the ideal orator is also always male and usually of privileged class.[2]

Defenses of women's preaching, then, belong in the history of rhetorical theory because they also enter the debate over the question "who is the ideal orator?" In *Women's Speaking Justified* (1666), Margaret Fell argues that the ideal orator or preacher is one who is gifted by God with the light, whether the person is male or female. Jarena Lee's *The Life and Religious Experience of Jarena Lee* (1836) defines the ideal orator or preacher as one who has been called by God—and if God calls "ignorant fishermen" (37) to preach, then he also may inspire women to preach. Lucretia Mott's "Discourse on Woman" (1849) suggests that, although men and women are different in nature, those differences do not affect the realm of preaching, and so women, possessing the ability to nurture souls, may also be preachers. In the *Life of Mrs. Ellen Stewart* (1858), Stewart decries the educated preachers who speak mechanically and holds up the uneducated and inspired (including women) as ideal preachers because they are proof of God's greatness. According to Catherine Booth in *Female Ministry* (1859), from nature and God women have been endowed with the qualifications to preach, as seen by the references in scripture to women's roles in the early church; only custom denies that women, too, might be ideal orators or preachers. In *Woman in the Pulpit* (1889), Frances Willard transforms gender restrictions into the qualities of the good orator: women's empathy and moral vision make them ideal preachers.

These women developed a strand of rhetorical theory related to sermon rhetoric, redefining preaching as testimony or holy conversation. Despite their shared arguments based on biblical interpretation, women published in a wide variety of forms, from Margaret Fell's epistle to Jarena Lee's spiritual memoir, from Lucretia Mott's oration to Ellen Stewart's conversion narrative, and from Catherine Booth's refutative pamphlet to Frances Willard's collage of men's and women's testimony.[3] It is in this religious strand of rhetorical theory, rather than in secular textbooks, that the language of women's rights enters rhetorical theory, for these women base their arguments on the right to religious freedom and liberty of conscience for women.

After a review of the history of the Reformation as a model for women's claiming the right to preach, this chapter considers representative English and American defenses of women's preaching by Fell, Lee, Mott, Stewart, Booth, and Willard.

The Reformation, Gender, and the Language of Rights

The Protestant Reformation simmered for a century in heretical groups who translated scriptures into the vernaculars and criticized the wealth and excesses of Roman Catholic clergy, but in 1517 Martin Luther hung ninety-five theses on a church door in Wittenberg and began a public debate that rapidly became a religious movement. By the end of the sixteenth century in Europe, England and many German city-states, as well as individuals in Catholic countries had converted to Protestantism, and Protestantism, under the influence of Luther, Jean Calvin, Huldrych Zwingli, and others, had become the Reformation, a religious movement that countered Roman Catholic doctrines with beliefs in the importance of faith over works, communion as a symbol not a transubstantiation of Christ's body, the right of individuals to read and interpret scripture in their own tongue, and a church as an institution guided by preachers and elders, not headed by priests and popes.[4] The Reformation, taking its name from the claim to return to the ways of the early church, was to some degree powered by Renaissance humanism, since that had provided the study of ancient languages and the textual studies that then enabled the vernacular translations of the Bible (Dickens, *Reformation and Society* 85, and *English Reformation* 64).

The Reformation generated a debate on rights more than a century before the Enlightenment debates on liberties of the seventeenth century that propelled the next century of European revolutions (Witte 20). The rights debated during the Reformation most important for this chapter are liberty of conscience and so religious liberty, the right to free speech and so to assembly and to publication (especially on matters of conscience), and the right to preach (when called by God). The original discussion of liberty of conscience and so religious liberty that Calvin outlined in *Christianae Religionis Institutio* (1536) was extended by Calvin's follower, Theodore Beza (Dickens, *Reformation and Society* 137; Witte 7–12). "Liberty of conscience," advocated by many Catholic as well as Protestant resisters to government regulation of religion, is the right of an individual to hold any religious belief as long as it is not expressed or acted upon in such a way that it runs counter to governmental laws; this belief eventually generated the rights to refuse to take an oath and to refuse to become a soldier, as matters of conscience. In England, John Foxe's *Acts and Monuments* (1563), the massive compendium of histories and trial records of English Protestant martyrs, is actually also an argument for various individual legal rights, especially the rights of a defendant to a speedy trial, to know what one is accused of, and to face the accusers. Peter Wentworth and the 1570s English Parliament, agitating for further religious reform, also began debates about the right to speak on religious issues, and so eventually on religious liberty and the separation of church and state (Dean). These European and English Reformation and Counter-Reformation debates influenced Nathaniel Ward's *Body of Liberties* (1641), and so the government of Puritan Massachusetts and eventually national American concepts of rights and liberties (Witte 14–15).

We can see most clearly how these Reformation debates that at first seemed to be only about men's liberties rapidly involved women. One early example directly related to the topic of women's preaching is a letter by Argula von Grumbach (1492–c. 1554) published as a pamphlet in Germany in 1523. An early Lutheran, wife first to Friedrich von Grumbach (administrator of the town of Diefurt) and then to Count von Schlick, Argula von Grumbach was a member of the Bavarian nobility. Influenced by the spread of reformist views from Wittenberg, studying Lutheran writings and rereading the Bible in their light, corresponding with reformers Martin Luther and Andreas Osiander, she was the first European woman to defend women's right to speak out on religious issues. She did so, however, as preface and support of her critique of the theologians at the University of Ingolstadt and defense of a young man, Arsacius Seehofer, whom the Ingolstadt college divines had forced to publicly recant as a heretic.[5] Circulated first in manuscript, her letter, printed with the accusations against Seehofer as a pamphlet under the title, *The account of a*

Christian Woman of the Bavarian Nobility whose open letter, with arguments based on divine Scripture, criticizes the University of Ingolstadt for compelling a young follower of the gospel to contradict the word of God, went through fourteen editions during the autumn of 1523. The preface, written by an admiring but anonymous Lutheran man, argues that her erudition and biblical knowledge, impossible for a woman, demonstrate "that her writing comes from the spirit of God and not from the instruction of others" (Grumbach 74).[6]

Grumbach is the first woman to employ the central sequence of arguments that recur throughout four centuries of Christian women's arguments to gain the right to preach publicly.[7] First, she acknowledges Paul's restrictions on women's speaking in church, but argues that these do not apply in her case because God has called her to speak. In the past, she says, she had kept quiet because of Paul's injunction in 1 Timothy 2:12, "But I suffer not a woman to teach . . . but to be in silence." Now, however, because no one else has been brave enough, she feels constrained to speak out publicly, citing Matthew 10:32: "Whosoever therefore shall confess me before men, him will I confess also before my Father" (Grumbach 79). The verse she cites helps her to redefine preaching as general testimony by a faithful Christian in the service of truth. As a consequence, she creates a category of confession, broader than the sermon, which includes persuasion in private life, where a woman has always been able to speak. From this standpoint, she can reach out to influence events through her letter, but within the traditional boundaries of political influence of the noblewoman. Besides building a scripture-based argument against an application of Paul's restrictions to all women, Grumbach cites a dozen biblical verses about God's use of the weak to overcome the strong, claiming that heavenly inspiration teaches her what to say (79–80). In addition, she lists women who have preceded her in church politics: those to whom Jerome wrote (Blesilla, Paula, and Eustocium), and those to whom Christ preached (Mary Magdalene and the woman at the well, 79). These three biblical arguments— the reinterpretation of Paul, the list of biblical women who preach, and the appeal to spiritual equality between men and women—will be rediscovered and repeated by most subsequent female defenders of women's preaching. At the same time, Grumbach is also pushing sermon rhetoric in the direction of confession and testimony, redefining discourse as modeled on conversation rather than public speaking, and using the gendered restrictions on women's speech as a means of persuasion.

In order to defend a woman's intervention in support of the young university student, Grumbach draws on Protestant hermeneutics: only God, not human power, gives understanding; if a judgment is not based on "God's commands" in the Bible, it has no validity (80). Citing Matthew 10:32 and Luke 9:26, she reminds her readers that the Bible excludes neither man nor woman (75). "What I have written to you is no woman's chit-chat, but the word of God," she reassures her audience (both the university officials and noblemen to whom she initially wrote, as well as the friends to whom the letter was shown in manuscript and the broader audience for the printed pamphlet); "and (I write)," she proclaims, "as a member of the Christian Church, against which the gates of Hell cannot prevail" (90).

Thus, even this early in the Reformation, Grumbach has understood the necessity of a special defense of women's right to the religious rights claimed by reformers for all Christians. In *Towards a Feminist Theory of the State*, Catharine A. MacKinnon traces the definition of gender as difference in the Anglo-American legal system and concludes that, because gender is defined as difference, gender issues do not legally fall under the basic principle of fairness, under which like is treated alike. Thus, argues MacKinnon, "difference defines the state's approach," and "Sex equality becomes a contradiction in terms, . . . an oxymoron. . . . Difference is inscribed on society as the meaning of gender" (216). Because women are produced by society as different through their education but pronounced different by nature, according to MacKinnon, there are two potential responses: one can argue that women are the same as men and so deserve what men have (220), or different from men in ways that result in appropriately different treatment (219). In either case, actual equality is not possible.[8]

Women who defend women's preaching have to figure a way around this stumbling block. Do they render women no longer different so that they can preach the same as men do? Do they acknowledge women as different and argue special benefits to women's preaching? On the issue of definitions of gender, there is a range of responses in the defenses of preaching we survey in this chapter, from Fell's claim to equality because all preaching is conversational testimony to Willard's proposal that women offer special benefits by serving as mothers of the church. In all these cases, however, redefining preaching as conversation changes the standards so that women may be seen as equal participants.

Margaret Fell: Women's Dissenting Rhetoric

Although there does not appear to be any influence of the Lutheran German pamphlet of Grumbach on Margaret Fell's English Quaker defense of women's preaching over a hundred years later, their arguments are remarkably similar in strategy and style. Margaret Fell (1614–1702) is the only woman treated in this chapter generally accepted as a rhetorical theorist, and her treatise defending women's preaching is included in several anthologies.[9] An early Quaker convert, an influential "preacher," one of the three central shapers of Quaker theology (along with George Fox and William Penn), she wrote *Women's Speaking*

Justified (printed in both 1666 and 1667), while she was in prison for holding Quaker meetings at her house.[10] Her defense of women's preaching rests on basic assumptions of her dissenting religious beliefs.

Women's Speaking Justified combines the genres of private letter to friends and public pamphlet on religious controversy. The religious pamphlet was used from the beginning of the Reformation but increased in popularity in England after 1640 because of the growing civil unrest which led eventually to the English Civil War. The controversial nature of Fell's topic is apparent from her first sentence: "Whereas it hath been an objection in the minds of many, and several times hath been objected by the clergy, or ministers, and others, against women's speaking in the Church; . . . how far they wrong the Apostle's intentions in these Scriptures, we shall show clearly" (61).[11] As in much religious controversy of the period, in this pamphlet Fell claims authority by imitating biblical style,[12] weaving biblical quotations into her own language: "And such hath the Lord chosen, even *the weak things of the world, to confound the things which are mighty* . . . I. Cor. i. And God hath put no such difference between the Male and Female as men would make" (61). Through the style of her treatise, she establishes herself as speaker of an inspired text, thus invalidating the assumption that gender renders her incapable of such speech.[13] Fell's pamphlet sets out what we will see are the three basic arguments in most defenses of women's preaching: she offers a refutation of a literalist reading of Paul's injunctions against women's speaking in church; she provides lists of biblical women who preached; and she argues that all are equal in God's eyes, both men and women.

Women who wrote in the Renaissance had to overcome the biblical authority that misogynist pamphlets invoked to silence them, especially the story of Eve's transgression and Paul's command for women's silence in church.[14] Fell rewrites Eve's story so that Eve is the one who begins the process of reconciliation with God—typically through her speech: "*And the woman said, The serpent beguiled me, and I did eat.* Here the woman spoke the truth unto the Lord" (61). Consequently, argues Fell, those who speak against women's speaking are siding with the serpent. Fell's pamphlet also refutes the Pauline injunctions (in 1 Corinthians 14, and 1 Timothy 2) against women's speaking in church, arguing that the apostle means not *all* women, but only women under the Old Law, who were not yet moved by their Inner Light (64–65). To make this argument, Fell develops in detail the Protestant principle of hermeneutics that holy writ be interpreted in its historical context and according to the intent and context of the speaker (64). Fell distinguishes between women not yet educated in the use of their Inner Light, who should not speak, from those, trained to listen for God's inspiration, who may preach: "Here he [Paul] did not say that such women should not prophesy as had the Revelation and Spirit of God poured upon them, but their women that were under the Law, and in the transgression, and were in strife, confusion, and malice in their speaking" (64).[15]

Fell also recuperates the Bible as an ally in the cause of women's preaching, constructing a tradition of women preachers that includes Mary Magdalene, Mary the mother of James, Aquila and Priscilla, Hannah, Queen Esther, Deborah, and others (63–64, 66–68). Fell is able to create a scriptural tradition of women's preaching because of her redefinition of preaching as conversation, prophecy, and advice, rather than public lecture. In the newly constructed Quaker institution of the Meeting, preaching is reconceived as sharing rather than lecturing, and in private rather than in public space.[16] Fell, however, sees yet a further connection to women's lived experience: most of her biblical examples concern what later Protestants call "witnessing," women talking to their friends and families about the spiritual events in their lives. My favorite from Fell's examples is Elizabeth's brief greeting to her pregnant cousin Mary (the mother of Jesus), which Fell renames "Elizabeth's sermon concerning Christ" (68). Fell's contribution to sermon rhetoric, then, is her redefinition of the category of preaching: using the Bible as authority for women's preaching, she must also redefine preaching to include advice and comfort spoken privately. Like the women of the previous chapter who modeled all discourse on conversation, the women who write defenses of women's preaching almost uniformly model preaching on more conversational forms of religious discourse—confession, testimony, or catechism.[17]

Fell thus addresses the problem of gender as difference in the same way that she counters Paul's restrictions on women: she argues that, in this respect, women are not different from men—God has given them equal potential as preachers, since both men and women may be inspired by Inner Light and since both men and women have experience in conversation and so may witness.

Despite Fell's redefinition of preaching as "private" conversation, her claim for women's preaching is not a conservative move reinforcing gendered roles, because both men and women among Quakers adopted this new form of propagating the Word. Thus, according to Fell, in the "True Church, sons and daughters do prophesy, women labor in the Gospel," and "the true speakers of men and women" "shall have the victory . . . over the false speaker" (69–70). Fell's gentry standing encouraged her to take her idea of conversational preaching as far as the king, to whom she frequently addressed letters and visits to request tolerant treatment of Quakers. Such a public use of this "private" form brings into question the whole notion of public and private gendered spheres.

Like Grumbach before her, Fell is anticlerical and antiestablishment. In a postscript (67–70), she points out that the very Anglican priests who deny women the right to speak get some of their best sermon material from women, from Elizabeth, Ruth, Esther, and Judith in the Bible. These "blind priests" "make a trade of women's words to get money by . . . and still cry out, 'Women must not speak. Women must be silent'" (69). Fell asserts that the custom of women's silence in church originates not in the Bible, but in the darkness of the years in apostasy under the Roman Catholic Church (66, 70).[18] It is not contemporary Quaker men who wish to prohibit women from their rightful voice in the church; it is the "False Church" (70). Conflating the practices of Catholic and Anglican priests, Fell tries to win the English lay audience she addresses away from the religious authorities who stand most adamantly against women's preaching and the Quaker sect in general.

Finally, Fell is the first woman to use the language of rights for women's preaching: *"the Jerusalem which is free, who is the Mother of us all, . . . the New Jerusalem . . . brings freedom and liberty, and perfect Redemption to her whole seed; and this is that woman and Image of the eternal God, that God has owned, and does own, and will own for evermore."* This passage, in context, signifies not only freedom from sin for both men and women, but also, more simply, freedom for both men and women to speak, so that the light of a purified Christianity "will shine throughout the whole earth" (66).[19]

Thus Grumbach and Fell, although almost certainly no direct influence on the women who will later rediscover these same arguments,[20] develop supports for women's preaching based on the Protestant Reformation emphasis on the spiritual equality of men and women, the limitation of Paul's restrictions on women to women who are not saved, and lists of biblical women who spoke publicly in support of their religion. In addition, Fell redefines preaching as conversation and proposes women's preaching as a God-given "liberty" or privilege. From the beginning of women's defenses of women's preaching, conversation as a model for all discourse, a conservative method of arguing based on the Bible, and a radical discourse of rights are intertwined.

Jarena Lee: Spiritual Conversation

A defense of women's preaching by a woman is not again published until the nineteenth century, and then there are many—consequently, this study is representative, not exhaustive.[21] We begin with Jarena Lee's 1836 *The Life and Religious Experience of Jarena Lee*, which records both her process of Christian conversion and also her call to preach. The autobiography employs the generic conventions of the conversion narrative and spiritual memoir as rhetorical arguments in favor of women's preaching and offers conversation as a model for the discourse of preaching.

An African American, Jarena Lee (1783–1850?) was born in Cape May, New Jersey, to parents who were free but poor, and so she was put out to service at the age of seven. She left service and moved to Philadelphia when she came of age. She was converted to Methodism in 1804 by Richard Allen, who later became bishop of the African Methodist Episcopal Church. She married Joseph Lee in 1811, a pastor for a small church in Snow Hill. After the death of her husband, in 1818 Lee returned to Philadelphia with her two small children and asked Bishop Allen for permission to preach; he discouraged her and told her that women might exhort but not preach in her sect. In 1819, she interrupted a minister's sermon to deliver her own message, and Bishop Allen, in the audience, at that time encouraged her, although she seems never to have been licensed to do more than exhort. She preached all over the Northeast and Midwest, from Baltimore, Maryland, to Dayton, Ohio, to Rochester, New York. In 1840 she joined the American Antislavery Society. She began printing her autobiography at her own expense in 1836 and enlarged and reprinted it in subsequent editions in 1839 and 1849.[22]

Lee makes her argument for women's preaching in two chapters of her autobiography entitled "My Call to Preach the Gospel," and "The Subject of My Call to Preach Renewed." However, her conversion narrative is throughout a defense of women's preaching because her call to conversion is also a call to preach (32), and so her treatise is also a kind of hybrid form: conversion narrative, spiritual memoir, and treatise using personal experience as evidence for a defense of women's preaching.[23] Lee compares herself to Paul, the great preacher and writer of the early church: her conversion was a sudden dramatic flash of light, like Paul's (34); her first mission to preach, like Paul's, was the most difficult because it was the town where she had lived before conversion (46).

Lee uses the conventions of the conversion narrative and spiritual autobiography to support her argument for women's preaching.[24] The conventional line of the conversion narrative, that the sinner feels terrible anguish until turned toward faith in God and salvation, becomes a specific example of God's requirement that women as well as men are called to preach. Lee hears a voice calling her to preach and sees a vision of a pulpit (the symbol of male episcopal authority) (35). When she tries to resist the call to preach, Lee feels anguish, but when she follows the call, she experiences peace (36). As she tells this story, she stops to critique the A.M.E. Church and all institutions that put earthly customs before spiritual duty: "O how careful ought we to be, lest through our by-laws of church government and discipline, we bring into disrepute even the word of life. For as unseemly as it may appear now-a-days for a woman to preach, it should be remembered that nothing is impossible with God" (36). While Lee offers this critique of the church as an institution, her treatise avoids the language of women's rights. However, her editor, William Andrews, hypothesizes her involvement in the A.M.E. women's group who demanded to be assigned pastorates at the 1850 A.M.E. Philadelphia conference (6); at the 1852 General Conference, a proposal to license women to preach was defeated by a large majority of the all-male delegates (7).

In her first discussion of the call to preach, Lee briefly covers two of the basic arguments that we have seen before: since Christ died for women as well as men, women are equal to men and may preach (36); rather than a long list, she advances Mary as the first preacher after Christ's death, since she brought word of his resurrection to the other apostles (36). Lee ignores Paul's injunctions against women's speaking in church.

Lee offers other arguments, however. If God can provide the inspiration for ignorant fishermen to preach (an allusion to the original apostles), she maintains, he can surely do so for women, as well (37). Adapting a convention of the conversion narrative, she describes herself as ill and despairing, yet kept from dying by the call to preach (40). She indicates her knowledge of sermon rhetoric in her description of Rev. Richard Williams' preaching: "He entered the pulpit, gave out the hymn, which was sung, and then addressed the throne of grace; took his text, passed through the exordium, and commenced to expound it" (44). She uses the technical terms of sermon composition—*text, exordium, expound*. But it is God who disposes her to preach, and she interrupts Williams: "he seemed to have lost the spirit; when in the same instant, I sprang, as by an altogether supernatural impulse, to my feet, when I was aided from above to give an exhortation on the very text which my brother Williams had taken" (44).

Elsewhere Lee tells us that she experiences the call to preach as "a fire shut up in my bones" (42), a quotation from Jeremiah 20:9: "But *his word* was in mine heart as a burning fire shut up in my bones."[25] The close similarity of this passage to a description in Nancy Towle's spiritual narrative suggests that Lee may herself have read Towle's *Vicissitudes* (1832), published the year before Lee started editing her journal for publication. Thus Lee may have seen herself in a tradition of women preachers defending their right to preach.

As in the description of interrupting Williams's preaching, Lee frequently employs the narrative strategy of anecdote as refutation to those who deny women the right to preach. Although Bishop Allen at first refuses Lee's plea for a license to lead prayer meetings, after he later hears her impassioned discussion interrupting a male preacher's sermon, he supports her call (44–45). When Lee leaves her sick son with a neighbor in order to preach thirty miles away, and a second time for an extended time with her mother, she presents her action as evidence of the holy nature of her call, not of her failure as a mother (45–46). Dramatically, in this pre–Civil War memoir, she tells the story of a man, a slaveholder, who comes only to heckle her, who tells everyone that colored people have no souls (46); so moved by her preaching is he that he begins to treat his slaves better and attends many of her prayer meetings (47). Thus Lee addresses difference in her defense of women's preaching along lines of both gender and race. For Lee, God's call erases these differences, not in the sense of making the woman like a man or the black like the white, but subsuming all differences in the larger categories of Christian and called-to-preach.

Like Fell, Lee defines preaching more as conversation than as public speaking. Despite her vision of a pulpit, Bishop Allen licensed Lee for prayer meetings rather than preaching, and Lee exhorted and held prayer meetings in a "private house" (42). The success of her conversational method is attested in an anecdote about a deathbed conversion, where "a very wicked young man," who "had generally attended our meetings . . . to disturb and to ridicule our denomination" (42), was brought to salvation at the last dramatic moment through Lee's exhortations and prayers:

> his sister came for me in haste, saying, that she believed her brother was then dying, and that he had *sent* for me. . . . While calling on the name of the Lord, to have mercy on his soul, and to grant him repentance unto life, it came suddenly into my mind never to rise from my knees until God should hear prayer in his behalf, until he should convert and save his soul. . . . There appeared to my view, though my eyes were closed, the Saviour in full stature, nailed to the cross, just over the head of the young man. . . . his eyes were gazing with ecstasy upward; over his face there was an expression of joy; his lips were clothed in a sweet and holy smile; but no sound came from his tongue; it was heard in its stillness of bliss, full of hope and immortality. Thus, as I held him by the hand his happy and purified soul soared away, without a sign or a groan, to its eternal rest. (43–44)

Thus Lee's call to preach is attested to by this scene of private prayer and personal, conversational exhortation that yet shows God's power conveyed through her.

Lee's treatise, therefore, adapts the conversion narrative itself as an argument in defense of women's preaching (since if God calls, women may not refuse) and sidesteps the problem of difference by claiming equality in God's eyes; and it eases the transition to women's preaching by defining preaching as conversation, exhortation, and prayer more than public oratory.

Lucretia Mott: Preaching as a Woman's Right

While it was important to note Jarena Lee's inventive use of the conversion narrative as argument in defense of women's preaching, we can see more clearly the connection between the language of women's rights and the form of the defense of women's preaching in Lucretia Mott's 1849 "Discourse on Woman." Mott was born Lucretia Coffin in 1793 and had six siblings. She grew up in Nantucket and

Boston and was educated at a Quaker boarding school, Nine Partners, in New York State. There she met and married James Mott and had six children by the time she was thirty-five. From 1830 on, she was a close friend of the abolitionist William Lloyd Garrison. Indeed, her husband transformed his import business from cotton to wool to avoid supporting slavery and was a member of the first American Anti-Slavery convention. Soon after, Mott founded the Philadelphia Female Anti-Slavery Society. In 1840 she met Elizabeth Cady Stanton at the World Anti-Slavery Meeting held in London, and, although neither was admitted to the meeting, the two became life-long friends as they watched from the balcony. They worked together most famously in 1848, at the Seneca Falls convention on women's rights.[26]

Mott begins her 1849 oration, "Discourse on Woman" (printed in 1850 in Philadelphia, where it was delivered) with the three central arguments of the tradition of defenses of women's preaching. Because men and women are equal in the eyes of God, she argues, they should be equal in the matter of right to preach (144–45). She lists biblical women from the Old Testament who were esteemed for their leadership—Miriam, Deborah, and Huldah (145)—and she lists women from the New Testament who were prophets—Anna, Philip's daughters, Priscilla, and Phebe (146). In a significant critique of biblical translation, she points out that the word applied to Phebe and translated "servant" is translated as "minister" when referencing men. Besides the arguments from equality and examples of biblical women's preaching, she also argues for an antiliteralist reading of Paul (146–47). Elsewhere Mott castigates the misuse of the Bible to support war, slavery, and the oppression of women (125). To these conventional arguments in defense of women's preaching, she adds an appeal to the practices of the early church: for the first two to three hundred years of Christianity, female elders and ministers were common (147); to the nineteenth-century audience, this argument was also an appeal to the principles of the Protestant Reformation, against the corruptions of the Roman Catholic priesthood. Like many other women's defenses of women's preaching, Mott's "Discourse on Woman" inveighs against ecclesiastical power and "hireling priesthood" (124, 131).

However, many historians might question my inclusion of Mott's oration in the genre of defenses of women's preaching.[27] Is "Discourse on Woman" a sermon defending women's preaching or an oration urging women's rights? It is both, I argue, and it consequently demonstrates the growth of a discourse of women's rights out of the genre of defense of women's preaching. As before, when women searched for a genre to hold the new ideas defending women's preaching and settled for the letter or the essay or the conversion narrative, so now Mott adapts the genre defending women's preaching to the new goal of urging women's rights.

Mott argues that the present sphere is *not* woman's ordained sphere, but one that restricts her from effectively doing good (147–48). We should be prepared, she argues, "to meet the assertion, so often made, that woman is stepping out of her appropriate sphere":

> This age is notable for its works of mercy and benevolence—for the efforts that are made to reform the inebriate and the degraded, to relieve the oppressed and the suffering. Women as well as men are interested in these works of justice and mercy. They are efficient co-workers, their talents are called into [prolific]²⁸ exercise, their labors are effective in each department of reform. The blessing to the merciful, to the peacemaker is equal to man and to woman. It is greatly to be deplored, now that she is increasingly qualified for usefulness, that any view should be presented, calculated to retard her labors of love. (147)

Mott further explains that, although men and women are different by nature, there is no need to exaggerate those differences into effeminacy in women. Instead, Mott would have women exercise and achieve strength (148–49). As she had listed biblical women who were prophets, Mott lists great female reformers who are still womanly—Elizabeth Fry, Dorothea Dix, and Grace Darling (151–52). Women, like men, she attests, should receive public recognition for intellectual accomplishments and scientific discoveries. Citing conservative men who desire uneducated women because opposites attract, she reverses the commonplace and posits a true union between men and women based on similarities, especially of education (153). Testing Mott's solution to the problem of women's equality against MacKinnon's theory, we see that Mott redefines the relationship between the sexes as one of similarity, not difference.

Explaining that contemporary women have only the right of petition,²⁹ Mott pleads for the extension of all civil liberties to women, and as rights, not privileges. Women should not have to promise obedience in marriage (155), should not be deprived of rights and property by marriage (157), should not lose the property they helped maintain at death of a husband (158–59), and should not be paid less than men for teaching (160–61). Women should have all political rights, including suffrage, the right to appropriate and useful employment (159–60), and the right to education equal to that of males, including college (160–61).

However, Mott's "Discourse" also makes an argument for women's preaching by its initial deployment of the conventional arguments of equality, examples of biblical women, and reinterpretation of Paul. Moreover, throughout the speech, while there is emphasis on women's rights, there is an equal emphasis on a religious career for women. Mott describes how, after the heady years of education, women's use of their abilities sink: quoting Catherine Beecher, she urges that women should use their talents not to crochet but to nurture souls: "We shall not so often see her, seeking the light device to embroider on muslin and lace (and I would add, the fashionable crochet work of the present day); 'but we shall see her, with the delighted glow of benevolence, seeking for immortal minds, whereon she may fasten durable and holy impressions, that shall never be effaced or wear away'" (149–50). In addition, Mott explicitly defends women's right to be preachers: woman's "exclusion from the pulpit or ministry—her duties marked out for her by her equal brother man, subject to creeds, rules, and disciplines made for her by him—this is unworthy her true dignity" (154).

Finally, like the women we have already discussed, and in keeping with her Quaker tradition, Mott views her discourse as modeled on conversation, not public speaking: "I have no prepared address to deliver you, being unaccustomed to speak in that way; but I felt a wish to offer some views for your consideration, . . which may lead to such reflection and discussion as will present the subject [of women] in a true light" (144). Thus Mott continues the tradition of women's defenses of women's preaching, not only in the list of arguments called on, but also in her reliance on conversation as a model for preaching, and her intermingling of a discourse of rights with a conservative reliance on biblical evidence.

Ellen Stewart: The Defense as a Hybrid Genre

While Lucretia Mott's "Discourse" is an oration on women's rights informed by the tradition of defenses of women's preaching, Ellen Stewart's 1858 conversion narrative and spiritual autobiography, *Life of Mrs. Ellen Stewart*, with accompanying epistolary debate, modifies a traditional form of the defense of women's preaching by a new and energetic political discourse of women's rights. In fact, Stewart's book reiterates her argument in several forms, creating a hybrid text of several different genres: conversion narrative/spiritual autobiography, sermonic treatise, biography of her husband, and epistolary exchange reprinted from a church magazine. Moreover, Stewart is aware of writing in a tradition and cites Mary Bosanquet's letter to John Wesley on women's preaching (139).

Ellen Brown was born July 15, 1792, to Hosea and Hannah Brown in Middlefield, New York, the oldest of fourteen children. She had only ten months of schooling, but her aunts tutored her at home with spelling and vocabulary games, while her mother taught the family the Bible and encouraged them to read and memorize verses. Ellen supported herself in service until she was twenty and then taught school in Seneca, New York, and in 1813 in Canandagua, New York. There she married Reuben Hickox, member of a Methodist Episcopal church, and they had seven children. While her husband at first decried her conversion to a different sect, he eventually supported his wife's preaching; but later he decided, without consulting her, to sell their farm and move them to

Ohio. After the deaths of her husband and the wife of a nearby minister, Cyrus Stewart (and the passing of a decent interval), Ellen married Stewart. Raised a Quaker, she had already become a Methodist, but after trying first Episcopal and then Reformed Methodist sects, she ends the book as a nonsectarian Christian.[30]

The bulk of the *Life of Mrs. Ellen Stewart* is a spiritual autobiography and conversion narrative, but even this narrative is interrupted by interpolations of letters, poems, and summaries of sermons. The biography is followed by a chapter that is a condensed treatise defending women's preaching but modulating into a discourse on women's rights in general, a chapter biography of Stewart's deceased second husband, and a chapter biography of her first mother-in-law, Caroline Hickox. In an appendix, Stewart reprints two epistolary debates that she conducted with men in a religious journal, the *Church Advocate*. In each genre melded together in this hybrid text, Stewart repeats her defense of women's preaching.

In the first long section, Stewart offers a narration of her life within the conventions of the conversion narrative and spiritual autobiography. Like the other women we have studied in this chapter, Stewart repeats the three basic scriptural arguments: men and women are equal in God's eyes (18, 101); the many women in the Bible who were recorded as preaching, praying, or prophesying indicate that women's preaching is legitimate (101); and a literalist reading of Paul's injunctions for women to be silent in church is inconsistent with many other places in the Bible where women's preaching is praised (17–19). Least emphasized is the list of biblical women in the conversion narrative, replaced by repeated scenes where Stewart herself is called. Especially interesting is Stewart's treatment of Paul. Instead of the deferential and careful resituating of Paul's words in an historical context, Stewart demands, "if the same Holy Ghost teaches the same gospel to females, and teaches them that they must preach it, who is Paul, or any other man, that they shall say they shall not?" (18).

Besides these foundational arguments in defense of women's preaching, Stewart appeals to a nostalgia for the early past of Methodism, patterned on the general nostalgia of Protestant sects for the early church. In her description of former Methodist prayer meetings, for example, she redefines preaching as communal conversation: "The preachers delighted to mingle with the people in their social prayer meetings, and all were like little children together. . . . [with] two or three exhortations follow[ing] each sermon" (23). Since sermons were generally by men, but exhortations frequently by women,[31] Stewart is looking back to earlier Methodism as a time when women had a more equitable role in the church. Connected to this utopian ideal of early Methodism is an anticlericalism that takes the form of a contempt for theology and seminaries: too much education in the male preachers causes stereotyped, routine preaching (47) and a loss of spirit: "they, who once thundered in the pulpit against a man-made and man-paid ministry, got up their Colleges and Seminaries of learning, that theirs might be as learned as the rest, and required a certain course of theological reading, of each traveling preacher. . . . in proportion as they rose in outward prosperity, they rose in a sense of self importance or denominational pride" (45). Under this argument about educated versus inspired preaching lies a second argument about gender: women were denied seminary training, and so even inspired women were gradually forced out of preaching. As a result, Stewart explains, "the preaching was not so powerful, and the people so warm-hearted as once they were, nor . . . our meetings were not so refreshing as when we used to meet in the lowly log cabin in the woods" (45–46).

Like many of the other women's defenses we have examined, Stewart's book deploys the conventions of the conversion narrative as a form of argument for women's right to preach: when God calls her to preach and she refuses, she experiences spiritual and physical malaise until she does God's will. Her life is told in the form of a spiritual "pilgrimage" (3): providence guided her even before her conversion, protecting her from an uncle who threatens sexual molestation (5–6); she wrestled in a spiritual struggle until she was "born again" (9–10); God's spirit called her to speak, but she held back, mistakenly adhering to her social duty as a modest female (12–13, 15–16); one pastor encouraged her (14), sending a mixed message, though, when he mocks another woman's speaking (17). Her conversion (17), her sanctification (32), her backsliding and renewed faith (35) are narrated not only as a struggle for salvation, but also as a struggle for the right to preach. For example, Stewart experiences her call to conversion as also a call to preach:

> Then did I hear "the still small voice" say, I will that you speak in My name; my flesh cried, anything but this. I thought, will it not answer as well to pray? But a feeling of horror passed over me; and I felt that under present circumstances, it would be mocking my Creator to his face. I remembered the wormwood and the gall, and that to obey was better than sacrifice; besides I had strong fears, if not obeyed this time, the gentle spirit would take its everlasting flight. Therefore I yielded and rose to my feet and began to speak. But now what a change, what a transition did I experience; light beamed upon me; love to God, for His great love to man, sprang up in my heart; sweet fellowship with His people, and melting compassion for perishing sinners; all these were felt while speaking with ease of utterance. (17)

Stewart casts her defense of women's preaching as God's call to her as an individual evangelist to preach and so argues for warmhearted, inspired preaching rather than educated, uninspired preaching. She reinforces her argument with biblical allusion, to Deuteronomy 29:18, which represents Israelites who turn from Jehovah to pagan gods as "a root that beareth gall and wormwood," and to 1 Samuel 15:22, which urges "to obey is better than sacrifice."

Much of this struggle is acted out as contention with her husband, and she feels "travel [travail] of soul" like the "pangs of labor" (60). However, God guides her, and despite even her children's antagonism to a preaching mother, she holds Sunday School in the summers of 1848 and 1849 (120–21).

More than any other of the authors of conversion narratives, Stewart offers an explicit analysis of the misogyny that denies her liberty of conscience and freedom to speak. It is Satan who attacks through the social stigma attached to women's preaching, she argues: "a female must encounter, on all sides, an inveterate prejudice, founded on a misconstruction of the scriptures. . . . I was ignorant and unlearned; and in assuming the awful responsibility of a public teacher, I feared I should teach wrong things, and mislead my fellow creatures. . . . Satan did not fail to attack me at every vulnerable point, telling me I had disgraced myself beyond recovery, and that all my husband's relatives and my own, were ashamed of me" (63–65). When her husband begins to support her preaching, but she is heckled by antagonistic men, she responds with a sermon that is also a defense of women's preaching (80–81). Stewart employs anecdotes for emotional appeal, telling the story, for example, of a woman driven insane because she was not allowed to preach (102).

Stewart's spiritual autobiography underlines this basic argument from generic conventions of the conversion narrative through adept use of biblical language: for example, she justifies writing her story by her purpose, to show what she has learned under "the chastising rod" of her suffering, so that others also will avoid being "cast out as a reprobate sinner, and as salt without savor, . . . trodden under foot" (4).[32]

But besides scriptural language, Stewart also borrows from the midcentury discourse of women's rights, for a second purpose of her story is to mark "the progress of free principles, within the last thirty years" (3). "Whatever He has capacitated females to do," Stewart argues, "they have a right to do, under the guidance and restriction of His word and Spirit" (18). Stewart extends this scriptural argument for the rights of women not only to preaching, but also to general human rights, such as property rights (96). She also broadens her defense of women's right to preach to other social rights: she holds mixed-race prayer meetings (84), joins the temperance movement (89–90), and leaves the Reformed Methodists when they unite with the proslavery Protestant Methodists (98).

Stewart ends the story of her life in 1853 but does not end her book. The next chapter is a sermonic treatise very like Catherine Booth's (as we shall see), arguing in defense of women's preaching, and rehearsing the traditional arguments. She argues from Old Testament citations that men and women were created equal, that, like men, women have power for good and evil (as exemplified in Deborah and Jezebel), and that both men and women are shown to prophesy (128, 130). She lists examples of women's preaching: Mary and Elizabeth in the gospels (131), and the women whom Paul praises—Phebe, Philip's daughters, Tryphena, Tryphosa, Priscilla, and Aquila. "Now, O great apostle!," she apostrophizes, "if you had only told us what those women did—what their labor was—how many cavils it might have silenced!" (134). Borrowing from arguments in favor of women's education, she further argues that we must elevate women and allow them to assume spiritual leadership because women must teach their sons (144).[33]

Stewart's brief treatise defending women's preaching also covers the traditional refutation of literalist readings of Paul's dicta against women's speaking in church. Stewart begins with Paul's positive commentary on women's participation in early Christianity (132). But she also adds a new approach to the revision of Paul, arguing that there has been general human progress since Paul's time: "Paul, though a good Christian and a great apostle, was but a man, and when not particularly inspired, wrote according to his own judgment, with the light of his age, which, admitting human progress, must have been far behind that of the present" (133). Stewart then points out the inconsistencies in Paul's pronouncements on women: Paul, for example, exculpates Adam but blames Eve, and much evil treatment of wives is founded on Paul's advice on women's subjection and subordination to their husband, when it is to God, not to men, that all are subject (133–37). Like many of the women we have previously examined, Stewart ties anticlerical sentiments to her revision of Paul, arguing that viewing the pulpit as sacred is a carryover from popery (132).

From the traditional arguments of defenses of women's preaching, modified by a new sense of the human fallibility of the scriptures, Stewart moves into a discourse of women's rights. Beginning with an argument for liberty of conscience (129, 137–38), she then mounts an appeal for women's "liberty, equality, and individuality" and "a mighty revolution" that will take humanity "far above and beyond the bigoted superstitions of our early education" (138). Like Mott, Stewart links to women's right to preach the further privileges of suffrage, property rights, and rights to children (139–41).[34]

The next, shorter section includes biographies of her second husband and her first mother-in-law. In the biography of her husband, Stewart cites her partner's authority in support of her cause, explaining that he had written a will because he thought the laws on widows' property rights unjust (146), and that he had urged her to write to the *Church Advocate* on the "religious liberty of females" (147). Such a gesture as part of her overall defense of women's preaching is strangely inconsistent—she draws on her husband's authority, but throughout in her argument for women's right to preach she is dissenting from men's authority. Stewart further presents the life of Carolina Case Hickox, her first husband's mother, as an example of an early female preacher (161) who was persecuted for her religion, forced out of Simsbury, Connecticut because she denied the Presbyterian doctrine of election (158).

Stewart repeats her arguments in defense of women's preaching in one more form, in two sets of epistolary exchanges, one with William Johnston, one with Rev. J. F. W. Sr., reprinted from the *Church Advocate* in her final section of the book, an appendix of her letters to journals and published sermons. In the epistolary exchange, she again reiterates the foundational arguments in defense of women's preaching. Stewart provokes the letters from the men, demanding a response to two letters she published in favor of women's preaching. When the men respond in opposition, citing Paul, she lists the women of the early church whom Paul cites (168): Anna, the woman of Samaria, and Priscilla (174–75); Deborah, Huldah, and Miriam (182); Tryphena, Tryphosa, Persis, Phebe, Priscilla, Mary, and the women visited at Pentecost with the spirit (183, 188). In answer to Johnston's claim that there is no scriptural precedent for commissioned female preachers, Stewart argues from the dictionary meaning of *evangelist* to a definition of *preacher* that would include the biblical Anna and the woman of Samaria (175). And in answer to the claim that Jesus only called male disciples and that no bishops or elders or deacons of the early church were female, she argues not all male preachers were called to be bishops or deacons or elders, either (183), and that "man" includes "woman" in biblical language (181). Thus Stewart is deploying gender limitation (the sexist nature of language) as a means of persuasion.

Her argument for the equality of women to men, however, is based not on scripture but on natural rights. In answer to J. F. W.'s proclamation of separate spheres for women, Stewart responds that women are equal to men except in strength (186) and calls on the republican principle, that all are free and equal (187). In response to William Johnston's appeal to Paul's injunctions, Stewart cites the inconsistencies in Paul's representation of women in the early church (175); in response to J. F. W.'s appeal to Paul's strictures, however, Stewart critiques her correspondent's method of argumentation through sarcasm instead of scripture (196) and denounces his literalist and misguided view of scriptures as supporting slavery and women's oppression (195–96). In addition, when J. F. W. denounces women's preaching and suffrage as violating women's sphere, she criticizes him for clinging to idols of biased assumptions (191). And she refutes him by reversing the gender of his arguments, showing that they must apply to men as well as women—if some men are faulty preachers, should men then never preach (193–94)? Like other women we have studied in this chapter, Stewart traces a superstitious awe of the pulpit, which is "only boards," to the errors of a corrupt Roman Catholicism (167, 184).

Most notably, Stewart takes an incisively historical perspective, pointing out that women were allowed to preach in the early days of many sects but were denied that right when these churches became established and more conservative (170).[35] Assuming conversation as a model for all discourse, she explains that in these sects private teaching, visiting the sick, and prayer are allowed to women—all not very different, after all, from public preaching:

> What is the difference, then, if teaching them to repent and believe in Christ, is preaching the Gospel, whether she preach it in Sabbath-school, in her family, . . . [as long as she] can devote her time, without infringing on any other duty, and believes herself called of God thereto. . . . I may teach two or three at a time, or the Sunday-school, or families; the Gospel and men will approve, and Christians and ministers praise me; but if I appoint a time and place to teach the same things, in public, it becomes a crime in their estimation. Though it furnishes me with the same breath and labor as an opportunity to teach a thousand. (183)

In these letters, furthermore, Stewart also mixes the traditional biblical discourse of defenses of women's preaching with the new discourse of women's rights. Indeed, she sees the nineteenth-century United States as approaching Apocalypse, with a battle for human rights as part of that turmoil (200). Citing the Constitution, she argues for women's "liberty of conscience" (167), and the "right" to answer the call of the Holy Spirit (169). Stewart challenges the idea that female preachers are exceptions—if one woman is allowed, she argues, all women are "entitled to liberty of conscience" (172). She views this "right of free speech" for women as extending to a voice in making laws (187). She invokes the American myth of history as progress and proclaims the dawn of a new era of human rights (192), foreseeing a better world when women achieve their rights, especially the right, based on liberty of conscience, to preach (197).

Stewart finishes off her epistolary opposition by outlining a sermon rhetoric that would not favor men over women as preachers. All preachers must have "a thorough knowledge of Scripture," but a knowledge based on "experimental . . . understanding [such] as the Holy Spirit gives" (206), rather than familiarity with biblical languages or commentary.[36] Persuasion will come not through the speaker's gifts, but through God's power: "The teaching or the doctrine of Christ, spoken in the Holy Ghost, always come with power and authority, commending themselves to every conscience" (206). While the "ability to read," "common sense," and "a tolerable gift in telling what they know" are important, "No book, nor all the books on theology, or any or all other subjects, can furnish such eloquence and oratory as the Bible" (206). Stewart thus addresses the problem of difference not by suggesting that women must be like men, or that women have a gendered capacity for preaching, but rather by reversing the requirements for preaching so that difference is an asset. Stewart uses the claim that uneducated preachers are inspired to redress the inequalities of a system where only men can be educated. Ironically, of all the authors of defenses of women's preaching, Stewart, one of the most radical, defending the right of the uneducated to preach, comes closest to writing the kind of sermon rhetoric that was part of the Euro-American tradition of masculine rhetorical education.

Catherine Booth: Reforming Exegesis

A similarly hybrid composition is Catherine Booth's 1859 *Female Ministry*. Catherine Mumford Booth (1829–90) was born in Ashbourne, Derbyshire, England, to Sarah Milward Mumford, a devout Methodist, and John Mumford, a coach builder, wheelwright, and lay preacher. The finances of the large family suffered when the father began to drink heavily. They moved to London, where Catherine met William Booth, also a lay preacher, when she changed her church membership to the Reformed Methodists. They were married in 1855 and for many years were Methodist evangelists. Booth began her preaching privately, speaking to female temperance audiences from 1857 on and took her husband's pastorate in 1860 when he fell ill and was moved to a clinic to recover. They had seven children, but Booth maintained a demanding schedule of preaching and writing evangelist pamphlets, and the Booths were crucial in the founding of the London Christian Mission, which was reorganized in 1879 as the Salvation Army, with William Booth as leader.

Catherine Booth wrote *Female Ministry* in 1859 in response to a pamphlet against women's preaching that specifically attacked a revival tour by the American Phoebe Palmer (who had also published defenses of women's preaching).[37] Booth's defense of women's preaching was thus part of a pamphlet debate, a refutation of a previous work, and also similar in length and organization to sermons. In addition, it testifies to the transatlantic nature of the tradition of women's defenses of women's preaching.

Booth structures her pamphlet around her exegetical method and the traditional three arguments in defense of women's preaching: the equality of men and women in God's eyes, a revisionist reading of Paul's strictures against women's speaking, and lists of biblical women who preached. After a brief introduction, she states her thesis: "not only is the public ministry of woman unforbidden, but absolutely enjoined by both precept and example in the word of God" (6).

Booth's pamphlet is hybrid both in its combination of exegetical method and the discourse of women's rights, and also its integration of long quotations from many men's works in the text (as in a long quotation from Dr. Barnes, 5).

Booth begins with the most difficult aspect of her task of persuasion—with a revisionist reading of the Bible and Paul that demonstrates a general call for women to preach. She first reviews scriptures that indicate women's participation in the early church. She then offers a revisionary reading of Paul's demand that women be silent in church: since Paul in 1 Corinthians 11:1–15 discusses appropriate attire for women who pray and prophesy, he cannot be forbidding entirely women's speaking, but only inappropriate speech. Booth adds the argument that Paul meant not all women but only those who were chatting and interrupting the service. She cites four Greek scholars on the meaning of the word *lalein* in this context, "to prattle" (8–9)—so women are not forbidden to speak in church, but forbidden to prattle in church. She instances Phebe, where *diaconon*, "deacon" or "preacher," is mistranslated as "servant" because of her gender (10–11), suggests that in some instances biblical advice no longer applies because of its historical limitations (as in the order of service in this same book of Corinthians). And finally, she rereads Paul's second restriction on women in Timothy, suggesting that Paul did not mean to forbid all teaching by women, but only such teaching as oversteps women's authority by contesting men's dominance. Since Booth allows teaching unconverted husbands, women's sphere is so broad, it would be difficult to overstep it. Like many of the women we have examined, Booth blames the misunderstanding of Paul that has silenced women on the Roman Catholic priesthood: "the love of caste and unscriptural jealousy [of] a separated priesthood" (19). Booth finishes by dumping the literalist reading of Paul into the dustbin of other "errors and contradictions," such as the universalist belief in the salvation of all, the Antinomian emphasis on faith alone, and the Unitarian belief in the entire humanity of Christ (25).

Into this refutation of a literal reading of Paul, Booth inserts reminders of the spiritual equality of men and women in the church: she quotes Dr. Taft on women's equal capacity as evangelical instructors (13); and she twice cites Galatians 3:28, that there is "neither male nor female" in Christ's service (15, 19). She buttresses her revision of Paul with lists of biblical women who preached or prayed or prophesied: in the New Testament, "Phebe, Junia, Philip's four daughters, and many other women" (15), Anna, the two Marys who first saw the resurrected Jesus, the women who shared the pentecostal experience with the men, Priscilla, Aquila, Tryphena, Tryphosa, and Persis (17–19); and in the Old Testament, Deborah, Huldah, the women who published the Lord's word in Psalm 68, and Miriam (15–16). This list of biblical female preachers is by Booth's time traditional. To the lists of biblical women, Booth further adds a list of contemporary women preachers[38] noted for feminine modesty: "the sainted Madame Guyon, Lady Maxwell, the talented mother of the Wesleys, Mrs. Fletcher, Mrs. Elizabeth Fry, Mrs. Smith, Mrs. Whiteman, . . . Miss March" (4), "Mrs. Mary Taft, Miss Elizabeth Hurrell, Miss Sarah Mallett, Mrs. Rogers, Mrs. President Edwards, . . . Mrs. Hall, Mrs. Gilbert, Miss Lawrence, Miss Newman, Miss Miller, Miss Tooth, and Miss Cutler," "Mrs. Palmer, Mrs. Finney, Mrs. Wightman, [and] Miss Marsh" (20–22). Of these contemporary or recent female preachers, Mrs. Fletcher was famous for her letter to John Wesley on the importance of women's preaching.[39]

Just as Booth argues that private capacities are similar to, not different from, public capacities, she also suggests that the private conversation and witnessing of women is like public preaching; in this manner, she uses conversation as a model for public discourse to bolster her claim that women may preach. Examples that Booth cites are Anna's conversation in the temple, a public place, and Mary's bringing the word of Christ's resurrection to apostles (17). "But the Lord gives the word," Booth proclaims, "and He will choose whom He pleases to publish it; not withstanding the condemnation of translators and divines" (16).

Like Stewart's and Mott's works, Booth's incorporates a language of women's rights. Indeed, her title declares the hybrid nature of her text: *Female Ministry; or, Woman's Right to Preach the Gospel*. Booth begins not with *scriptura sola*, but with an argument distinguishing nature from custom:

> Making allowance for the novelty of the thing, we cannot discover anything either unnatural or immodest in a Christian woman, becomingly attired, appearing on a platform or in a pulpit. By nature she seems fitted to grace either. God has given to woman a graceful form and attitude, winning manners, persuasive speech, and, above all, a finely-toned emotional nature, all of which appear to us eminent natural qualifications for public speaking. We admit that want of mental culture, the trammels of custom, the force of prejudice, and one-sided interpretations of Scripture, have hitherto almost excluded her from this sphere; but, before such a sphere is pronounced to be unnatural, it must be proved either that woman has not the ability to teach or to preach, or that the possession and exercise of this ability unnaturalizes her in other respects; that so soon as she presumes to step on the platform or into the pulpit, she loses the delicacy and grace of the female character. Whereas, we have numerous instances of her retaining all that is most esteemed in her sex, and faithfully discharging the duties peculiar to her own sphere, and at the same time taking her place with many of our most useful speakers and writers. Why should woman be confined exclusively to the kitchen and the distaff, any more than man to the field and workshop? (3)

Women are restricted from preaching by custom, Booth argues, but it is not unnatural for women to preach, for women have natural and God-given qualifications for successful public speaking. Booth discards the assumption of separate spheres of responsibility in the church by looking at biblical passages that confirm women's participation in the early church (15), and exults that women are at last "overstepping those unscriptural boundaries" (14). Moreover, Booth returns to the language of women's rights in her emphatic conclusion: "We have endeavored in the foregoing pages to establish, what we sincerely believe, that woman has a right to teach. . . . If she has the right, she has it independently of any man-made restrictions which do not equally refer to the opposite sex. If she has the right and possesses the necessary qualifications, we maintain that, where the law of expediency does not prevent, she is at liberty to exercise it without any further pretensions to inspiration than those put forth by that male sex" (25). Booth handles the problem of difference by laying out the qualifications for male preachers and demonstrating that women possess those qualifications—that in this respect, women are like men. But she also revises the terms of definition, arguing that private is not different from public, but similar: thus if the woman can do the work of spiritual comfort in the household, she can also do it on the platform (4, 13–14). A woman, according to Booth, does not lose "delicacy and grace of the female character" when "she presumes to step on the platform" (4). Intertwining the discourse of rights with an exegetical method of argumentation, Booth also further develops the idea of conversation as a model for all discourse in her account of preaching.

Frances Willard: Difference as Defense

Like Ellen Stewart's, Frances Willard's defense of women's preaching is a hybrid text, merging the genres of argumentative treatise and letters. But Willard takes an extreme stand on the issue of women's difference.

Frances Willard (1839–98), born in New York and raised in Wisconsin, home-schooled but also educated at Milwaukee Normal Institute and North Western Female College, was a social activist, served as dean of women at Northwestern University, worked for woman suffrage and helped found the WCTU, the Woman's Christian Temperance Union, becoming its most successful president. After breaking off her engagement with a man who eventually became a Methodist bishop, Willard engaged in a series of passionate friendships with women who lived and traveled with her and supported her work. In the WCTU, Willard oversaw development of effective techniques of social protest and public demonstration for women, teaching women public speaking and parliamentary procedure and extending WCTU social activism into child care, school lunches, unions, and antirape and anti-child-abuse legislation.[40]

Willard published *Woman in the Pulpit* in 1889. In this defense of women's preaching, she weaves together her own words with letters and essays from male and female preachers, to argue once again for the benefits of having women preach. Whereas Margaret Fell and others after her had adapted an inspirational style and collaboration with scripture to achieve authority, Willard devised a method more in keeping with nineteenth-century rationalism and American republicanism. Rather than divine authority, Willard draws on the republican and presbyterian authority of democratic testimony by the best of the citizenry, quoting letters from several countries and from twenty-one men and eleven women in defense of women's preaching.[41]

Willard's treatise is organized around the three foundational arguments defending women's preaching. In the first chapter of *Woman in the Pulpit*, Willard constructs an argument against a literal reading of the Bible, refutes the arguments to deny women the role of preacher based on Eve's fall or Paul's injunctions to silence, and begins her lists of famous examples of women in the Bible who preached. Willard offers a revisionist Paul, ridiculing literalist readings of the Bible (17) through a humorous story about a church where only men sang in the choir because women had to be silent, and through a grim survey of proslavery biblical misreadings (18). After giving examples of prescriptions in the Bible that are never followed literally, such as those against costly attire in church (19–20), she explains that men have read their biases into Paul, and especially the unfair subjection of women (22). Like Stewart, Willard posits that interpretation changes, influenced by historical time and place (23), and sets out a table of inconsistencies in Paul's letters, citing two scriptures proving women's public participation in the early church for every one criticizing it (27–28). In any case, Willard argues, Christ, not Paul, is the ultimate authority (40). Like defenses of women's preaching reaching back to Fell's, Willard's calls on anticlerical sentiment to turn sympathy against literalist readings: she bitterly decries men's protection of their "ecclesiastical prerogative" (38) and attributes opposition against women's preaching to "priestly intolerance" (40).

In the second half of the first chapter and in the second chapter of *Woman in the Pulpit*, Willard argues that women demonstrate their faith as apostles in the scriptures, so that there is a kind of history of women's preaching. Willard furthermore introduces philological arguments to reinforce her lists, explaining that Phebe being called "servant" is a mistranslation for "minister" (28), and reasoning that what is termed "prophesy" in the Bible is what we would today call "preaching" (30–31). These supporting arguments are familiar ones by Willard's time. In the tradition of women's defenses of women's preaching, Willard lists biblical women who preached: Anna, Phebe (28), the women who received the gift of inspiration at Pentecost (33), Miriam, Hannah, Esther, Judith, both Marys, Martha, Lois, Eunice, Tryphena, Tryphosa, Persis (33–34), the Samarian woman, Joanna, Susanna, and the daughters and the handmaids who, Paul promises, will prophesy (40–44). Willard also lists contemporary women preachers (63), including quotations from the defenses of women's preaching of Catherine Booth (103) and Phoebe Palmer (106). Thus we have seen British evangelist Catherine Booth defending American evangelist Phoebe Palmer, and American evangelist Frances Willard citing both Booth and Palmer, creating a transatlantic community of women preachers in conversation with each other.

Willard adds to these traditional appeals an argument based on her view of women's essential nature, maintaining that preaching is particularly appropriate to women because they more effectively appeal to moral sentiment. Moreover, she claims that motherhood is not in conflict with a life of spiritual guidance, but in keeping with it. "The mother-heart of God will never be known to the world," pronounces Willard, "until translated into terms of speech by mother-hearted women" (46–47). Indeed, Willard deploys the ideology of gendered spheres to support women's appropriateness for the career of preaching. "Men reason in the abstract," maintains Willard, "women in the concrete" (47). But "Religion is an affair of the heart," and reasoning from concrete experience may better move the audience (48). The role of preacher, Willard claims, will not disrupt woman's role at home (54–55), for indeed, the roles of mother and minister are complementary by nature: "If the refinement, sympathy, and sweetness of the womanly nature, as men describe it, fit women especially for the sacred duties of the pastoral office, and these qualities are raised to their highest power by the relationships of wife and mother, as all must grant who have not forgotten the priestesses of their own early homes and present firesides, then, other things being equal, that woman who is a mother and a wife is, above all others, consecrated and set apart by nature to be a minister in the household of faith" (65). Arguing that it is mainly the ecclesiastical hierarchy of the centuries of masculine domination in the Catholic church that excludes women, Willard urges United States Protestants to restore women, who lie "prostrate under society's pitiless and crushing pyramid" (51). Thus Willard opposes "ecclesiasticism" (52), and exhorts men to let the women who are called to preach, who are already preaching all over the globe, back into the established church: man must ask woman to join him; "he . . . must swing wide the door to the throne-room of government, and bid us share his regal seat as joint rulers with him of this republic" (61).

Finally, throughout these first two chapters, Willard argues that men and women are equal spiritually (39), or even that women are actually superior, more fitted to be ministers because of their holiness and purity (41). Christ called women, as well as men (44), Willard explains, and women as well as men may be filled with the Holy Ghost (60).[42]

Like those of the other women of this chapter, Willard's argument is founded on the concept of conversation as a model for discourse. In the words of a woman quoted in one of the introductory letters, Willard puts forth Miss Colby's experience as a template: "My public talks, or lectures," the female missionary to Japan explains, "were simply my women's meetings enlarged" (11). Women's meetings in the nineteenth-century church were not held in the public space of the sanctuary but in smaller rooms or even women's parlors. Thus Willard sees women's preaching as an extension of her domestic experience in conversation; indeed, she claims, a woman is "set apart by nature to be a minister in the household of faith" (65) and "speaks . . . with the sacred cadence of . . . [a] mother's voice" (48). Willard follows nineteenth-century conventions in seeing the women, especially mothers, as central to the household's emotional economy and suggests that these same skills can be transported to public preaching: "that blessed Gospel ministry, through which her strong yet gentle words and work may help to heal that heartache, and to comfort the sinful and the sad 'as one whom his mother comforteth'" (62).

Willard extends her theory of republican preaching into the form of her defense, buttressing her own arguments with the testimony and arguments of others. She begins her treatise with three letters by men in support of women's preaching, refutes the arguments against women's preaching (especially literalist readings of Paul), advances her own arguments, offers a whole chapter of testimony from male preachers, as well as a chapter of testimony from women preachers, and concludes with a debate between two men occasioned by her argument first published in a journal.

The form of collage that Willard employs for this argument has special advantages. First, it reproduces on the page the integration of the church that Willard advises. In the introduction, for example, Willard chooses men's voices: she reprints letters supporting her position in favor of women's preaching by famous male divines (by Dr. T. De Witt Talmage, Rev. Joseph Cook, and Dr. Joseph Parker).[43] But square in the middle of the introduction, quoted at length by Rev. Cook, is a letter from Miss Colby, a Japanese missionary, outlining how her teaching English led gradually to women's Bible meetings and then to her preaching, when the Japanese men asked to join in. Second, the form of collage for argument in favor of women's preaching allows more room for what Kenneth Burke calls "identification," audience alignment with the voice of the text (19–21). While Rev. Cook bases his argument for women's preaching on the social construction of women's roles, and thinks we must decide on the basis of "prolonged experience" (Willard, *Woman in the Pulpit* 12), Dr. Parker bases his argument on an essentialist view of women's spiritual gifts—women have "the sacred tact, the melting pathos, the holy patience, the exquisite sympathy . . . the omnipotent-weakness," which makes them naturally good preachers (15).

Like Stewart's, Willard's whole book started as articles and responses, an exchange of letters, in a religious journal, in Willard's case *The Homiletic Monthly* (5). Willard makes particularly bold use of this principle in her final section of *Woman in the Pulpit* by publishing a lengthy letter by Dr. Henry J. Van Dyke refuting her views, and then an even lengthier letter by Prof. L. T. Townsend defending women's preaching. In a rhetorical move typical of the women in this study, but nonetheless full of irony, Willard defers to men's final authority in order to conclude her argument for women's right to speak out. Dr. Van Dyke argues through historical examples of evil women that women have no special qualification for the ministry; that their gendered gift of speaking from the heart is a dangerous gift (compared to men's reasoning abilities) to bring to preaching; that motherhood precludes them from preaching; and that the Bible both implicitly and expressly excludes women from the ministry. Prof. Townsend counters that women have special qualifications of reasoning ability (like men), but also "quicker intuition" and "tenderer sympathies" than men (133); that only *some* women are precluded by their responsibilities as mothers from preaching (136–42); that implicit exclusion is not sufficient warrant (illustrated by the *reductio ad absurdum* that women are not shown receiving the Lord's Supper, and so . . . [146]); and that women are explicitly recorded, even by Paul, as preachers, deacons, and prophets in the early church (149–50). Willard appropriates her opponents' words in order to certify her republican voice: letting all voices be heard, those in favor of women's preaching rationally win out.

Willard thus assumes that a great part of her audience will be hostile to the idea of women's preaching and constructs her argument not straightforwardly, but interwoven with refutation and what Aristotle calls "inartistic proofs"— testimony from witnesses. Willard has good warrant for making this assumption. In the early 1860s, she broke an engagement to a young man, Charles Henry Fowler, who later became a Methodist minister (Bordin 34–35) and, eventually, president of Northwestern University just after it merged with the Evanston Ladies College, of which Willard had been president. Willard was made dean of women, with lifelong tenure. The two administrators did not get along. One major issue that divided them was evening prayers for the women's college. The women had always held their own prayer service, which Willard often conducted. When the women moved to the new building in 1874 as part of the Northwestern campus, the new president refused to allow the women to conduct their own service, and the role was given to the college steward, a clergyman (63). Willard resigned. She must have felt special satisfaction in her later preaching on the Moody revival circuit.

Willard avoids the terminology of women's rights (except for support of suffrage in a letter by one of the men, 69–70) in favor of the more conservative discourse of a gendered sphere that fits women for the role of preacher. Still, she states something tantamount to a claim for women's rights through a moving pathetic appeal—Willard explains that she writes this book because she herself was initially forbidden by Methodists to answer the call and so failed in her duty: "But even my dear old mother-church (the Methodist) did not call women to her altars. I was too timid to go without a call; and so it came about that while my unconstrained preference would long ago have led me to the pastorate, I have failed of it, and am perhaps writing out all the more earnestly for this reason thoughts long familiar to my mind" (62). Willard pleads not to let other "younger women who feel a call, as I once did," suffer so (62). She makes this argument with the practical understanding that her audience of church members is three-fourths women (25).

Throughout her text, Willard makes arguments for women's right to preach, for suffrage (52, 69–70), and for dress reform (64–65), but without using the discourse of women's rights. In a particularly sly move, she quotes a man on woman's competence to vote as analogy to her competence to preach (69–71), at a time, of course, when women had neither of these rights. Framing his feminist argument, Willard dampens the language of rights in favor of a strategic essentialism that allows her to suggest women, as mothers, may speak for both men and women:

> It will be easy to trace the analogy between the Senator's reasons why mothers should vote to the reasons why mothers should also preach—if they desire and are qualified to do so. . . . The average preacher almost never mentions women. "A man must do so and so." . . .—this method of discourse is [as] familiar to women's ears as the Doxology or Benediction. But when women themselves speak, they represent not world-force so much as home-force; the home includes both man and woman, youth and maiden, boy and girl; hence it is natural to women to make all feel themselves included in the motherly utterance that not only remembers but recognizes all. (69–72).

In *Woman in the Pulpit,* Willard lets other voices speak along with her own, in order to be heard. Willard separates men and women into their own chapters—creating quite literally in her book the separate spheres of nineteenth-century Anglo-American social life. Yet she argues against this doctrine for preaching, demonstrating a tension between her commitment to social change and an essentialist view of women's gender as naturally nurturing. Moreover, in the very structure of her book, a print forum drawing attention to the inclusion of men's and women's voices, she overthrows the ecclesiastical hierarchy of institutionalized religion and creates a model for a presbyterian, republican church that would include women as ministers as a matter of course. While Willard is among the more conservative on the view of women's essential nature, she is among the more radical in her claims for women's right to speak out—indeed, her view of the difference of women is her defense of their right to preach.

Conclusion

Defenses of women's preaching by women thus take a variety of generic forms: conversion narrative/spiritual autobiography, epistle, sermon, and treatise. Almost all of them reiterate three basic biblical arguments, although it is not until the nineteenth century that they realize they are thus part of a tradition and begin to cite each other. These works almost uniformly cite scriptures showing men and women as equal in God's eyes, list biblical women who were preachers, prophets, and ministers, and refute literalist readings of Paul by placing his commands for women to be silent in a specific historical context or by harmonizing their readings through citing his praise of women elsewhere. In addition, in the early treatises, women often redefine preaching as testimony, catechism, or prayer meeting, thus giving up the public space of the pulpit for feminine modesty, and in the later defenses, the argument yet rests on the assumption that women's domestic conversation is a model for public preaching.

Nevertheless, from the mid-nineteenth century onward, these women know very well that they want the right to speak publicly from the pulpit and to be ordained preachers, often arguing against the restrictions on the pulpit as a relic of corrupt Roman Catholic practices. Moreover, many of these women's defenses attack anonymous male priests and preachers who preach against women's preaching or proclaim misogyny from the pulpit. This thread responds to women's realization that the church they are part of is a patriarchal institution that denies women's rights. Ironically, then, it is not in the humanist strand of women's takeover of rhetorical theory where the language of rights first enters the discussion of women's speech, but in these defenses that rely heavily on conservative biblical arguments.[44]

These works by the women who defend women's preaching further experiment with rhetorical argument based on collaborative authorship and dialogic authority. In their study of collaborative composition, *Singular Texts / Plural Authors: Perspectives on Collaborative Writing*, Lisa Ede and Andrea Lunsford distinguish between the problem-solving, discrete tasks of hierarchical collaboration and the "fluid," "multivoiced" shared explorations of dialogic collaboration.[45] The women we have studied in this chapter experiment with forms of argument based on collaboration. The earlier writers collaborate with scripture, fusing their arguments with scriptural quotations and gaining authority from biblical language. Later writers construct texts that approach collage, copying into their books the letters, arguments, and poems of others. In general, then, women's defenses of women's preaching construct texts that represent themselves as corrections of biblical misinterpretations and democratic discussions of citizens' rights. As we saw at the end of the last chapter, in the discussion of Jennie Willing's advice on "Talking," the defenses of women's preaching align themselves with other strands of women's rhetorical theory, taking conversation as a model for preaching, and eventually intertwining into women's theory a discourse of rights.

4

Elocution: Sentimental Culture and Performing Femininity

By the mid-nineteenth century, conversation as a model of discourse, the gendered nature of communication, and women's rights to public speaking were intertwined in a transatlantic women's tradition of rhetoric in women's rhetorical theory. However, besides conduct rhetoric and defenses of women's preaching, nineteenth-century women also wrote elocution handbooks that added to this tradition a theoretical consideration of women's bodies as means of persuasion. These handbooks provided vocal exercises and calisthenics to guide the performance of emotions in public displays such as oral reading and pantomime. As taught to girls and women in the nineteenth century, elocution was preparation for a young lady's role in conversation, as well, and so conversation was also a model for women's public elocutionary performance.

In the second half of the century, sentimental culture, emphasizing the public display of emotion, was already associated with women. In elocution, the performance of emotion through voice and body, sentimental culture found ideal expression, and the women who took over the teaching of elocution found a new freedom and control over themselves. As Carol Mattingly has observed, the body, because of gendered restrictions on women, was "the greatest barrier women speakers faced" (*Appropriate[ing]Dress* 135). Despite the association of sentiment and sympathy with gendered constraints on women's roles in the nineteenth century, elocution offered women an avenue into public speaking and a means of powerful physical training that countered the passivity of the nineteenth-century ideal of delicate femininity. In elocution handbooks, women reimagined women's bodies not as weak and soft, but as strong and powerful.

After an opening section defining elocution and linking it to sentimental culture, in this chapter I analyze elocution texts by four women (with briefer references to other texts by women), explicating their theories of sentimental performance art and practice: two by Anna Morgan, actress and director, whose treatises discussed elocution as a foundation for dramatics; two by Genevieve Stebbins, forerunner of modern dance, whose many handbooks represented elocution as creative movement; one by Emily Bishop, developer of modern physical education and physical therapy; and two by Hallie Quinn Brown, African American elocutionist and professor at Wilberforce College, whose early handbook offered elocution for parlor and stage performance, and whose later textbook treated elocution as preparation for public speaking.[1] These texts were chosen because they represent the major directions that this art of bodily performance and public reading took in the nineteenth century.

Elocution and Sentimental Culture

Elocution was the most popular form of Anglo-American rhetoric for over a century. In the eighteenth century, as the focus of rhetoric changed from emphasis on the training of public orators to emphasis on the development of taste in the audience, delivery was separated off from rhetoric as a specialized art of oral reading or recitation.[2] In this art of elocution, middle-class Anglo-American vernacular readers were taught correct pronunciation, vocal control, bodily grace, dramatic gesture, and expressive reading. In the eighteenth century, in texts like Thomas Sheridan's *Lectures on Elocution* (1762) and John Walker's *Elements of Elocution* (1781), the art of reading aloud was developed into a set of rules and exercises as a means of training for public speaking and public entertainment.[3] In the nineteenth century, besides Sheridan and Walker, American elocution was influenced primarily by the theories of the French teacher of acting François Delsarte (1811–71), published after his death by his students. Delsarte retained the rules and exercises of traditional elocution, but rationalized them by an epistemology based on Emanuel Swedenborg's mysticism, applying Swedenborg's principle of the trinity as basis of all life to the physical, mental, and spiritual effects of elocution.[4]

By the mid-nineteenth century, elocution permeated middle-class United States culture. Children in public schools studied techniques for reading aloud and presented programs to parents that included recitation and physical movement drills. Printers published collections of poems and excerpts for reading aloud at school or home or on civic occasions. Adults registered for classes and went to lyceums, chautauquas, and public lecture halls to hear famous elocutionists. Middle-class families read to each other for evening entertainment and pronounced "pieces" for family or church gatherings, and women put on public performances, reciting literary passages and performing pantomimes or synchronized physical movement pageants.[5]

Indeed, although there has been little scholarly attention given to them,[6] women were a major force in the late nineteenth-century elocution movement, taking and giving lessons, founding schools, organizing local performances, touring as elocutionists, and writing textbooks.[7] In her essay "Five Private Schools of Speech" discussing the post–Civil War era, Edyth Renshaw documents participation by women across the nation in the elocutionary movement: the partnership in performance, schools, and publications of Rachel Hinkle Shoemaker and her husband, J. W. Shoemaker; Rachel Shoemaker's successful leadership of the National School of Elocution of Oratory from 1880 to 1915 in Philadelphia after her husband's death (303–4, 311–12);[8] the partnership of Jessie Eldridge Southwick and her husband, Henry Lawrence Southwick in the teaching at, and eventual management of, the Boston School of Oratory (304); the founding of the Columbian School of Oratory, Physical Culture, and Dramatic Art in Chicago by Mary Blood and Ida Riley, and their collaboration in writing textbooks (305–6, 315);[9] the founding of the School of Elocution and Expression by Anna Baright in Boston, and the merger with S. S. Curry's private practice in elocution to create the School of Expression when the two teachers married (306, 322); and the founding of the School of the Spoken Word in Boston and the publication of an elocutionary handbook by Carol Hoyt Powers and her husband, Leland Powers (307, 318–20). In *Self-Expression and Health: Americanized Delsarte Culture* (1892), a late nineteenth-century elocution handbook, Emily Bishop suggests that by her time women were the majority of students in elocution classes: "such classes being usually composed of grandmothers, mothers, and daughters—with an occasional gentleman" (x).[10] Moreover, Genevieve Stebbins, in *The New York School of Expression* (1893), promotes her school to women who desire a career in teaching elocution, printing an advertisement that represents the ideal elocution teacher as "a lady whose voice and manners shall be an inspiration to all pupils . . . the authority for pronunciation in the school . . . capable of directing the gymnasium . . . [and of reading] in an agreeable, unaffected manner" (11).

Despite the importance of elocution to nineteenth-century United States culture, historians have generally disparaged it as an unfortunate detour from effective rhetorical practice. Bahn and Bahn, for example, judge that "Antics of emotional display, devoid of real feeling, were prevalent in this era" (154), and Brenda Brown concludes that "this system reduced the study of rhetoric to the stilted expression of emotion through learned (and practiced) bodily gestures and positions" (214). This dismissive attitude toward elocution most probably results from its association with sentimental culture and with women and is epitomized in the parodic representation of the Mayor's Wife and her statue-posing performance club in the musical *The Music Man*.

Sentimental culture arose in the eighteenth century from a combination of forces.[11] Rooted in an epistemology and moral philosophy based on the impressive power of emotions and sense experience,[12] the growth of a middle-class reading public in England and the United States, and the reorganization of the family around the figure of the self-sacrificing mother, sentimental culture migrated in nineteenth-century United States culture by means of its association with women from post-Romantic poetry to the midcentury novel, and, I argue, into late nineteenth-century elocution, the rhetorical display of emotion.[13]

In sentimental culture, affection is seen as the basis of society (Halttunen 51; Dobson 266),[14] and emotion is associated with moral value and social reform.[15] Sentimentalism finds its expression in "the communication of common feeling" (Todd 4) and "celebrates human connection, both personal and communal," especially through shared loss (Dobson 266).[16] Sentimental culture promotes not the autonomous self, but "the self-in-relation," emphasizing the values of family and community (Dobson 267). According to Todd, the "sentimental virtues" are "benevolence and compassion," and women are their guardians (19); and according to Bennett, sentimental culture for women was also allied with "domestic ideology" and "evangelical Christianity" (xxxvi). Halttunen suggests that sentimental culture rests on a central paradox: the ideal of sentimental society is sincerity, the open and honest expression of emotion and the self, but paradoxically, one has to keep oneself under complete control to prove such sincerity through moral earnestness—that is, the social codes of its acceptable performance must be learned. For the latter half of the century, I argue, but beginning even earlier, elocution became the means, especially for women, of *managing* the self and the body in order to perform these social values (the way physical exercise is such a means of management now for both men and women).[17]

Historians and literary critics have posited that sentimental culture (which emphasizes the values of sympathy and emotional connection) had its heyday in middle-class American society and its poetry and fiction, especially that by women, from about 1820 to 1850 or 1860, disappearing after the Civil War.[18] In this chapter, however, I show that sentimental culture, still associated with women, migrates to elocution after the Civil War and remains a strong influence until elocution disperses at the turn of the century into more specialized training in acting, creative movement and modern dance, physical education and physical therapy, and public speaking. Anna Morgan explains elocution for women as performing emotional control; Genevieve Stebbins describes elocution as an emotional semiotics; Emily Bishop explores the nerve force that results from women's physical development through elocution; and Hallie Quinn Brown represents elocution, the rhetorical display of emotion, as a means to power through persuasion. All of them offer women empowerment to resist traditional feminine roles through control over their own bodies. Thus elocution, which begins as a means of domesticating women for parlor conversation, ends by preparing them for public performance. Now let us look more closely at each of these theorists of elocution to determine the particular ways in which they inflect the alliance of elocution, conversation, and sentiment.

Anna Morgan: Performing Emotion

Anna Morgan was a professional elocutionist, trained by Steele MacKaye. She eventually ran her own studio in Chicago, helping to found the "Little Theatre" movement.[19] Morgan's *An Hour with Delsarte* (1890) is an elegant volume, illustrated by her students, written in a narrative style, beginning with elocution as social performance and culminating in dramatic training. Morgan's *The Art of Speech and Deportment* (1909) is a hefty tome in a catechetical format of question-and-answer, linking elocution as training for social mobility with a rehabilitation of dramatic arts as high culture.

The origin of elocution in classical rhetorical delivery (training in "action") is clear in Morgan's adjuration that the body "preaches" the self to the audience and in her charge to her students (the motto to the first illustration) to "Let my sorrow *plead* for me" (*Hour*, inside cover, my italics). Yet, as in many of the works we have examined in this study, Morgan's elocutionary handbooks predominantly present communication as modeled on conversation.[20] "Gesture is the language of nature . . . comprehensible to people of every tongue" (58), Morgan advises; "the eye . . . translates with . . . fidelity the nicest shades of thought and feeling" (46–47). Elocution is an art in the sense that conversation is, a cultivated exchange that evokes social bonds: "[Elocution] is the idea, feeling, or emotion speaking through cultivated mediums that touches the subtlest chords of harmony. When it is remembered how much meaning can be conveyed by a timely and responsive look, or the significant movement of the head or arm, what a language the perfected whole must speak!" (114–15). Indeed, for Morgan, "the rare and perishable gift of conversation" (*Art of Speech* 28) is "the most important though least heeded department of the art of expression and is capable of great refinement" (16).[21] Conversation thus becomes a means to social mobility because it is the major avenue to display cultivation, the currency of social mobility.

Morgan's theory is a product of sentimental culture. *An Hour with Delsarte* gives a dignified overview of François Delsarte's philosophy (based on the aesthetic and moral power of emotion), sentimentalizing it even further. Morgan reviews Delsarte's division of the soul into intellectual, vital, and emotional states, but argues that "The seat of sentiment is the emotive nature, which is the source of the highest emotions of the soul" (27). This emphasis on emotion, sympathy, or sentiment, and the consequent theorizing and reflecting on sentiment, are central to elocution as presented by women theorists.[22] Justifying her art, sentimental-fashion, as "natural" and centered in feelings, Morgan suggests that "Gesture is the immediate revelation of the being. . . . the touchstone to the character, . . . the language of nature" (58). In *The Art of Speech and Deportment*, Morgan lends the emotions even more importance, as the avenue to perception of the beautiful, thus creating a sentimental aesthetics (7). Yet, paradoxically, Morgan advises that "we must free the body from the stiffness of individuality by yielding it up to the claims of universality" (*Hour* 15), imagining that elocution places the speaker or performer in relation, as well, to the Platonic universals of great art.[23]

But emotion does not equate with loss of self-control in sentimental culture, or in Morgan's theory of elocution. In *An Hour with Delsarte*, Morgan suggests that the purpose of elocution is making the body "subservient to the master, the will" (8), clearly demonstrating this goal of disciplining the self and body. Morgan further pronounces that one must know how the voice is produced because "knowledge is power" (*Art of Speech* 136), and she proposes that "those only are great who have so disciplined the body that it has become the servile creature of the soul" (*Hour* 11), connecting her theory of physiology to moral purpose. Moreover, Morgan demonstrates the social anxiety that motivates this desire for disciplined control over the body when she argues that "People form their estimates of our character [read *social status*] . . . through the bearing of our entire bodies" (*Hour* 11).

In its attention to social regulation of the body and the politeness codes of middle-class deportment, Morgan's theory draws on the tradition of conservative conduct book rhetoric for women that we have traced in chapter 2 of this study.[24] For instance, in *An Hour with Delsarte*, Morgan admonishes her students that "Good reading is a recommendation, just as good manners are a passport" in society (67). But her texts step beyond the strictures of feminine gender codes in their emphasis on the physicality of emotion. Morgan offers breathing exercises, voice exercises, posture and movement exercises, and exercises in gesture as coded emotional and moral response. "A well-poised head . . . bespeaks a well-ordered mind," she suggests, and reveals the training in gender role and social manner that she is offering in her comment that "a person of a sympathetic nature who is full of trust and tenderness will habitually incline the head forward" (*Hour* 96). This passage in Morgan also bears out Halttunen's conception of sentimental culture as based on a sincerity that is, ironically, performed rather than instinctive. Indeed, elocution texts by women, in similar fashion, seem to teach comportment, the social codes of gender, but in actuality teach women that such performance is an impersonation, and that the goal of study is physical strength and control. In *Gender Trouble*, Judith

Butler argues that "gender is a kind of persistent impersonation that passes as the real" (viii), that identity is a signifying practice (145), and that gender is always performative, constituting the self (136). Poor performance of gender is punished by social disapproval, but such enforcement suggests that getting the gender "wrong" (140–41)—as in parody, hyperbole, dissonance, internal confusion, and proliferation of identities (31)—may be a means of protest, showing that gender is arbitrary, imposed. Elocution texts by women, such as that by Morgan, instruct and regulate the performance of gender, but also resist it in the interest of a "human" ideal of health, grace, and bodily strength.[25]

Many of Morgan's exercises might be described as practicing the self-in-relation-to-others, a central focus in sentimental culture. For example, sitting gracefully is important not only in itself, but mainly in relation to others, for "to put others at ease you should be at ease yourself" (*Hour* 100). In *The Art of Speech and Deportment*, Morgan has a whole chapter on manners as bodily performance (19–49)—opening a door, entering a room, shaking hands. But this handbook also includes other advice on social relationships, praising conversation as "the true delight of human intercourse" (34) and listing what is appropriate (and inappropriate) for young women in social interactions with young men (44–45). In addition, Morgan assigns moral purpose through moving the emotions to the bodily signals of elocution: "When the breast heaves and swells under the stimulus of some noble impulse we know that the mental has invaded the emotional nature, and stirred the being to the projection of some lofty purpose" (49). The "projection of lofty purpose," originating in the speaker's moral feelings, must then affect the audience as moral persuasion, according to Morgan.

Despite passages that are similar to conservative conduct book rhetorics, Morgan's handbooks also resist the constraints of traditional feminine roles. Halttunen points out that sentimental dress was constricting—tight sleeves, tight corset—and that this earlier period saw American women less active physically (78–79).[26] Elocution was thus a radical departure or revision of sentimental culture. If we consider illustrations from Morgan's *An Hour with Delsarte*, we can see that Morgan is offering women release from certain physical, social restrictions. In one illustration, the girl with bad posture, before elocution lessons, is also wearing tight sleeves and a corset (*Hour*, opposite 12). Her hips are pushed forward and her back is pushed out of line by the high-heeled shoes she is wearing, and her face is held expressionless. Corsetted, she is, as Wendy Dasler Johnson puts it, "bound up by conventional expectations" (216). In a later illustration, the girl participating in elocution lessons is in flowing robes, uncorsetted, and with sleeves free for movement (*Hour*, opposite 28). Her arms are akimbo and her back is straight despite the expressive, challenging posture of her body, while her facial expression suggests independence (her chin is raised and her head pulled back) but socially engaged (her eyes are clearly fixed on someone outside of the frame). The moral of the contrast in these two illustrations is clear: elocution gives young women self-possession, in the full sense, or, as Morgan explains in *The Art of Speech and Deportment*, "elocution . . . is the expression of yourself" (13).[27] As depicted in Louisa May Alcott's *Eight Cousins* (1875), the corset and constricting, unhealthy female attire in the nineteenth century constituted a crucial issue in women's rights. Morgan's view of elocution provides young women, then, a means to resist such constraints: a method that eschews "rigid . . . formula" (*Art of Speech* 56) and "which adds force and meaning to our every movement" (*Hour* 8).

From Morgan's perspective, elocution allows her female students freedom from the constraints of feminine ideology, and the female body consequently becomes a site for resisting them. "The body is but the outward symbol and development of the real or inner self" (*Hour* 11), Morgan explains, and she studies the body as the agent of expression (35–36). But that does not mean that using the body to express the self is merely natural; instead, it requires the rigorous training of elocution to achieve self-mastery, to enable the body to be the means by which the soul "manifest[s] itself to the outer world" (*Hour* 25). In *An Hour with Delsarte*, for example, Morgan gives women instructions on the discipline of sitting in one motion: "settle pliantly backward, touching the back of the chair at the waist-line first, and successively each joint in the articulations of the back until the neck is reached and the head falls easily into a restful attitude" (100). In the word *pliantly*, this description calls up nineteenth-century feminine stereotypes of feminine acquiescence; but the degree of control required and the attention to backbone suggest strength, and both of these also suggest self-expression, although self expressed through a body employed as an artistic medium.

In *Excitable Speech: A Politics of the Performative*, Judith Butler explores the power that *embodied* speech achieves in communication: "Is the one speaking merely speaking, or is the one speaking comporting her or his body toward the other. . . . As an 'instrument' of a violent rhetoricity, the body of the speaker exceeds the words that are spoken" (12–13). Elocution allowed nineteenth-century women the power not only of controlling and resisting the enactment of gender, but also of developing rhetorical force through their bodies. As Morgan comments, the art of elocution offers "the possibility of adding strength and expression to our movements, as well as grace and ease" (*Hour* 8). If women were defined by their bodies, then they also in elocution might use their bodies as instruments of persuasion.

Morgan's elocution theory is further empowering in the way it steers the art of elocution in the direction of dramatic training, using emphasis on manners as a way of making the dramatic arts acceptable instead of scandalous for young women (*Art of Speech* 22–23). In *An Hour with Delsarte*, many of the illustrations are titled with quotations from Shakespeare, and the final chapter concerns "The Stage." In *The Art of Speech and Deportment*, the examples for the section on voice come mainly from Shakespeare, and Morgan includes chapters on "Platform Manners," "The Development of Drama," and "On Rehearsing." Morgan's theory thus merges elocution with the art of acting, recuperating the theater as a respectable career for young women.

Linking acting to these middle-class and feminine roles, Morgan further offers public display through acting to women as a respectable social role in sentimental terms, for "the function of the body is to reflect the soul" (*Hour* 110). Halttunen sees movement to parlor theatricals as signaling the end of sentimentalism (182), but I see it as sentimentalism migrating into elocution. Elocution and parlor performance train women for bourgeois social performance and deportment, just as college education trained men for their middle-class social roles. But these venues of "private" performance ironically also become steps in the expansion of women's sphere.

Genevieve Stebbins: Emotional Semiotics

Genevieve Stebbins was a professional actress in New York who studied elocution with Steele MacKaye and later founded her own schools in Boston and New York. Moreover, she was principal of the New York School of Expression, housed in Carnegie Hall. At the Madison Square Theatre, she presented "Delsarte Matinees" that included readings, dance, pantomime, statue-posing, gymnastics, and dance dramas, which became models for women's exercise groups and modern dance.[28] In *The Delsarte System of Expression* (1894), Stebbins elaborates Delsarte's system through philosophical principles adapted from Swedenborg and Ruskin, through the addition of yoga breathing exercises, through exercises based on classical statuary researched in museums across Europe, and through routines modeled on dance and religious rituals observed throughout Europe and the Middle East.[29] Her "Eastern Temple Drill," for example, is based on Muslim and Druse religious practices, "The Carmen" on traditional Spanish dance forms, and "The Amazon" on Greek statuary (*Genevieve Stebbins System* 84, 109–10).

Like Morgan, Stebbins characterizes elocution in sentimental terms. For Stebbins, the movements of the body reflect the affections: "Excitement or passion tends to expand gesture; Thought or reflection tends to contract gesture; Love or affection tends to moderate gesture" (*Delsarte System* 121). "Art," says Stebbins, with a characteristically sentimental definition, "conquers all hearts in moving the sentiments" through a "power irresistibly sympathetic" (xvi); it is "heart-work, not head-work" (79).

Stebbins claims that elocution teaches a "semiotics," a science that decodes the signs that represent emotions, and an "aesthetics," an art that represents universal truths through the forms of sentiment (57–58). Semiotics, for Stebbins, is, furthermore, a science of correspondences, in the sense that the physical forms of voice and gesture are "spoken from the heart" so that "the material form . . . correspond[s] to the inner form" (61); as a consequence, the appropriate sign will arouse in the performer, and through her, in the audience, the sentiment signified (62–64); and thereby, "signs of expression tend through reflex action to produce states of mind" (*Genevieve Stebbins System* 12). In her analysis of the semiotics of emotional delivery, Stebbins thus represents elocution as a rhetoric of the emotions expressed through the body.

Emphasis on affection as social bond and emotion as motive for moral reform are especially strong in these women theorists of elocution. In her study titled *Gender and Rhetorical Space in American Life*, Nan Johnson cautions that such emphasis on sentiment was limiting, for "the cultural message promoted by parlor rhetorics is that women should be associated with the performance of sentimentality" (39–40).[30] In many of the elocution handbooks by women, however, rather than the constraints of domestic life, the communal relationships expressed in elocutionary exercises result in connection to the wider life of the community. Stebbins, for example, described herself as forgoing matrimony in favor of "Art, Oratory, and Social Reform" (*New York School of Expression* 22).

In *The Delsarte System of Expression*, Stebbins urges her pupils, "Cultivate your mind and heart. For the expression of noble emotions, one must feel noble emotions" (40).[31] Employing an agricultural metaphor to suggest that the work is "natural," Stebbins also links emotions to moral persuasion. In *The Genevieve Stebbins System of Physical Training*, Stebbins defines elocution as the art of "training the body easily to express a beautiful soul, or vice versa, training the body to right normal expression—that through reflex action a sickly spirit may grow into uprightness" (14). Such a definition suggests that conversation rather than public speaking is the model for discourse in this emotive rhetoric. Stebbins's analogy between health and virtue, moreover, seeks to collapse into each other the well-trained body and moral well-being. This emphasis on control and moral management of self and body explains why young women would be allowed, in this restrictive culture, to pursue an art that claims, as Stebbins does in *The Delsarte System of Expression*, to "free the channels of expression, [so] the current of nervous force can thus rush through them as a stream of water rushes through a channel" (11).

But as the last quotation suggests, Stebbins's handbooks also may be read as training in resistance against the constraints of the traditional feminine role, especially in her emphasis on creative movement and physical education.

Stebbins's exercises in *The Delsarte System* include physical stretching and calisthenics for all the parts of the body, breathing exercises, exercises in walking and standing in character or for different emotions, pantomimes, and statue-posing.

Additionally, the pantomimes are exercises in emotional responses: greeting someone for whom you feel affection, registering a protest, reacting to the presence of an object. For example, after explaining that "Excitement or passion tends to expand gesture," that "Love or affection tends to moderate gesture" (168), and that "gesture shows the emotional condition from which the words flow, and justifies them" (170), Stebbins offers a pantomime to practice this relationship of emotion to gesture as it would be used in conversation:

> Door opens. Eyes turn right toward object entering. Head follows in rotary motion, leveling gaze on object. Face assumes an expression of delighted surprise. Titillation of eyelids. Head lowers slightly toward object in tenderness . . . shoulder rising in opposition. Movement creeps down upper arm and turns eye of elbow toward object, thus asserting tenderness. This movement has slightly bent forearm as it hangs from elbow decomposed. Now unbend forearm. Rotary movement of wrist turns hand into relative attitude . . . then expands in conditional attitude . . . , affection. (177)

The Genevieve Stebbins System of Physical Training (1898) takes elocution in the direction of creative movement, gymnastics, and dance and argues that elocutionary exercises, emphasizing "breathing . . . relaxation . . . energizing" (15), will increase mental health (a claim many modern psychologists would agree with). Half of Stebbins's book covers exercises that teachers can lead their classes in, and half offers "drills" that teachers can use for graduation or school performances for parents. The program for classroom use consists of an hour's worth of exercises: respiratory exercises; exercises for legs, arms, trunk, and head; marching; and more respiratory exercises—in modern terms, an admirable warm up, exercise, cardiovascular workout, and cool down. The advice Stebbins gives on breathing exercises sounds remarkably like modern yoga: the goals of such exercise consist of "breathing, with right thinking; relaxation, with conservation of energy; energizing, with creation and direction of energy" (*Genevieve Stebbins System* 15).

Stebbins's philosophy, though, pushes movement and exercise toward a spiritual aesthetic defining creative movement: she divides movement into the material form one can see and the spiritual form that is the energy that motivates it, arguing that "living power" results in "living motion" (*Delsarte System* 33) and that the outer expresses the inner (34). In *The Delsarte System*, the examples Stebbins cites are not theatrical but sculptural (classical statuary, 71–72, and the Elgin marbles, 75–76); and in *The Genevieve Stebbins System*, many of the exercises for performance are based on dance (the minuet, 115–18, and the flamenco, 103–10).

Stebbins's elocutionary training for women offers resistance to nineteenth-century gender ideology, emphasizing strength of body for women, not elegantly weak femininity. In *Gender Trouble*, Judith Butler observes that "Gender is the repeated stylization of the body" (33). In Stebbins's development of physical exercises for girls' public performance based on Greek statuary, we see such stylization, but in her choice of images of Amazons we see, at the same time, resistance of gender coding. In *The Genevieve Stebbins System of Physical Training*, Stebbins provides a series of exercises suitable for teachers to use with their students for public performances as well as strength training; but rather than graceful domesticity, the girls perform "The Roman Drill," "called the Amazon from its generally athletic nature, and because its figures are principally studies from Amazon statues in the Vatican, Rome" (110). The stances for this pantomime include "Running Amazon," "Amazon drawing the bow" (111), "Amazon heaving a rock," "Wounded Amazon," "Amazon charging," "Amazon retreating" (112), "Amazon with broken bow," and "The Amazon's vow" (113). While this exercise depends on performing femininity, it also depends on getting it wrong—performing hyperbole, dissonance, multiple identities (both nineteenth-century school girl and warlike Amazon). In this exercise, Stebbins's performance of gender is also a challenge to gendered ideology.

Thus elocution for women is training in preparation for social mobility, but undercut by the very physicality of the training. In *The Genevieve Stebbins System of Physical Training*, for example, Stebbins claims to help women to achieve "Relaxation [which] recuperates power through . . . repose" (33). Repose is a quality in keeping with the calm and sympathetic feminine ideal of the nineteenth century, but power is a quality infrequently associated with that ideal. Admittedly, there are some affinities with conduct rhetoric in Stebbins's handbooks: "people of higher class have a gamut of expression subtler than those of the lower" (*Delsarte System of Expression* 48). But much more often there is resistance to gender ideology: "Observe me. I start in the defiant attitude, vital force flowing to toes before I move; rigid knee. I feel 'how manly I am.' Each advance step strikes the heel hard on the pavement, the torso dragged after" (80–81). Parodying manliness, elocution for women, in Stebbins's view, is more resistance to gender ideology than training in it.

Emily Bishop: Performing the Self through the Body

Emily Montague Bishop (née Mulkin) (1858–1916), who studied with Stebbins, was head of the physical education department of the Chautauqua Institute in Chautauqua, New York, and also a lecturer, an elocutionist who pioneered political readings from U.S. Senate speeches, and an author of self-help and elocution handbooks.[32] Besides *Self-Expression and Health: Americanized Delsarte Culture* (first edition, 1891), which went through many editions, Bishop also published *Seventy Years Young* (1907), and *Daily Ways to Health* (1910). *Self-Expression and Health* (in the revised edition of 1895), analyzed here, is a handbook that steers elocution toward the basics: physical exercises, health practices, and attitude adjustment. The handbook is dedicated to her pupils, which Bishop indicates are mainly women (x, 30), and it alternates chapters of theory, or "Lesson Talks," with chapters of exercise. The theoretical chapters are heavily indebted to Delsarte, which the title declares, but also to Herbert Spencer, William Hogarth's aesthetics (3), and Friedrich Froebel's theories of education (183). The final chapters move into original territory by applying physical exercises to alleviation of women's muscle pain, headaches, insomnia, and nervousness.

Like most of the rhetorical theorists we have studied in this chapter, Bishop takes conversation as a model for all discourse. "Expression develops faculties as exercise develops muscles" (184), Bishop explains, for talking (like breathing, eating, walking, and moving) is a natural operation of life (171). The goal, then, is "to spontaneously express [one's] best self" (188), and to that end, Bishop recommends voice exercises as part of a healthy regimen that dissipates the repression that leads to tension and nervous disorders (196–97). Furthermore, Bishop adapts conversation to the purposes of physical therapy, recommending the exercise of "Guarding the words" in response to depression: "try to express physically . . . lightness of spirit" (175).

While other women theorists turn elocution to the purposes of public speaking, modern dance, and drama, Bishop's adaptation stresses physical education (ix), women's health, and the advantages of physical therapy for women in their stressful contemporary culture. Bishop develops an empirical theory that pictures elocution as promoting the development and use of the "nerve force" which in most middle-class Americans is inhibited by "*tension or over-nervation*" (60–62). "Keeping nerve-force in the muscles when there is no legitimate use for it," she cautions, "is like keeping up steam in a locomotive days before it is to be run. Tension is unnatural as it is wasteful." Along with the steam engine, she uses the analogy of the telegraph: "Every quality of thought sends a corresponding quality of vibration over the nerves." The body responds to tension with "physiological effects," and "every mental affection is followed by change in the chemical nature of [bodily] fluids" (68).

Bishop's handbook provides exercises to correct "over-nervation," especially to relax shoulders, deepen breathing (74), and encourage yawning, for "Yawning is helpful in overcoming nervousness and insomnia. Yawning and laughter are natural—albeit involuntary—gymnastics" (81). Health is thus the result of "self-expression" rather than "repression" (182–83).

Like the other texts considered in this chapter, Bishop's handbook situates elocution in sentimental culture. "Every movement is the manifestation of a thought, of an emotion, or of the unconscious action of some nerve-centre" (24), Bishop explains. She further teaches "motion as related to emotion or a mental state" and provides not only "gymnastics of exercise" but also "gymnastics of expression," which promote "growth of the mental and the emotive natures" (25). She stresses the interdependence of inner feelings and outer body in the Delsartean Law of Correspondence (27), seeing the shoulders, for example, as a measure of the passions (89). She warns that "People are impoverished in their vocabularies of feeling by too little, or the wrong use, of organs of expression" and urges her students to cultivate "expression of higher feelings" (187) and to relax so that the physical body may freely express their sentiments (42).

Indeed, a main goal of Bishop's exercises for women is bodily freedom, which for her is a means of resisting gender ideology. The purposes of her elocution exercises include "muscular freedom," "invigoration," "harmony of movement," strength, flexibility, and "power through breathing" (14–16). Her exercises, she claims, develop "poise, or equilibrium; freedom, or elasticity; strength, or control" (28) and ultimately transform feminine weakness into womanly strength (29). The woman who performs Delsartean elocutionary exercises, Emily Bishop claims, becomes a "self-possessed person [who] forgets the body when using it and thinks only of the object of its use" (34). Such women are able to maintain "habitual, easy control of their bodies" that allows them to achieve "an important emancipation." The soul of such a woman, Bishop imagines, has the "freedom" to express its "inner power" (35), and such a woman achieves "power through control" (111). Bishop urges her students to practice exercises thirty minutes every day, but to put the principles into practice at all times: "*living the truth* in bodily expression . . . is the only telling practice" (13), she suggests, by which she means *performing* the self through the body.

Repression is harmful, Bishop argues, because the self suffers "confinement" (186–87). She encourages her female students to avoid restrictive clothing so that they can breathe deeply (84), joining in the nineteenth-century feminist campaign against corsets. She recounts the poignant response of a beginning student, "a woman [who] says, 'I want to get possession of myself. My body is really an incumbrance, I never know what to do with it'" (31). Bishop's goal is thus to free women from the physical limitations of gender ideology: "When by self-knowledge and self-discipline, women gain habitual, easy control of their bodies, they will have achieved an important emancipation" (35).

Furthermore, Bishop views women as restricted not only in dress and movement but also in occupation and ambitions: too many American women are "narrowed in a narrow sphere," she laments (134). She sees elocution as a means to counteract such political constraints on women, as well: "The fountain of rejuvenescence is fed by human sympathies" and by "general interests," Bishop argues, and the goal of elocution is to prepare "women [to] lead broad lives" (133–34) and to retain youthfulness through such communal activity. Bishop imagines that her exercises, giving women strength, will move then from the gymnasium into "literary, social, church, and reform movements" (133). Finally, she hopes that a woman who studies and enacts the principles of elocution will metamorphose from "conventionalized woman" bound by "constraint" to "her emancipated, physically free sister": "We need to free ourselves," she urges, "from such bondage if we would be genuine and self-respecting" (114).

Hallie Quinn Brown: Persuasion through Display of Emotions

Hallie Quinn Brown was a middle-class African American woman who attended Wilberforce College in Ohio, became a professional elocutionist, and had a long career in teaching, college administration, and elocution, eventually achieving the position of professor at Wilberforce. Brown was a feminist and activist and helped found the National Association of Colored Women, eventually serving as its president.[33] In *Bits and Odds* (c. 1880),[34] Brown defines elocution in a brief preface and assembles readings (many with political purposes) for performance on stage or in parlor. In *Elocution and Physical Culture* (c. 1908), probably written and self-published for her students at Wilberforce, Brown borrows from Delsarte the notion that elocution allows vocal expression of the moral, intellectual, and spiritual, and she outlines a course in physical training that also uses techniques from classical delivery. Indeed, Brown suggests that the goal of elocution is to "co-ordinate . . . body and voice . . . with the spiritual" (7).

Like the other women whose handbooks we have analyzed in this study, Brown sees conversation as the model for all communication. For example, she suggests that the elocutionist must be "as earnest and sincere upon the platform as we are in private conversation" (*Elocution* 21) and maintains that even "in . . . daily intercourse with society" all speakers use the full range of musical capacities of the voice (24).

Like Morgan's, Stebbins's, and Bishop's theories, Brown's theory is permeated with the values of sentimental culture and is especially influenced by Delsarte's sentimental reworking of elocution. According to Brown, the elocutionist "must feel and then express those feelings," and the purpose of elocution is "to play at will on the chords of the popular heart" (*Bits and Odds* 5–6). In *Elocution and Physical Culture*, Brown quotes Delsarte: "'If you would move others, put your heart in the place of your larynx.'" Brown also maintains that "Every word and sentence should have its proper proportion of emotion equally distributed by the speaker," suggesting the mechanism by which feeling might be circulated for social good (28). Delsarte is certainly, for all these women, a source of the sentimental emphasis on emotion,[35] but each develops Delsarte's philosophy and teaching in original ways. In part, this emphasis on sentiment in Brown seems to be a feminization of the power of speech. For example, Brown expatiates on "The mother-tone [that] runs like a scarlet thread through the lullabies of many primitive peoples, . . . the first cry of babyhood, of mother-love, of home-love and home-longing" (*Elocution* 15–16). Such a vision claims the power of speech for women and for African Americans through citing historical origins.

The emphasis on common feeling in sentimental culture is especially pertinent to elocution, where the elocutionist as reader always mediates in relationship to text (and its author) and audience. As Brown explains in *Bits and Odds*, the elocutionist is concerned with "giving forth those thoughts and feelings of his own mind, suggested by the expressed words of another, and causing the listener on the other hand to start the kindred chords vibrating in unison with his own" (5). Thus the elocutionist binds together the author's words, her own emotional response, and the audience's expectations, aiming to create social harmony.[36]

Elocution finds one of its important venues in Christian evangelism. Brown's chapter "Bible Reading" in *Elocution and Physical Culture* constructs a sentimental framework for such art: "Sincerity, sympathy, emotion, soul—better these with no art, than the highest art without these qualities" (37). In addition, the cultural work of elocution might include social reform and expression of dissent. For Brown, it is the soul, not the body, which is moved by emotions (28), and she cautions her students, "Never . . . be enslaved to thought alone, but yield to feeling when it predominates" (23). Seeing sentiment as the basis of moral feeling and conscience, Brown advocates Bible reading so that "the heart, as well as the mind, shall be trained to the love and the practice of every virtue" (35). And the final line of Brown's handbook is "Let your motto be heart-work not head-work" (39), a familiar motto of Delsartean elocution that Stebbins had also cited.

We can see as well the influence of sentimental culture on Brown's *Bits and Odds*, a collection of readings for public performance with a brief preface on elocution. The readings, like sentimental culture in general, emphasize the moral force of emotion, the bonds of community, the effect of loss, the domestic virtues, and the power of evangelical Christianity. Among the readings included are a prose piece and a poem on the death of a child, as well as an anonymous poem about Mrs. Garfield rushing to her husband's side after Lincoln's assassination; such poems help nineteenth-century American society to negotiate the terrible emotional trauma of a 50 percent infant mortality rate and the public tragedy of civil war and presidential assassination. The readings also include a poem in which Christ saves a child from fever, the father from shipwreck, and the mother from freezing to death as she gallantly tries to ring the warning bell for ships; Brown thus reveals her assumption that elocution may serve the work of Christian evangelism. Since Brown further cautions that elocutionists must "have a sympathetic nature, but should be able to control . . . emotions" (6), we can see that the dramatic performance of these readings, besides the emotional work, also models stoic emotional control and rigorous discipline of the voice and body to the audience. Finally, the collection also includes an anonymous poem about John Brown and another titled "The Black Regiment," Frances Watkins Harper's "The Dying Bondman" about the evils of slavery, Joaquim Miller's "The Sioux Chief's Daughter," an anonymous antialcohol prose piece, and an anonymous poem about the poorhouse, as well as humorous dialect pieces from German, Negro, and Irish speakers. The cultural work of these pieces seems to be social reform, and reform along the very issues that nineteenth-century women cut their political teeth on: abolition, temperance, institutional reform, social services, and education for immigrants and newly freed African Americans.

Brown's theoretical analysis of elocution is similar to Bishop's and much more pragmatic and scientific than the theories of Morgan and Stebbins. In *Bits and Odds*, Brown divides elocution into an art of expression and a science of vocal physiology. She thus approaches elocution as interdisciplinary, a cross between science and art, and it is in this context that we may understand Brown's advice to discipline the body in order to achieve bodily freedom: "Elocution is the art of expressing thoughts and sentiments in the most natural manner. But elocution is also a science. It embraces the study of the respiratory system and the construction and management of the vocal organs" (5). Indeed, *Elocution and Physical Culture*, compared to many other handbooks (such as those by Morgan), contains more specific exercises and more detailed explanations of the workings of the body and less theoretical material on the aesthetics and spiritual goals of elocution. The study of anatomy, Brown explains, "will enable us to give expression through the body" (10). Adapting the metaphors of her newly mechanized age, Brown conceives of the body as a speaking machine: the "motor" is the chest, the "vibrating element" is the larynx, and the pharynx and mouth are "resonators" (16). Through training and managing the body, Brown argues, breath and speech become "the chief source of power" (14). Brown discusses vocal hygiene for several pages, outlawing alcohol, smoking, and wool scarves (in favor of silk), as well as repressive clothing, such as corsets. As a result of such training, Brown claims, elocutionists live longer and healthier lives (38–39).

Like Morgan, Stebbins, and Bishop, perhaps even more than these three white women, Brown resists the constraints of traditional feminine roles both in the physicality of her theories of elocution and in her adaptation of elocution to preparation for public speaking for her students. Through training in elocution, she is also resisting the place assigned to African Americans in her culture. Alongside her emphasis on conversation as a model for discourse, Brown grounds elocution firmly in the tradition of rhetoric and public speaking in her handbooks. *Elocution and Physical Culture*, for instance, frequently addresses the reader of the handbook as "the speaker" (14, 38), and the venues Brown imagines for her pupils are the "pulpit" and the "platform" (21). In *Bits and Odds*, Brown even suggests that elocution goes beyond oratory: "Oratory is limited. The province of the orator is to convey to the listener his own ideas and to convince the listener at will while he has his ear. The elocutionist has a broader field. . . . The elocutionist must attain the expression of nature . . . [and] through culture he must make many varieties of expression his very own. . . . We cannot connect thought and its verbal symbols by secret links with our own thoughts and emotions. To do this and interpret them to the listener is the sole province of the public reader" (5–6). Similarly, in *Elocution and Physical Culture*, Brown argues that oratory is a higher art than poetry, music, and sculpture because it links elocution and action (i.e., delivery, 30).

Indeed, Brown's *Elocution and Physical Culture* accomplishes three things at once: it describes a program of exercises for voice, posture, and gesture; it summarizes human physiology of speech and eighteenth- and nineteenth-century theories of gesture as a "natural" language of emotions (6);[37] and it provides excerpts from theories on rhetorical delivery from many theorists, especially Cicero and Delsarte. From Cicero, Brown borrows the ideas that delivery, the most important element of oratory, harmonizes body and spirit (6–7), that imitation is key to developing one's own style (20), that successful orators feel themselves the emotions they wish to evoke in their audiences (28), and that philosophical study not nature is the basis of true oratory (31). From Delsarte, Brown adapts the idea of gesture as the language of nature (6), the emphasis on emotions as the main force behind eloquence (28), the nine aesthetic "laws" of gesture (8), many of the exercises, and the assumption that elocutionists must practice until their responses appear natural (20). Brown adds to the traditional elocution manual a chapter on Bible reading (35–37); many of her students at Wilberforce would become preachers in the A.M.E. church, and both male and female students might end up in need of public speaking skills as social activists. Thus, unlike Morgan's emphasis on drama, Stebbins's on creative movement, and Bishop's on physical education, Brown is directing the training in voice and gesture toward the classical end of public speaking.[38]

Public speaking as the goal for elocution is so important because Brown intends her students, both men and women, to be prepared to use their skills in the cause of African American civil rights: "The aristocracy of eloquence," she proclaims, "is supreme and in the land of the free can never be suppressed" (*Elocution* 28). In particular, in a late nineteenth-century African American culture where community revolves around the church, Brown envisions a minister who can lead his or her people politically as well as spiritually: "A well furnished minister is among heaven's most precious blessings to a free, self-governed people" (36).

Indeed, Brown promises her students self-mastery. The word *master* appears frequently in Brown's works: her program of physical and mental exercises is designed to bestow mastery of a discipline on the student, and more importantly, mastery of self. Houston Baker has described late modernist African American writers as achieving "mastery of forms and deformation of mastery" (15–16).[39] Brown conceives of elocution as a mastery that will similarly help to deform mastery. "But let us remember," she cautions, "when we have mastered these difficulties and made ourselves proficient, we are bound by the strong law of *Obligation*. Obligation to the man who is down. The vision and the cry from Macedonia are as real and vivid today as they were to the apostle Paul—They come from those who sit in darkness, not only in foreign field, but at our very door—from delta, canebrake, cotton field and rice swamp. Be prepared to carry the message" (Untitled speech, 176). Brown reminds her audience in the post-slavery United States that there is still work to be done and that elocution will prepare her people for that work of persuasion to gain equality. In this passage and in others, power is defined not as dominance for Brown, but as self-mastery in concert with the powers of others.

In an early journal, Brown promises the reader "the odds and ends of a travelling career, begun March 16th in the year of our Lord 1881, by a girl who has an idea that she is not a cipher nor a figurehead" (Diaries 1). This passage describes Brown's method of self-construction throughout her career by means of analogy to making a quilt: through elocutionary training and performance, piecing together the odds and ends of a fragmented life into a tool for self-control and social influence. It is also Brown's method of adapting her sources: she weaves together such disparate elements as classical rhetoric, Delsartean elocution, theories of evolutionary development, and a spirituality arising from her African Methodist Episcopalian religion. She draws from works on eloquence by Cicero, Quintilian, and Augustine and frequently cites Delsarte, "the master-teacher" (*Elocution* 7, 30).[40] She formulates her conception of education along the lines of evolutionary child development taken from progressive white educators (*Bits and Odds* 5; *Elocution* 6).[41] And she sees education as supported by a Christian foundation, "The study of the Word" (*Elocution* 35).

But she also synthesizes and revises these materials and thus masters them: her theory proposes physical and mental exercises designed to prepare speakers to be instruments of spiritual powers; exercises arranged scientifically in stages to imitate the original evolutionary development of speech in humans, from gesture to voice to articulation; and powers mastered so that they will only be used ethically. Her theory allows her to piece together and claim her whole heritage—classical, African, and United States—and so to validate her self as a whole, free, speaking person.

Conclusion

These theoretical works on elocution by women are important because they help to explain the movement of women's politics from parlor entertainment in the earlier nineteenth century to public speaking on such a diversity of causes as abolition, religion, temperance, and suffrage later in the century.

If we borrow a question that Jane Tompkins in *Sensational Designs* asks about sentimental fiction of the mid-nineteenth century, we might ask, "what kind of cultural work is elocution doing?"[42] As we have seen, elocution provides release to emote for a very uptight society and yet also reinforces domestic ideology about the control of the body that all gentlefolk, but especially women, were expected to maintain. In this way, elocution reinforces training in the performance of gender, but may also become a site of resistance to gender ideology.[43] Because elocution exercises freed women from restrictive clothing and aimed at bodily strength, elocution was also one site where women intervened in the process of learning to perform gender "correctly." In elocution handbooks, women reimagined women's bodies not as weak and soft, but as strong and powerful.

In her study of sentimental culture as represented in conduct literature, Karen Halttunen argues that the parlor became a third sphere between the public and domestic, a place where sincere women could counteract "hypocritical" men and have moral influence over others (59), "a stage setting for the genteel performance" (101). For these women who performed, taught, and theorized elocution, the parlor and parlor entertainment skills were also a step toward broader social roles for women. It is no accident that women's education blossomed in parlors, in reading groups and conversation parties, that women's activist movements of the nineteenth century—abolition, women's rights, temperance—began in parlor meetings, that the first women speakers generally began speaking in parlors to all-women audiences. Elocution, which originated as training in conversation, reading aloud, and social deportment, by the end of the nineteenth century was also an avenue for women to self-control, to public performance, and to social activism. Thus elocution adapted conversation as a model for all discourse.

As Joanne Dobson points out, the most central values in sentimental culture were "sympathy, affection, and relation" (283). Elocution was connected to sentimental culture because it carried domestic values into the public sphere. Although these sentimental qualities were tied for women to domestic ideology, that does not mean that the women who composed elocution theory and texts were conservative. Even though defending sentimental poetry, Bennett still assumes, for the period of 1820 to 1860, that sentimentalists and bluestockings were in different camps (xliii). Moreover, Nan Johnson concludes that "The power of that institutional stature [of parlor speaking] was wielded in the service of a highly conservative agenda of gender behavior—not in the service of expanding public rhetorical opportunities for women as well as men" (*Gender and Rhetorical Space* 46).[44] These conclusions do not hold for the second half of the century, when both conservative and radical women moving into the public sphere used sentiment as their prime persuasive tactic—think of the success of the sentimental propaganda of the temperance campaign, which expanded into a wide range of social reforms, including kindergartens, child care for working women, laws against rape and abusive husbands, women's property rights, and labor reform. The incorporation of sentiment into pulpit rhetoric also aided women's entry into preaching, in many sects, as well. In the late nineteenth century, elocution empowered many American women because it offered them, through the avenue of bodily expression of emotion, control over their own bodies and, tentatively, entry to the public sphere. Elocution did not die out, but transmuted, becoming part of twentieth-century public speaking, theatrical performance, modern dance, and physical education. In the guise of elocution, sentimental culture lasted the rest of the nineteenth century for women, disappearing eventually into public speaking, drama, and modern dance and gymnastics.

With the development of elocution aimed at women, the tradition of women's rhetoric espoused in handbooks for several centuries came to its full development. Characterized by conversation as a model of discourse, acknowledgement of the gendered circumstances of communication, defense of women's rights to speak out, and attention to the body as means of persuasion and control, women's rhetorical theory had, by the end of the nineteenth century, developed a parallel theory to men's rhetorical theory. By the end of the nineteenth century, as Carol Mattingly puts it, "women [had] deftly negotiated" the territory of "cultural restrictions . . . in order to reimagine themselves in a world more conductive to their needs" (*Appropriate[ing] Dress* 13). Ironically, however, once public speaking by women was accepted, the need for such a theory of women's rhetoric ceased. In composition textbooks by women at the end of the nineteenth century, addressed to mixed audiences, women compositionists, as we shall see in the conclusion, returned to the male model of public speaking.[45]

Conclusion: Composition Textbooks by Women and the Decline of a Women's Tradition

By the end of the nineteenth century, there was a firmly established women's tradition of rhetorical theory devised by women. It had been developed not in rhetoric textbooks but in humanist treatises and dialogues on women's education, conduct manuals for women, defenses of women's preaching, and elocution handbooks. Taking conversation as a model of discourse, acknowledging the gendered circumstances of communication, defending women's right to speak publicly, and claiming an embodied rhetoric for women, this tradition helps explain women's political success and the growth of women's organizations in the nineteenth century, as well as the development of a diversified rhetorical tradition that spoke to different segments of the educated public. At the end of the nineteenth century, however, this women's tradition created by women rhetorical theorists simply disappeared, as thoroughly as the first English colony in America on Roanoke Island. What happened? This chapter concludes the story of a rise and fall of a women's tradition and answers the question of its disappearance by examining composition textbooks.

The disappearance of a women's tradition of rhetoric can be explained partly by examining composition and rhetoric textbooks by women. During the second half of the nineteenth century in the United States, women at last began to write textbooks for public schools, academies, and even colleges, and for mixed-gender audiences. Concurrently, women gradually acquired some equality with men in public forums for speaking and writing, and women's experiences in communication become more and more similar to men's. By the last quarter of the nineteenth century, many women as well as men were educated in rhetoric, and, until college, in the same schools. Women as well as men were preaching, or at least "exhorting." Women as well as men were elocutionists. Women as well as men were speaking out on political topics. And women, even more than men, were teaching.

At the end of the nineteenth century, when women begin to publish composition and rhetoric textbooks, they were writing not only for a female audience, but for both boys and girls, and women were the majority of public school teachers in America. Consequently, conversation as a model for all discourse becomes much less important to women's conception of communication, while remaining central in the realm of pedagogy.

This chapter, then, gives a brief overview of the rise of women teachers of composition and their publication of textbooks and an explanation of the reasons those books did not, in general, offer the conversational rhetoric of the women's tradition we have seen established over the course of several centuries.

The scholarship on women's composition textbooks has concentrated on college textbooks by Gertrude Buck and Mary Augusta Jordan. In this chapter, I treat these textbooks in the context of women's overall production of composition handbooks during the course of the century. For nineteenth-century women, the high school or academy was often their final schooling, and many academies offered both high school level and college level coursework. If we add these many textbooks, we have a much richer sense of women's theories of communication. I have not chosen textbooks that were the most popular, but rather ones that represent the range of possibilities, for women published rhetorical grammars (Elizabeth Oram, Nelly Knox, and Lucy A. Chittenden), classical rhetorics (Harriet Keeler and Emma Davis), belles lettres handbooks (Virginia Waddy, Sara Lockwood, Elizabeth Spalding), and empiricist textbooks (Frances Lewis, Gertrude Buck).[1] I researched these texts, expecting to find that women were strongly influenced by the women's tradition of rhetoric that had preceded the rise of composition. But conversation as a conceptual model for communication is rare across all these texts, except in those that emphasize pedagogy.

The exception is Mary Augusta Jordan's college-level handbook, *Correct Writing and Speaking*, which I treat at length. Jordan's handbook for women seems intended as a substitute for college and combines the latest work in philology with the women's tradition of conversational rhetoric: it treats the history of English, advice on public speaking, but also guidance in conversation and letter writing, and throughout the book the author contests the correctness of the theory of language popular in men's textbooks of this time period. Jordan thus also challenges the popular list of modes of discourse by her emphasis on conversation and letter writing and suggests a collaborative relationships between speaker and audience—quite a difference from the men's tradition.

To conclude this study, we will take an overview of the tradition and consider the ways that it was merged into mainstream composition studies, especially in the model of conversation for pedagogy.

Women Teachers and Composition Textbooks

Women's admission to the writing of textbooks on rhetoric and composition depended on several things: the increase of women teachers in elementary and high schools during the nineteenth century, the migration of literacies from privileged to less privileged groups after the Civil War, and the changeover at the end of the nineteenth century from an emphasis on oral persuasion to an emphasis on composition.[2] In current literacy studies, definitions of literacy have rapidly mutated in the last twenty years: a most helpful contemporary scholarly definition is Deborah Brandt's: "literacy [is] not the narrow ability to deal with texts but the broad ability to deal with other people as a writer or a reader" (*Literacy as Involvement* 14).[3] Brandt has also argued that literacy migrates because it is passed on not only through dominant educational institutions, but also from mentors to less privileged readers and writers. She analyzes the ways that contemporary women "filch" literate tools "from more educated, higher-status men," and the means by which "dominant forms of literacy migrate" causing a "subversive diversion of literate power."[4] This chapter argues that women writing rhetoric and composition handbooks during the second half of the nineteenth century appropriate literacy from elite masculine sources in quite similar ways and divert literate power toward women and less privileged social classes. This chapter furthermore traces the merging of conversational rhetoric from the women's tradition into the mainstream teaching of rhetoric in composition textbooks, where it is housed mainly in discussions of the use of conversation in pedagogy.

Composition in the nineteenth century seems to have been viewed as a private activity even when it addressed a public audience and was therefore more appropriate than public speaking to women's education. By the end of the nineteenth century, the majority of public school teachers, and so the majority of composition teachers in the United States, were women.[5]

Once women became teachers of composition and writers of composition and rhetoric textbooks, one would expect that there would be carryovers from the women's tradition of rhetoric that had grown during the last several centuries, that conceptions of rhetoric and conversation as a model of discourse would have migrated from humanist treatises on women's education, defenses of women's preaching, conduct book rhetoric for women, and elocution handbooks to composition teaching and textbooks. But that is not exactly the case. Instead, as women's position changed, as women moved into public roles as speakers and teachers and writers, the necessity for a domestic conception of rhetoric decreased. Elementary and high schools were transformed into coeducational institutions; while there are occasional gendered assignments, with subjects for composition classified as male or female, textbooks by women nevertheless assume they are preparing both girls and boys for similar tasks of public communication.[6] A brief overview of women's composition textbooks will demonstrate the absence of conversational rhetoric as a main component of composition teaching.

But first, a definition of composition would be helpful. One might suppose that there is no need for a definition of composition, that its meaning is transparent. But the transformation of education in communication from a public-speaking to a text-based program and the concomitant widening of the audience for education in communication during the nineteenth century changed meanings of rhetoric drastically. For this reason, Linda Flower's definition in *The Construction of Negotiated Meaning* helps us understand that change: for Flower, composition is "a literate action," a "problem-solving process shaped not only by available language, practices, partners, and texts, but by the ways people interpret the rhetorical situation they find themselves in, the goals they set, and the strategies they control" (2). "Grounded in the social purposes" of a literate practice within a "discourse community" (23), writing is "constructive," transforming "knowledge in purposeful ways"; it is also a "negotiation," juggling "conflicting demands" and choosing among "alternative goals, constraints, and possibilities" (2).[7]

The early rhetoric and composition textbooks by United States women employ a close study of grammar, sentence structure, and figurative language to teach writing as a generative and problem-solving process. As the title of Helen J. Robins and Agnes F. Perkins's textbook declares—*An Introduction to the Study of Rhetoric: Lessons in Phraseology, Punctuation and Sentence Structure* (1903)—to many nineteenth-century Americans, rhetoric was the study of what we would call rhetorical grammar or, more often, current-traditional rhetoric.[8] These early rhetorical grammars by women are joined midcentury by women's textbooks aimed at high school and academy students that adapt empiricist or belletristic or classical rhetoric for learning composition.

The first American composition textbook by a woman, *First Lessons in English Grammar and Composition with Exercises in the Elements of Pronunciation, Words for Dictation, and Subjects for Composition*, published by Elizabeth Oram in 1846, belongs to this tradition of rhetorical grammar. Oram was an artist and a teacher in New York City from 1815 to 1847.[9] Aimed at an audience of public elementary school children, Oram's textbook is meant to be used when students are learning physically to write: her preface instructs the teacher to dictate the whole book to students in small sections,[10] and it is organized to teach children, through imitation, progressively larger linguistic units—first letters, then syllables, then parts of speech, and finally sentences. The preface to Oram's handbook promises to convey to students "principles which lie at the foundation of the structure of our language" and to help children operate, in written form, "the machinery [of speech] that makes the soul visible" (ii). This textbook thus promises language as a means of generating meaning, but does not take conversation as the main model of discourse.

Other rhetorical grammars serve similar purposes. Mrs. N. L. Knox (catalogued under Nelly Lloyd Knox Heath), in *Elementary Lessons in English for Home and School Use, Part First: How to Speak and Write Correctly* (Teacher's Edition), published in 1885, emphasizes correctness in speaking and writing, but does so through inductive principles, influenced by Johann Pestalozzi's "object teaching" philosophy of education.[11] For example, Knox recommends that teachers arrive at the abstract concept of *noun* by holding up a variety of objects and that teachers define *noun* only after several days' experience with the concept, as the name of objects—persons, places, and things (pt. 1, 4–10). "It is what the child does for himself," Knox suggests, "not what is done for him, that really educates him" (pt. 1, ix). In part 2, composition is introduced through sentence generation based on grammatical principles. Thus Knox teaches grammar and composition as a means of generating meaning but does not draw on the tradition of women's rhetoric based on conversation as a model of discourse, despite her progressive pedagogy.

Miss Lucy A. Chittenden, in *The Elements of English Composition: A Preparation for Rhetoric*, published in Chicago in 1886, develops a whole model of teaching composition based on the generative sentence exercises of grammar-rhetorics: exercises at every stage that require students first to imitate and then to generate according to specific guidelines. Her title page tells us that she is a teacher of English language and literature in an Ann Arbor high school, and she aims her volume at "the lower grades of High School" to help students who are not yet prepared for the study of rhetoric "to avoid the blunders, if not to acquire the graces of composition" (iii). However, Chittenden builds her program of composition teaching not on correcting mistakes but on generating and varying sentence structures (revising sentences, for example, by adding noun clauses or adverbial clauses or independent clauses, 10–14). In her introduction, Chittenden explains that her exercises are designed to move students from "reproduction" to "original" composition, step by step (iv–v); and for higher-order composition, she uses the same model, asking students first to learn a template for outlining, for example, then to fill it in, and then to compose an original essay with these discourse conventions in mind (24, 39, 53, 169). Like Oram and Knox, Chittenden thus uses generative grammar to teach composition as generating meaning, but does not employ conversation as a model for discourse.[12]

Even when we consider the larger manuals by women for high school and academy composition teaching, there is little evidence of the importation of ideas on conversation as a model of discourse from the women's tradition of rhetoric that we have been examining. *Elements of Composition and Rhetoric, with Copious Exercises in Both Criticism and Construction* (1888) by Virginia Waddy (née Waddey), aimed at high school students, combines belles lettres rhetoric with American patriotism. The title page announces that the author is a "Teacher of Rhetoric in the Richmond High School, Richmond, Va.," and the circumstance that Waddy's maiden name, Waddey, is the same as her publisher's name suggests that her textbook was a family publication. Waddy includes a long section on grammar, drawing on the rhetorical grammars of earlier in the century, but also underpins her discussion of composition with the belles lettres principles of the "graces of Rhetoric," the importance of taste (iii), style as self-expression (117–96), and the sublime (257–65). Her reading choices suggest she is molding republican citizens: she instructs her students to avoid using French, Latin, and other foreign phrases (121), and she uses American prose as her default model, with excerpts from Ralph Waldo Emerson, Nathaniel Hawthorne, John Webster, Washington Irving, and Oliver Wendell Holmes (although she also uses some British examples). She further includes student examples. In Waddy's textbook, however, we see conversation as a model of discourse only in a vestigial form: the history of rhetoric, she explains, has developed from oral public speaking to written composition (1), but conversational language is yet the basis of good composition style (294).

Inductive Lessons in Rhetoric by Frances Lewis, published in 1900, draws on empiricist and belles lettres rhetorical traditions combined with progressive pedagogy and addresses an audience of high school students (iii). Lewis promises to discard formalistic teaching of rhetoric and to show teachers how to teach inductively and directly from literature (iii–iv) to produce students who "think independently" (viii). Lewis borrows ideas from George Campbell's popular *Philosophy of Rhetoric* for her explanation of the rhetorical importance of the association of ideas and to teach the figures of speech catalogued according to Campbell's laws of resemblance, contiguity, and contrast (41–59).[13] Following Alexander Bain, Lewis's section on paragraphs emphasizes unity and arrangement (21–27), and her chapter on rhetorical force (36–85) is reminiscent of William Whately's approach to rhetoric. Such borrowing from previous textbooks is not unusual; Carr, Carr, and Schultz argue that all nineteenth-century composition textbooks are compilations (154, 205). In addition, Lewis's handbook covers the empiricist genres of exposition, argumentation, and persuasion.

The empiricist rhetorical theory in Lewis's *Inductive Lessons* is melded with a belles lettres interest in style, and the literary canon is mined for examples (especially Twain, Whittier, Dickens, Shakespeare, George Eliot, Helen Hunt Jackson, Elizabeth Stuart Phelps, and Henry James). Lewis does not posit conversation as a model for all discourse, but instead significantly develops the sections on public speaking topics for composition, covering persuasion in depth (246–56), especially the use of feelings (251). Her understanding of composition as the social construction of negotiated meaning is apparent in the political nature of the topics she suggests for themes: topics for argumentation include many issues related to citizenship and immigrants—women's vote, equal pay, child labor, capital punishment, lynch law, vivisection, Chinese immigration, socialization of railroads, and labor strikes (243).

Textbooks by women for academies and high schools during the nineteenth century are eclectic rhetorics that combine ideas from the rhetorical grammars, empiricist and belles lettres rhetoric, and object pedagogy. As women achieve the rights to public speaking and published writings, there is less and less distinction between the experiences of men and women in communication. When women finally begin to write composition and rhetoric textbooks, they are the majority of American public school teachers, and they are addressing a mixed audience of girls and boys. As a consequence, the importance for women theorists of conversation as a model of discourse fades and becomes vestigial, affecting (as will be seen later in this chapter) teaching methods, but not communication theory.

Mary Augusta Jordan's *Correct Writing and Speaking*: The Last of Its Kind

It is worth examining the major exception to the disappearance of the women's tradition of conversational rhetoric in composition textbooks by women to see what composition studies might have looked like if the women's tradition had been more fully incorporated. Mary August Jordan's *Correct Writing and Speaking* (1904) was addressed to an audience of women and was published in a national series called "The Woman's Home Library."[14]

Mary Augusta Jordan (1855–1921), educated at Vassar College, was a professor at Smith College, a white all-woman secular college opened in 1875.[15] Her experience at women's colleges helps to explain her preservation of the women's tradition of conversational rhetoric in her handbook for women who are attempting the equivalent of a college education through home-study. Her eclectic study combines masculine and feminine traditions of rhetoric and language study: eighteenth-century belles lettres rhetoric and the new science of linguistics from the men's tradition, and conversational rhetoric from the women's tradition.[16] Moreover, she critiques the 1892 Harvard Report calling for more attention to correctness in composition: making room for her nonstandard students and maintaining that there are "many ways that persons of intelligence have of expressing themselves" (9), Jordan draws on both men's and women's traditions to argue that correctness is not possible for such a mutable force as language change.

In *Correct Writing and Speaking*, Jordan borrows from the men's tradition in order to subvert one of the main purposes of elite male education: exclusivity. Her adaptation of belles lettres rhetoric, for example, undermines the emphasis on taste as cultural signal of class status by pluralizing taste. In her chapter titled "The Office of Criticism," Jordan cites Matthew Arnold, the Victorian helmsman of belles lettres criticism, only to disagree with him. Instead of Arnold's the "best that is known and thought," Jordan wants an Americanized, democratic, and reception-based[17] criticism that consists of "a disinterested effort to learn" (75) and eclectic, wide-ranging reading:

> The taste for the best may come to be as arrant a convention as the thought-less preference for one's own way simply because it is one's own, and may be as unintelligently maintained. The charms of grace, flexibility, and variety can not be had except as the expression of constantly renewed comparison of one's own methods with those of all sorts and conditions of men; for there can be no doubt that English expression, written and spoken, is a debtor to the Jew and the Gentile, the Greek and the Barbarian. In other words, mental alertness, catholicity of taste, rigid self-discipline, patient experiment, and humility in self-reference, are absolute requisites in the work of the student of English. (80–81)

English style, and so American taste, Jordan maintains, originates in the melting pot of diverse languages and cultures and is consequently a range of individual interests rather than a template of rigid conformity. "The disinterested effort to learn," Jordan suggests, "is the best that the plain man can get out of his own life, or hand on to others. Through it the humblest life takes on the splendor and thrill of creative effort" (78). Instead of the best of the elite, Jordan rejects a normative view of taste and promotes a democratic one, the best judgment of each individual literate person. Nevertheless, for Jordan "taste" does not consist in mere self-expression, but in learning eloquence through comparative reading (80): "catholicity of taste, . . . self-discipline, patient experiment" (81). While correct English is not possible, good English consists of "hospitality to ideas and . . . energy of self-development" (81). Thus in her handbook, Jordan offers a democratized belles lettres rhetoric accessible to all republican citizens: "The average citizen in the United States aims to have a mind of his own, and among other furniture for it, he covets means of expression. The dictionary helps him to find out what he means and to say his mind" (228).

Jordan draws on the new science of linguistics and histories of the English language to debunk the eighteenth-century men's elocutionary tradition that advocates correctness in pronunciation according to pronouncing dictionaries. She pits the "Guides to Pronunciation" against the many dialects of English (10–11), makes fun of Sheridan's treatise on elocution (33), denounces pronouncing dictionaries as "a sorry lot" (35), and, instead, quotes the modern linguistics expert A. J. Ellis on phonetics for three straight pages (54–56). After a brief survey of the history of English with samples (in original spelling) of Anglo-Saxon, William Tyndale, Sir Thomas More, and Ben Jonson, Jordan concludes that there is no standard pronunciation (25), no such thing as "purity of speech" (26), and clinches her argument with the authority of Samuel Johnson (27). Jordan concludes her pluralist discussion on "The Standard" by confirming that there is "no standard English . . . no one correct way of writing or of speaking English," but "there are many ways of attaining correctness" (36).

Thus *Correct Speaking and Writing* is actually a text denying the title: there is no "correct" or standard English (36, 71), because language changes and individuals express themselves individually (83–87). Jordan consequently opposes the dominant trend in college composition theory written for men: after the "Harvard Report," published in 1892, which criticized students' grammatical errors, correctness became a major goal of most composition textbooks (Kitzhaber, 73–77, 346–52). Jordan is quite aware of the class basis for the desire to speak "correctly" (101, 103),[18] and she revises the concept of "correctness" out of her understanding of her audience of women: either reading at home with no education, or contained within the home after college, the readers of "The Woman's Home Library" were expected to speak "correctly," as if they belonged to the class of their husbands, when they did not have the same education as their husbands. Since there is no "correct" English, then, one learns to speak and write by "study, discipline, and practice," not by rules (100), and the person who has knowledge, curiosity, and moral values will speak best (229).

Revising the men's tradition of belletristic rhetoric and linguistic science for women's use, Jordan also draws on the conversational rhetoric of the women's tradition. *Correct Writing and Speaking*, says the editor of the Woman's Home Library series, should appeal "to women who do not mean to let their weapons rust, nor to abandon intellectual pursuits because they have daughters at school" and to "Women's Clubs, where it may provoke discussion" (4). Jordan further acknowledges her feminine audience by alternating masculine and feminine pronouns to include women readers: on one page she writes, "a letter . . . should [not] compel the reader to cudgel her brains" (239), and two pages later, she asserts, "The careful writer will read and study the work done by successful writers of his own and other times" (241).[19] This study has traced the growth of a women's tradition of rhetoric through humanist treatises on education, defenses of women's preaching, conduct book rhetorics, and elocution manuals. Jordan draws mainly from conduct book rhetoric, but we can see some influence from the defenses of women's preaching and elocution handbooks, as well.

Conversation,[20] not public speaking, is Jordan's model for all discourse: "The good talker" is the "background for the serious business of life" (57), and despite American prejudice against eloquence as insincere, "Probably talk enters into more forms of social activity at the present time than in any former age" (58). The "art of oratory is near extinction," replaced by newspapers and pamphlets (64), Jordan argues, and the goal of good speech should be "free conversation," not an "imposed litany" of faddish expressions (11).

For Jordan, taking conversation as a model of discourse requires revising the "kinds" of discourse that she inherited: the familiar descriptive, narrative, expository, and argumentative, or the classical praise/blame, legal, and deliberative. Rather than these public forms, she classifies private forms of discourse, including conversation; in this way, her handbook is similar to many conduct books aimed at women during the nineteenth century. Like Madeleine de Scudéry in her humanist dialogues and like Hannah More and Lydia Sigourney in their conduct books, Jordan constructs a rhetoric of conversation: "*Fair play* may be offered as the brief advice for the conduct of private conversation. Don't force the tone of your voice, nor your subjects, nor your interests on the company. If your voice is tired, at least consider whether you have given anybody else time for the proper exercise of hers" (232). Offering conduct book advice on conversation, Jordan suggests that wit should be "pleasure giving" and should never consist of a joke at another person's expense (185). Jordan enlarges the feminine principle of self-effacement into a general principle of social harmony: "Be careful not to sacrifice to your own feeling of interest in what you are saying or thinking, or to the expression you are making of yourself, the convenience and pleasure of others in working out similar expressions of themselves" (234–35). How improbable such a sentence would be in a nineteenth-century rhetoric directed at men![21]

Jordan extends the boundaries of conversation as an artful form to areas of women's experience usually left silent, implicitly acknowledging the functions that middle-class women and lower-class servants have in common: "Don't fear to speak politely and interestingly to those who happen to serve you. The relation might be reversed" (235). Jordan addresses, I think, the shifting class position of middle-class women in her culture, at one moment "master" of servants, at another moment, servant to the masters. Jordan offers very specialized advice for women that recalls the conduct book tradition. She commiserates with women for their lack of formal training in public speaking (66–68) and recommends rules of thumb for diction (183–89) that lead to a critique of women who allow their children to be raised by a bored nurse (191). Jordan also suggests that degrees of friendship are reflected in conversation etiquette: "The familiar intercourse of intimate friends permits, by common consent, waste of time, display of personal weakness, or the expression of strong feeling that should never be imposed on general society, even in private" (233). The puzzling phrase "general society, even in private" is perhaps a code, indicating a woman in company with male family members.

In addition, Jordan acknowledges the socialization of women, representing it as a nonacademic education comparable to that of elocution: "Few women are ignorant of the education they have undergone in the effort to fit themselves for the discharge of their purely private obligations. It probably takes as many years to learn to keep one's temper with an exasperating companion as it does to acquire control of the pitch and carrying tones of one's voice" (67–68). I read *companion* as a code word for "male," perhaps as specific as "husband."

Even for speaking in public, Jordan takes the interaction of conversation as a model, in ways that are reminiscent of the defenses of women's preaching. "The audience is not to be dominated, cajoled, or bullied," Jordan insists. "It is to be interpreted, and made to know its own self in terms of something else than prejudice, or passion, or lazy self-indulgence. . . . The successful speaker of the present will use all his art to enable him to discern the signs of the spiritual forces coming into action in his presence. His aim will be to conserve them, to let as little as possible real energy go to waste" (69). The phrase "spiritual forces" recalls defenses of women's preaching, where even while women are claiming public preaching for women, they nevertheless dissipate anxiety by citing God's inspiration as their warrant. In addition, the model for speech in this passage from Jordan is based on conversation, not public discourse, and revises the goal of classical rhetoric—persuasion—into the goals of social harmony and self-knowledge. I read this, in the context of Jordan's culture, as a feminization of rhetoric—despite the masculine pronouns in this passage—one that comes dangerously close to enforcing the status quo of rigid gender roles for women: "unselfishness" is a quality of Jordan's ideal speaker (229). To apply Rachel Blau DuPlessis's words on nineteenth-century women writers to Jordan, "Being a [speaker] is . . . reinterpreted as self-sacrifice for the woman, and thus aligned with feminine ideology" (87). Although it comes close to enforcing gender roles, Jordan's theory does not, because her description of the relationship of speaker and audience is also an acknowledgment of composition as negotiated meaning, of the speaker as "medium" (70).

According to Jordan, "women may be said to have come into entirely new duties and new responsibilities" in the area of "public speech" (66). She is quite conscious of creating a new body of knowledge for women, and she even makes fun of Eliza Farrar's earlier conduct book rhetorics, scornfully combining Farrar's titles to advise that "When all the lessons have been done, . . . the scholars settle down to a type of social intercourse that has a medium vastly different from the King's English or the 'Young Lady's Epistolary Guide'"(57). [22]

Building a theory of rhetoric for women, Jordan treats letters, and even diaries. She argues that discourse lies on a continuum from private to public, and that letters are "closest to the personal character of the writer" (60), diaries and journals being a subgenre of letters (238). She sees letters as, at once, a personal "gift" (61, 238) and potentially a published literary form (61)—she cites Esther Edwards (63) and Lady Mary Wortley Montagu (24) as examples, along with many men. Jordan notes a new style of "suggestiveness in contemporary letters" (61), and sets forth standards for this private-public genre: letter writing requires "skill in presentation, vividness of detail, choice of significant subject matter, evidence of delicate and precise knowledge of the reader's taste and character, and just so much revelation of the writer's self and interests as shall really serve the reader's" (62). She uses the model of conversation for such writing: "In a letter, as in conversation, the other person should be left something of the topic to deal with. Letters should not be simply 'unpublished works,' but part of a pleasurable give and take, of suggestion, comment, interested question, and generous self-expression. The form might be after this sort: Something about me, something about you, something about the wide world" (239). It is in such a context that she justifies the necessity of (women) learning to write well: "Nearly everybody professes hatred of writing. Yet nearly everybody admires and enjoys good writing in others and depends upon it as one of the consolations or resources of life" (237). The subtext that I hear in Jordan's text is her preparing her women students through this writing to support friendships made in a hometown or at a college, over long years after they are separated by marriage.[23]

Jordan's *Correct Writing and Speaking*, then, is not exactly a college composition textbook, but rather a handbook addressed to women who are excluded from college but desire an education in speaking and writing equivalent to that of the college-educated. While the composition textbooks of other women addressed to a mixed audience reveal the disappearance of conversation as a model for discourse, Jordan's handbook, addressed to women, offers it as a main principle. Jordan merges conversational rhetoric with men's belletristic and linguistic studies in order to critique contemporary trends, citing correctness as a firm standard for composition and communication. Her handbook thus suggests one direction the field might have taken if more of the central features of women's conversational rhetoric had been incorporated into the study of composition.

Remnants of Conversation

This study has traced the rise of a transatlantic tradition of women's rhetoric from the seventeenth century through its decline by the end of the nineteenth century. This is not a continuous history, but a series of moments where particular expository genres were taken up by women and used to promote conversation as a model of discourse. There is nothing inherently feminine in this model, but it resulted from the particular domestic roles women were required to play in these Anglo-American societies. This tradition of conversational rhetoric arose because it served women's interests in learning to communicate over the course of these centuries when women of the upper and middle classes achieved some education: while women were denied full participation in college education, public speaking, and published writings, they still communicated in conversation, letter writing, reading aloud, speaking at social events, public prayer and even sometimes preaching, and they developed means of training themselves for these rhetorical purposes. In humanist dialogues and defenses of women's education in the seventeenth century, women developed a concept of conversation as a model for all discourse. In conservative conduct books of the eighteenth and nineteenth centuries, women helped to construct a theory of gendered spheres of rhetoric that both enabled their communication in conversation and letters and also—perhaps—restricted their participation in public speaking. However, the rise of parlor entertainments and parlor politics among women is perhaps partially a successful result of such restrictions. In progressive defenses of women's preaching from the seventeenth to the nineteenth centuries, women modified conceptions of the sermon to include testimony and argued for women's rights to public speech, especially preaching. In elocution handbooks of the nineteenth century, women studied voice and bodily movement and learned poise for domestic occasions, but also delivery for public occasions.

Though most of this tradition based on conversation as a model for discourse did not enter the mainstream of composition textbooks, and so faded, it nevertheless influenced nineteenth-century study of composition in ways that are still important today. In many composition textbooks by women, conversation becomes a model for pedagogy: the teaching of writing depends on conversation and dialogue. This final section of the study examines a few representative examples of this merger of conversational rhetoric into the mainstream of composition studies.

Sara E. Husted Lockwood (1854–c. 1902) published *Lessons in English, Adapted to the Study of American Classics: A Text-Book for High Schools and Academies* in 1888. As the title declares, this textbook addresses an audience of students in academies and high schools and their English teachers, and it assumes the teachers will be female—the English teacher is called "she" (280). Lockwood was herself a high school teacher. Born in Bridgeport, Connecticut, she gradu-ated from New Haven High School (called "Hillhouse High School" on the title page of *Lessons*) in 1873 and taught there from 1874 to 1890.[24]

Lessons in English is a composition textbook in the tradition of the belles lettres rhetoric of Hugh Blair and many previous English and American hand-books. Lockwood's goal, she tells teachers in the introduction, is to develop in students "a critical literary taste" and "Power of thought and facility of expres-sion," as well as "a broad general culture" (v). Students progress through several genres of composition until they are able "to exercise [their] imagination, de-pending entirely upon [their] own taste and ingenuity" (323–24). Rather than canonical European literature and culture, however, Lockwood's text features American literature; she establishes a canon in a final chapter containing bio-graphical sketches of Washington Irving, Henry W. Longfellow, John Greenleaf Whittier, Nathaniel Hawthorne, Oliver Wendell Holmes, James Russell Lowell, and William Cullen Bryant. Lockwood combines this belletristic approach to composition with progressive teaching methods, using the pupils' own com-positions as models (297–99).

In teaching methods, then, the concept of conversation as a model of dis-course enters Lockwood's text.[25] One exercise she suggests is collaborative writing: "Good results are obtained by having parts of this work done by the class as a whole, the teacher writing upon the blackboard at the dictation of various pupils" (xvi). She urges that teachers bring in elocutionary techniques to coach students in reading aloud in "natural, conversational tones" (xvi). In Lockwood's text this interest in conversation as a model for discourse extends to some modes of composition: students' sentences should be "pleasing . . . [to] the ear" (205); and "in writing, as in speaking [students should employ] courte-ous habits of expression" (272). The section on letter writing sounds very like those in conduct books: the letter is a "conversation" (272), and a letter writer should "write as you talk" (272).

Harriet L. Keeler and Emma C. Davis's *Studies in English Composition with Lessons in Language and Rhetoric* was published in Boston in 1891 by a national press, Allyn and Bacon, and went through two more editions, in 1892 and 1900. Born in 1846, Harriet Louise Keeler taught as a teenager in Cherry Valley, New York, then took an A.B. at Oberlin College in 1874 and an LL.D at Western Re-serve University in 1913.[26] She served as superintendent in the Cleveland public schools from 1871 until 1879 and again in 1912, and taught at Central High School from 1879 to 1909.[27] All we know of Emma C. Davis is that she must have taught with Harriet Keeler in the Cleveland public schools.[28] Designed for high schools and preparatory schools that have weekly exercises in composition, *Studies in English Composition* covers four years' worth of lessons (iii). An amalgamation of belles lettres and classical rhetoric, this textbook takes a strong stance against the correctness school of composition: "the spirit and thought of any exercise are more than the technical dress, and . . . if the former are developed, the latter will not be wanting" (iv). In its progressive pedagogy, Keeler and Davis's slim volume shows the influence of Oberlin.

While *Studies in English Composition* does not theorize conversation as a model for communication except in letters, the textbook puts into practice such a pedagogy: oral reproduction and recitation are encouraged as teaching tools throughout the volume. Students are asked, for example, to condense longer stories for oral reproduction (8). In the section on letter writing, Keeler and Davis evince a pragmatic skepticism about the letter writing tenet to "write as you speak" (46): although they urge that "a letter of friendship is a conversation on paper" (47), they nevertheless give exceptions to this rule of thumb: don't overdo emotions, avoid colloquialisms (46). A further use of conversation as a basis for pedagogy may be seen in their recommendation of starting beginning writing assignments with observation: students observe and orally describe a game of tag, a bird building a nest, street musicians, before they then individually write compositions on fishing, nutting, camping, and shopping (3–4, 6–7).

Elizabeth's Spalding's *The Problem of Elementary Composition: Suggestions for Its Solution* was published in Boston by D. C. Heath & Co. in 1896. Rather than a rhetoric composition handbook for students, this book is a guide for elementary school teachers, giving ideas for "elementary composition" (1). Elizabeth Hill Spalding (1854–c. 1909) took her A.B. at Vassar in 1874, and after marriage, lived and taught at Pratt Institute in Brooklyn, New York.[29] Spalding's *Problem of Elementary Composition* combines belles lettres composition taught to cultivate "judgment and taste" (74), classical rhetoric and lessons on figurative language and amplification, and progressive pedagogy. It is addressed to public school teachers, especially female one-room schoolhouse teachers.[30]

Like Lockwood, and like Keeler and Davis, conversation as a model for discourse has been relegated to pedagogy—but pedagogy is the centerpiece of Spalding's volume. "Education is progressive" (114), Spalding announces, and, indeed, her treatise promotes progressive educational principles, maintaining that students must experience confidence and delight in the classroom (4).

Spalding stresses "community work" or collaboration as a learning technique (1, 86): students in groups, for example, write songs to known tunes (2), and the class as a whole records their achievements in scrapbooks as a way of self-publishing students' writing (11, 13, 25–26). Spalding's use of group work aids students in understanding composition as the social construction of negotiated meaning. Group-writing letters, for instance, teaches neighborliness, as well as communication: "write a school-letter—a simple, brief little letter, contrived by putting all the heads together; a letter neatly written out, and actually sent somewhere—to another school? . . . There is a sense of neighborliness born of a letter and its quick reply" (6).

Conversation as a model for all discourse is a central tenet of this teaching philosophy, for it generates thought for writing, Spalding argues, "The writer believes that composition work need not be restricted to the production of written themes, but that it may include speaking as well as writing, work by a little community as well as work by individuals, and interesting conversations to rouse thought and deepen feeling" (1). In addition, oral exercises always precede written composition in her lesson plans (38, 75, 86). She urges teachers to use conversation to generate story writing for students (22):

> Suppose we had read a little from *Uncle Tom's Cabin*, making the extract easily intelligible by means of our own explanations. That might call out the question, "What is it to be a slave?" You will readily see how interesting and profitable a conversation with this for its topic might become. For the first time, the children might behold their own fetters, and they might break some of them; and the thought of helping those enslaved by poverty, or crime, or appetite, or disease, thus germinating, might in later years bear fruit in fine actions. (23)

Indeed, as this passage shows, Spalding sees conversation as the foundation of good teaching and social reform.

A final example of the migration of conversation as a model of discourse to pedagogy is Gertrude Buck (1871–1922). Buck has received a great deal of attention as the exceptional woman who published early college composition textbooks.[31] But for our purposes, she is one among a group of women who wrote composition textbooks that emphasized conversation as an element of pedagogy.

Having taken her Ph.D. at the co-ed University of Michigan and having taught at Vassar College for women, Gertrude Buck published five textbooks, several theoretical treatises, and many articles on pedagogy in which she revised sources in "scientific" progressive education theory by men like John Dewey and William James.[32] Buck felt free to adapt this psychological theory to her own subject of composition, arguing for an organic, developmental model of learning language and writing. Her emphasis, like those of male theorists, was on formal composition and public speech, but she started in the classroom with informal dialogue and written exercises, and she used conversation as a model for teaching and learning writing, a model adapted as a result of her new audiences of students at co-ed Michigan and female Vassar.

In her earliest work, *The Metaphor: A Study in the Psychology of Rhetoric* (1899), a philosophical exploration of the figure, Buck outlines several of the tenets on which she establishes all of her work: language is social, communication between a speaker and a hearer, or a writer and a reader;[33] language is in the process of evolutionary development both for the entire society and also for the individual speaker; and understanding and, consequently, education is based on an evolutionary psychological model rather than a mechanistic one. In this work, we can see clearly the influence of the women's tradition of rhetoric: "The theory that discourse is self-expression has reference only to the speaker: the hypothesis that it is persuasion makes the hearer all-important. When discourse is regarded as communication the two factors in the process are equally emphasized" (80). Buck here specifically critiques public speaking (persuasion) as a model and argues, instead, for the give and take of conversation as the foundation of discourse.

However, like Lockwood, Keeler and Davis, and Spalding, Buck emphasizes public speaking, not conversational rhetoric, as the norm, but also like these other women writers of composition textbooks, Buck advocates a pedagogy that centers on conversation and dialogue. *A Course in Expository Writing*, authored by Buck and Elisabeth Woodbridge and published in 1899, adapts empiricist rhetoric to college composition, stressing exposition as "conviction gained through sense-experience" (4), and defining it as communication "to make language take the place of experience" (1). *A Course in Argumentative Writing*, also published by Buck in 1899, similarly adapts empiricist rhetoric to persuasive writing, emphasizing psychology and privileging the inductive method (iii) and the student's "own first-hand observation and thought" (iv). In *A Course in Expository Writing* Buck also offers conversation as a model of pedagogy: for example, she explains that an oral debate on whether or not Lady Macbeth elicits sympathy from her audience prepares students for composing an essay on the character of Lady Macbeth (iv).

A Course in Argumentative Writing interweaves conversation as a teaching technique throughout. Buck advocates oral debate before writing (vii) and recommends taking examples for teaching from daily conversation (1). The exercises for argumentation include asking students to analyze their conversations with their friends for the elements of the argumentative process: "Write a . . . list of all the conclusions to which other people have recently tried to lead you. (Recall sermons and public addresses of any kind as well as private conversations.) Did you accept the conclusion in each case? If so, why? If not, why not? Would you have accepted it if the speaker had given you different reasons?" (8). Buck encourages a progressive pedagogy, recommending a subject matter for writing close to students' interests (iv, vii), oral debate in class to establish a purpose and sense of audience for writing outside of class (vii), and an inductive pedagogy that allows students to infer the principles by which they will then later compose (153–58). In the debate course that she designs, "students themselves take charge of the course" (168).

Buck is a fitting end to our study, which began with seventeenth-century humanist dialogues and defenses of women's education by women that envisioned conversation as a model for all discourse. Along the way, we surveyed conservative eighteenth- and nineteenth-century conduct book rhetoric that nevertheless gained women a public voice through parlor conversation and letter writing; and nineteenth-century elocution handbooks that offered poise in the parlor and confidence on stage and platform. We examined seventeenth- to nineteenth-century defenses of women's preaching that insinuated women into preaching by redefining preaching as conversation and at the same time radicalized women's rhetorical theory by arguing women's right to public speaking, especially on religion. In Buck, as in the other composition textbooks we have considered in this conclusion, we see how far women ventured from their beginnings in conversational rhetoric, for Buck advocates an empiricist, psychological rhetoric and public speaking for both sexes. Nevertheless, remnants of a women's tradition of conversational rhetoric remain in the composition pedagogy of Buck and other women writers of composition textbooks for mixed audiences.

Implications

By the end of the nineteenth century, defenses of women's education and women's preaching are no longer needed as women achieve the right to public speaking. Conduct book literature for women continued to be written, but as elementary education was extended equally to both sexes and women were admitted to college, conduct book literature lost its function of homeschooling and retreated to its other purpose of etiquette manual. Elocution dispersed into drama, modern dance, physical education, and public speaking, and training in reading aloud for family and community became an anachronism (especially with the popularity of the new invention, the radio). Women who wrote composition textbooks addressed an audience of mixed gender and assumed both men and women would be sending letters, speaking publicly, and as adults reading and writing for business and pleasure: the most widespread model of the literate adult, after all, was the female school teacher.

But in its heyday, conversation as a model for discourse in a tradition of women's rhetoric enabled nineteenth-century women to maintain the fiction of the private woman while participating in public political discussion, especially in abolition, the temperance movement, and social reform.[34] In their theory, women had constructed a transatlantic tradition of women's rhetoric that paralleled men's classical tradition. The women's tradition emphasized conversation as a model for all discourse, collaborative and consensual communication, and the art of listening; it acknowledged the gendered nature of communication and took gender as a means of persuasion; it explored techniques of embodied rhetoric in elocution. It challenged the traditional modes of discourse in its emphases on conversation and letter writing, and it offered an alternative view of the relationship between speaker and audience or writer and reader. But when women began to speak in public and write composition textbooks, they laid this tradition aside.

The disappearance of conversational rhetoric was a loss that recent developments in composition studies make apparent. Rhetoric and composition theory would have benefited from a strand that concentrated on dialogism, collaboration, and consensus during communication. Twentieth-century rhetoricians missed an opportunity when they cast off elocution as sentimental instead of incorporating the bodily language of emotions into public speaking. And certainly, an art of listening might have developed into methods of training conflict negotiators much sooner. In addition, in turning away from an all-women audience, women who theorized communication often also abandoned examples of women writers in favor of the male canon.

But this historical women's tradition, no matter how defunct, yet is important for our understanding of the history of rhetoric and composition because conversation is such an important model for our current classroom pedagogy. Let me cite just two examples, and any composition teacher will be able to think of others. In his famous article "Inventing the University," David Bartholomae describes a first-year student's grappling with academic writing in this way: a student "has to learn to speak our language, to speak as we do, to try on the peculiar ways of knowing, selecting, evaluating, reporting, concluding, and arguing that define the discourse of our community. . . . they have to invent the university by assembling and mimicking its language" (403). In this article, Bartholomae is offering conversation as a model for discourse, but also as a model for pedagogy. He is addressing composition teachers, and he is advising us that we need to help our students extend themselves into the community of the university through imitating its languages and conventions of reasoning, and we need to help our students become aware of the codes that define written academic conversation.

Similarly, in a recent guide to teaching composition, Suzanne Clark and Lisa Ede promote talking as a basis for composition pedagogy: "Talking about writing and writing about talking, students begin to weave a network of connections between speech and the written language. . . . Talking makes the community of students literate about their shared experiences. Talking also leads students to collaborate with one another, to be excited about one another's work, and to see writing as a social act rather than a solitary one" (10). In this teacher's guide, Clark and Ede are advocating that we, as teachers, relinquish some of our authority in order to allow students to conduct their own conversation in the classroom, and so learn how to adapt that academic, informed conversation as a model for their writing. In doing so, they are echoing Gertrude Buck, Mary Augusta Jordan, and many other women theorists. While there is not a direct link from the women's tradition of rhetoric to these examples of contemporary composition pedagogy, nevertheless, we can yet learn something about our own teaching practices from a tradition that taught women how to enter the conversation.

NOTES

WORKS CITED

INDEX

Notes

Preface

1. See Berlin, *Writing Instruction*; Kennedy, *Art of Persuasion*, *Art of Rhetoric*, and *Greek Rhetoric*; Murphy; and Howell, *Logic and Rhetoric* and *Eighteenth-Century British Logic*. For a brilliant critique of the Kennedy-Howell-Corbett school of history of rhetoric, see Berlin, "Revisionary Histories" 112–14. See also Poulakos 1–2, for his evaluation of Kennedy; Vitanza viii–xi, for his dialogue with Kennedy; and Crowley, "Let Me Get This," for her survey of the debate on historiography (1–8), as well as her definition of *constructionist* history, which presupposes that "categories such as 'human nature' and 'rhetoric' are produced and modified within the discourse of a given community or culture in accordance with current social or political requirements" (10).

2. The traditional histories of rhetoric do not, in general, treat any women theorists, since they concentrate on the textbooks of formal masculine rhetorical education. In his massive *Eighteenth-Century British Logic*, Howell revealed the effect of the development of the "new science," what I have called "empiricism" in this study, on eighteenth-century logic and rhetoric; these influences transformed rhetoric from an art into a science and refocused emphasis in the discipline on the psychology of the audience, rather than the invention of arguments; nevertheless, British rhetoric had four different lineages in the eighteenth century, according to Howell—a reinterpretation of classical rhetoric that includes all canons, stylistic rhetoric, elocution, and the new empirical rhetoric (for a brief survey of these, see 696–98). Howell mentions no women rhetorical theorists in his study. In his groundbreaking study, Kitzhaber pointed out that early nineteenth-century college rhetoric (for men) reworked and merged the belletristic rhetoric of Scotsman Hugh Blair and the psychological rhetoric of George Campbell, modified by the new science of linguistics; this rhetorical direction was overwhelmed at the end of the century by the demand for correctness generated by the 1892 Harvard Report, and rhetoric became a discipline devoted to the mechanics of grammar, paragraphing, and the four forms of discourse—description, narration, exposition, and argumentation. Berlin followed Kitzhaber, but divided nineteenth-century American writing instruction into four periods: early classical, Scottish psychological, romantic

(emphasizing Emerson), and current-traditional (emphasizing correctness). Although both mention Gertrude Buck, who wrote composition textbooks, Kitzhaber and Berlin set the direction of scholarly exploration of nineteenth-century writing instruction by considering only college composition texts (almost all by men) or writings of famous men (like Emerson). In *Nineteenth-Century Rhetoric*, Nan Johnson has explored the synthetic nature of American rhetoric, which combines classical, psychological, and epistemological concepts in textbooks for composition used in colleges; again, since she studies the most frequently used college textbooks, she is in actuality describing men's rhetoric. This trend of considering college textbooks, and so mainly men's texts, has continued in otherwise admirable studies of nineteenth-century Bostonian rhetoric by Broaddus and of the college tradition of composition by Brereton and by Crowley in *Methodical Memory*. Such preselection of materials, however, distorts conclusions. For example, although Brereton includes Luella Clay Carson's "Compilation of Standard Rules and Regulations Used by the English Department of the University of Oregon" (1898) in his sourcebook (one of only five women out of over fifty entries), he considers her list as a precursor for college handbooks, rather than realizing that women as normal and high school teachers had been compiling such lists for several decades before Carson. For such lists, see. e.g., Knox; Lockwood; and Keeler and Davis.

Introduction: Adding Women's Rhetorical Theory to the Conversation

1. Here I allude not only to Aristotle's definition of rhetoric—"the discovery of the available means of persuasion" (*Rhetoric* 24; 1.2.25)—but also to Ritchie and Ronald's use of his definition for the title of their collection, *Available Means*. See esp. xvii: "Our decision to title this collection with Aristotle's famous definition of rhetoric . . . reflects our desire to locate women squarely within rhetoric but also to acknowledge that their presence demands that rhetoric be reconceived."

2. Besides Hull, see Hannay, introduction, esp. 1–5; Grafton and Jardine, esp. 37–38; and Beauchamp, Hageman, and Mikesell, introduction xxiii–xxvi, xxxix–lxxvi.

3. Examining the accounts of the rhetoric of Frances Willard, Susan B. Anthony, and Elizabeth Cady Stanton, Nan Johnson found that even for these women "the parlor [was] woman's proper rhetorical world" (*Gender* 119), for in their rhetoric, the nation was their home, and their children in crisis, needing a mother's intervention; female rhetors represented themselves as good housekeepers cleaning up the nation (121–25).

4. See, e.g., Brody on virility as an aspect of classical and Anglo-American rhetorical style.

5. In *"We Are Coming,"* Logan analyzes Maria Stewart's prophetic oratory, Frances Harper's construction of communities of interest, Ida B. Wells's use of graphic description to motivate distanced audiences, Fannie Williams's appeal to identification in divided groups, Anna Julia Cooper's tactics of arrangement when addressing male audiences on women's issues, and Victoria Matthews's responses to the exigence of constrained rhetorical situations. See also Logan's essays: "Rhetorical Strategies," "Literacy as a Tool," "Black Women on the Speaker's Platform," and "'What's Rhetoric Got to Do with It?'"

6. In *Well-Tempered Women*, Mattingly argues that women's temperance rhetoric mixed conservative appeals to feminine roles with progressive ideas, emphasized women as victims to shield women orators from public criticism, and focused on the

warrant that women had the right to protect their homes. Similarly, in *Appropriate[ing] Dress*, Mattingly uses the debate about women's dress during the nineteenth century as rhetorical theory by women that addresses the difficulties women have with cultural constructions of the body on the speaker's platform and explains how women nevertheless devised means of constructing a usable ethos through dress despite society's fears of women who showed themselves on public stages. Women used modest Quaker dress, bloomers, cross-dressing, and "womanly" attire to make audiences sympathize with them or to attract audiences with their celebrity.

7. In *Imagining Rhetoric*, Eldred and Mortensen analyze Hannah Foster's connection of literacy to republican prosperity and morality; Judith Murray's defense of intellectual property against plagiarism; Mrs. A. J. Graves's championing of belletristic rhetoric against the activist rhetoric of female reformers; Louisa Tuthill's creation of a new Christian belletristic rhetoric opposed to the extreme liberatory rhetoric of woman suffrage; Almira Phelps's advocacy of self-reliance for women and composition as self-expression; and Charlotte Forten's paradoxical juxtaposition of exhortation to Christian patience and admiration of abolitionist rhetoric.

8. See also Berlin, "Revisionary Histories" 113.

9. In "Revisionary Histories," reflecting on historiography, Berlin cautions that we must avoid the fallacious plot of "heroic rhetoricians with the courage and wisdom to change" (138).

10. I am taking the term *counterdiscourse* from Fraser, "Rethinking": "*subaltern counterpublics* . . . are parallel discursive arenas where members of subordinated social groups invent and circulate counterdiscourses" (67).

11. Carole Blair agrees, cautioning that pluralism is not the same as multiple stories (419).

12. In "Revisionary Histories," Berlin further advises that in revisionist history we are constructing "contingent narratives" (117, 121, 124).

13. In "Regendering the Rhetorical Tradition," Glenn sums up the relationship between gender and rhetorical history in this manner: "To regender rhetorical history, then, is to imagine gender as an inclusive and nonhierarchical category of analysis for (1) examining a wide range of rhetorical performances by sexed bodies; (2) denaturalizing the concept of sexual differences; (3) investigating the sociocultural construction of male and female, of masculine and feminine; (4) revitalizing our thinking about the (in)appropriate roles and opportunities for sexed bodies, particularly in terms of rhetorical performance; and, finally, (5) writing both women's and men's contributions and participation into an expanded, inclusive rhetorical tradition" (29).

14. I developed this definition, and a justification for it, in my introduction to the anthology *Rhetorical Theory* xiv–xv. But see also Bordelon, *Feminist Legacy,* on Gertrude Buck's view of rhetoric as communication rather than more narrowly as persuasion (65).

15. On the range of meaning of the term *conversation*, see Peter Burke, *Art of Conversation*, 90–92.

16. See also Berlin, "Revisionary History" 144–45: "in writing rhetorical history it is not enough to locate and consider rhetorics that reproduced the ideology of the established power structure," for there is always "opposition"; there are always "competing rhetorics"; and Royster and Williams, who point out the danger of erasing narratives of African American composition studies in sweeping histories of rhetoric and composition.

17. See, e.g., Gregory Clark, *Dialogue, Dialectic, and Conversation.*

1. Humanist Dialogues and Defenses of Women's Education:
Conversation as a Model for All Discourse

1. I term this dialogue "mid-seventeenth-century" because, while it was not published as a dialogue until 1680, it was revised from a conversation in Scudéry's novel, *Artamène, ou Le grand Cyrus* (Paris, 1653), v.10, bk. 2:712–32, in the episode known as "The History of Sappho." For a slightly different working out of the materials of this chapter, see Donawerth, "Conversation," "'As Becomes a Rational Woman,'" and "Politics of Rhetorical Theory." For the classical notion (in Isocrates, Cicero, and Thomas Wilson) that language is civilizing, see Donawerth, *Shakespeare* 10 n11.

2. On women and humanism, especially women's use of rhetoric, see the works in the Other Voice series edited by King and Rabil, especially their introduction to the series, "Other Voice" xi–xxxi; Donawerth and Strongson, introduction 9–16; Fedele; Aragona; Marinella; and Schurmann. See also Donawerth, "Oratory and Rhetoric." These women are not all humanists in the sense of being learned in Latin and Greek; on "vernacular humanism," see Boutcher.

3. Habermas further argues that the late seventeenth and early eighteenth centuries saw the development of a "public sphere" at the border between domestic privacy and absolutist monarchical authority (2–3, 12, 30) where the rising class of bourgeois discussed public issues of taste and politics, a discussion that became increasingly powerful during the eighteenth century and influenced political decisions (2–3, 23, 41). This sphere was constituted from an educated reading public of men of property but not aristocratic rank (23). Preceding this development, publicity was deployed by monarchs to display their power (13), but once this discussion began in reading circles, table societies, salons, and coffee houses, as well as in the new newspapers and journals (21–25, 41–43), publicity became a means of furthering a critique of the absolutist state (51, 54), according to Habermas. While this public sphere was actually composed of propertied, educated, middle-class men, its success depended on the fiction that it was constituted of all rational, unbiased human beings in consensus (51–52). Feminists and culture critics have critiqued and revised Habermas's theory so that it might better explain the political involvement of women and lower-class men. See, e.g., Fraser, "What's Critical about Critical Theory?" 262–72, which makes the point that citizenship depends on a capacity for consent and speech that is tied to education and is often denied to women and, indeed, that the role of the citizen would be better described as "the masculine citizen-speaker role"; see also Landes, esp. 97–99, 109–10; and McDowell 7–12. I wish to further complicate Habermas's model by suggesting that the rhetorical theory of the women examined in this chapter, in the form of humanist dialogues and defenses of women's education, demonstrates that public discussion, the creation of a public sphere, began earlier than the late seventeenth century and that middle-class, gentry, and aristocratic women were extremely important to its development. Defenses of women's education (including rhetoric) increase during this period because there now resided a new power in reading, since it prepared a person to participate in civil society where literary issues and politics were discussed.

4. On the humanist genre of the dialogue, see Snyder viii, 6–10; and Smarr 1, 29–30, 98–153, 283–86.

5. On salons, see Lazard ch. 16, 291–308.

6. For early modern women who published in humanist genres—dialogues, epistles, and orations—see the Other Voice series of translations and editions, general editors

Margaret King and Albert Rabil, published initially by the University of Chicago Press and now by the Centre for Reformation and Renaissance Studies, Toronto.

7. On the biography of Scudéry, see Aronson; and Donawerth and Strongson 21–29. On the biography of Cavendish, see Kathleen Jones; and Battigelli. On the biography of Makin, see Teague, "Identity," and *Bathsua Makin*. On the biography of Astell, see Perry.

8. Besides Lougee, on the salon see also Maclean 141–54; Stanton; Beasley 47–52; Goodman 2–9, 90–135; Harth 179–93; and Donawerth and Strongson 14–16.

9. Habermas has argued that humanism failed to generate a critique of absolutism because royalty, most famously in the case of Louis XIV, absorbed their energies into courtly display, into the representation of publicity rather than into public discussion (9–14). I wish to suggest, instead, that the salon and women who published rhetorical theory in the middle seventeenth century were not passively incorporated into royal display, but deployed display (especially the rhetoric of praise) in order both to situate themselves in a position of influence and to critique patriarchal and sometimes monarchical power. Indeed, the woman question may be one area where public discussion first arose, as early as the sixteenth century. On the pamphlet controversy on women or the *querelle des femmes*, see esp. Henderson and McManus 173–88; Joan Kelly; and Malcolmson and Mihoko Suzuki. As we shall see, in varying ways, Madeleine de Scudéry, Margaret Cavendish, Bathsua Makin, and Mary Astell published rhetorical theory that was part of public discussion of several issues: the right of a woman to an education according to her class, the limits of patriarchal (and monarchical) authority, and the nature and proper process of communication.

10. Except for the preface to *Fictional Orations*, all of the Scudéry works cited in text and the page references cited parenthetically are from *Selected Letters*. For French versions of these materials, see Scudéry, *"De L'air Galant," Choix de Conversations*; and the seventeenth-century French editions available on microfilm. When I say that women take intellectual control of conversation in Scudéry's dialogues, I do not mean that they use conversation as an occasion for individual performance as do the men in earlier Renaissance treatises on conversation, such as Baldassare Castiglione's *The Courtier*; there is much more give and take and collaborative exploration in Scudéry's dialogues than in Castiglione's, where the women serve as audience to the long speeches of debate by the men. For a history of conversation as an art in Europe, see Peter Burke, *Art of Conversation* 89–122; for an extremely useful survey of men's writing on conversation in the Renaissance and eighteenth century, see Ann Cline Kelly.

11. The translation of the preface to *Famous Women, or Fictional Orations* is taken from *Les Femmes Illustres or the Heroick Harangues of the Illustrious Women*, trans. James Innes; spelling has been modernized.

12. See the four-way analogy linking rhetoric, cosmetics, cookery, and sophistics, as opposed to dialectic/justice, gymnastics, medicine, and legislation in Plato, *Gorgias* 26–27; 465.

13. Similarly, in Letter 53, Scudéry compares rhetorical style to women's fashionable attire: "Your style is like those beauties who always appear fashionable and attractive whether they are dressed up or not at all" (52). See also where the letter writer makes fun of pompous writing constructed of memorized set-pieces: it is "like wearing a scarlet scarf on top of rags"; "such people are dwarves in high heels" (53). On appropriating the sophistic for feminist rhetorical theory, see Jarratt, *Rereading the Sophists*.

14. Similarly, in *Amorous Letters*, the letter writer throughout expresses her own anxiety about lacking a sufficient education to write entertaining letters, thus raising

such an anxiety in the readers of the volume, which will be presumably alleviated by learning from this formulary rhetoric how to write letters; see esp. Letter 54: "Please . . . do not stop writing to me, even if this person is not deserving of your letters. They will serve me as textbooks" (54).

15. Maclean explains that *"préciosité"* offered seventeenth-century women who participated in the salons and belles lettres

> a system of existence conceived of as an antidote to their plight as wards and wives . . . the purification and enrichment of language, [and] the creation of a self-conscious intellectual élite. . . . The *précieuse* develops essentially feminine qualities, such as "finesse," elegance, sensibility; she is neither pedantic nor unlearned, but "savante" . . . ; she exists in a universe in which love is deified, but only that love which has been purified from constraint, from consideration of convenience and financial gain, from the dangers of habit and monotony. . . . where marriage is always just out of sight (152–53).

16. The three most popular Renaissance humanist Latin genres are the letter, the oration, and the dialogue—all forms that Scudéry adapts to the vernacular.

17. Stanton has argued that the seventeenth-century French rhetorical ideal of the *honnête homme* was defined by the elite space of the *cabinet,* or salon; the conversational literary form as an indication of aristocratic leisure; and the classical names, the "crypto-classical morphology" suggesting "emulation of an idealized past, a mythical place distant from the everyday, contingent world" (81, 83, 91).

18. Also see Cicero, *De Officiis,* 1.3.37:

> Conversation, then, in which the Socratics are the best models, should have these qualities. It should be easy and not in the least dogmatic; it should have the spice of wit. And the one who engages in conversation should not debar others from participating in it, as if he were entering upon a private monopoly; but, as in other things, so in a general conversation he should think it not unfair for each to have his turn. He should observe, first and foremost, what the subject of conversation is. If it is grave, he should treat it with seriousness; if humorous, with wit. And above all, he should be on the watch that his conversation shall not betray some defect in his character. This is most likely to occur, when people in jest or in earnest take delight in making malicious and slanderous statements about the absent, on purpose to injure their reputations. The subjects of conversation are usually affairs of the home or politics or the practice of the professions and learning. Accordingly, if the talk begins to drift off to other channels, pains should be taken to bring it back again to the matter in hand—but with due consideration to the company present; for we are not all interested in the same things at all times or in the same degree. We must observe, too, how far the conversation is agreeable [*delectationem*] and, as it had a reason for its beginning, so there should be a point at which to close it tactfully.

19. In "On Speaking Too Much or Too Little": "Undoubtedly, [there] are people who now and then conceive more or less appropriate things . . . but whose words so completely tangle their thoughts that one cannot guess what they wished their listeners to grasp . . . There are others . . . who only explain themselves poorly because they do not themselves understand [what they are talking about]. Thus not only are they searching for the words they wish to say, but also for the ideas they wish to think." On Aristotle's categorization of sophistries, see *On Sophistical Refutations.*

20. In "On Speaking Too Much or Too Little": "It is necessary to adopt the language of well-bred people." See also, "On Wit" (*Selected Letters* 120), where Euridamia maintains that even jokes must be in "the language of well-bred people." Scudéry is paraphrasing Quintilian's definition of *usage*: "the agreed practice of educated men" (1:133; 1.6.45).

21. In "On Speaking Too Much or Too Little," a contrast is drawn between "those who regulate their speech by what they read" and those "who frequent the company of gentle-folk" in order to learn the art of conversation; and "On Wit" 128: "those to whom Nature has given a certain [art] . . . should not desire to attempt anything more, for it is true that the art that might perfect [such talent] could also sometimes spoil it." On the debate on nature vs. art (or imitation), see, e.g., Cicero, *De Oratore* 1:265; 2.21.89 ; and Quintilian 1:19; 1.27.

22. On competition and warfare as metaphors for rhetoric in men's rhetorical theory for the classical and renaissance eras, see Rebhorn 23–79.

23. On compliments, graciousness, and elegant self-presentation as the art of the courtier, see Whigham.

24. See Jarratt, *Rereading the Sophists* 74: "instead of moving in the direction of fixing a law of logic, [the sophists'] works seem designed rather to call attention to the ways patterns of reasoning came to be accepted."

25. Antigene hints that Sesostris is fabricated in his over-precise description of his sources and their dating as 15,660 years old — "Everyone laughed at a date so long ago" (*Selected Letters* 132) — and in his explanation that there are *two* Sesostris the Greats, one well known, and this earlier one newly rediscovered (132–33).

26. On the Fronde, see Beasley 43:

> There was no one overriding purpose, except perhaps a general hatred for the regent's [Anne D'Autriche's] foreign-born prime minister, Mazarin. . . . the parliament instigated the troubles in 1648 with a series of decrees designed to call royal authority, especially the role of the prime minister, into question. . . . A second wave of protest and rebellion, termed . . . the princely Fronde, added to the revolt and enlarged the sphere of participants. This group . . . incited the peasants in [their] principalities to civil disobedience. The princes' primary objective was to profit from a relatively weak regency to increase their own power. They opposed Mazarin and sought to replace both the regent and the prime minister with a leader from among their ranks who could rule both the country and the young Louis XIV more to their satisfaction.

27. On the development of this opposition, see Fleming 122–23.

28. On "The Female Academy," see Gweno Williams 98–99.

29. Selections from Cavendish, *The Worlds Olio* (London, 1655), with modernized spelling, are reprinted in Donawerth, *Rhetorical Theory* 46–58. A male humanist who wrote encyclopedias, for example, was Thomas Elyot, transferring classical knowledge into the vernacular.

30. Cavendish, *The Worlds Olio*, dedication to "My Lord," William Cavendish, Duke of Newcastle, Margaret's husband, fol. A2^r. See also bk. 2, "Epistle," fol. 04^v, reprinted in Donawerth, *Rhetorical Theory* 57: "But language should be like garments, for though every particular garment hath a general cut, yet their trimmings may be different and not go out of the fashion; so wit may place words to its own becoming, delight, and advantage, and not alter language nor obstruct the sense, for the more liberty we have with words, the clearer is sense delivered."

31. On women's writing as "natural," as opposed to men's writing as artful, see Jensen 25–45. On manuals of cookery addressed to women as an audience in the Renaissance, see Tebeaux, esp. 168. See also Hall 171: "In Continental Europe, production and use of cookbooks were a masculine affair. In England, however, male authors both dedicated their cookbooks to, and assumed their books would be read by, women. . . . Thus, printed cookbooks and domestic manuals have specific class, as well as gender, valences. Like other forms of courtesy literature, they preserve the fiction that they are writing for aristocratic audiences, offering their upwardly-mobile women readers a peek into the status competitions and consumption patterns that they wished to emulate."

32. In contrast to my reading of Cavendish, Sutherland examines Cavendish as a rhetorician deliberately experimenting with the masculine forms of oratory and science writing but sees her "as a practitioner of rhetoric rather than as a theorist" ("Aspiring to the Rhetorical Tradition" 255).

33. Spinning, turning raw wool or flax into thread for weaving cloth, was a main occupation of women in Cavendish's day.

34. On the sophistic trope that language (and rhetoric) are the basis of civilization, see, e.g., Isocrates 5–9 ("Nicocles") and 253–57 ("Antidosis").

35. Compare Cavendish's use of sophistic rhetorical theory, especially the social purpose of speech and the emphasis on *kairos* or timeliness of speech, to Susan Jarratt's present-day adaptation of sophistry to feminist composition theory, in *Rereading the Sophists*.

36. See Beck and Lanser, 86: "Androcentric thinking—which in our day usually masquerades as scientific objectivity—is rewarded in the woman scholar, while thinking within a gynocentric frame of reference is dismissed as emotional, subjective, specialized, or intuitive—i.e., not scholarly as the patriarchs have defined the term. As a result, many female thinkers have been reduced to parroting the patriarchy or remaining silent. The writings of women who are struggling to define themselves but have not yet given up a patriarchal frame of reference may betray a tension so strong as to produce a virtually 'double-voiced' discourse." In her introduction to Cavendish, *Blazing World*, Lilley takes another tack to this inclusion of disparate points of view in Cavendish, insightfully arguing that we read her as a "hermaphrodite," who "combined masculine and feminine elements in a parodic masquerade of gender" (xii–xiii).

37. I am indebted to the argument of Hilda Smith that seventeenth-century rationalism allowed women to reformulate the terms under which they combated their inferior position; Smith, however, sees Makin as a conservative (*Reason's Disciples* 13).

38. See also Makin 29. All citations of this work refer to the edition compiled by Frances Teague, but I have modernized spelling and punctuation. For those excerpts that are reprinted in Donawerth , R*hetorical Theory,* the page reference is given in brackets .

39. Astell, *Serious Proposal, Parts I and II* (4th ed., 1701), 6. All citations of this work refer to the 1970 reprint of the 4th edition (1701) but with modernized spelling. If the quotation is included in the excerpts from Astell in Donawerth, *Rhetorical Theory,* the page number will follow in brackets.

40. I think that a major model for Astell's college is Mme. de Maintenon's Saint-Cyr, a school for girls founded in 1686, that attempted "to counter the social processes at work in polite society" (Lougee 173; see also 172–95). Scudéry's *Conversations* was used as a textbook at Mme. de Maintenon's school from 1686 to 1691; see Goldsmith, *Exclusive Conversation* 66. Astell's hope for a women's college was not realized immediately because she underestimated English anti-Catholic sentiment against the Continental

education of girls in nunneries: it was rumored that an anonymous lady was about to donate the funds to establish Astell's college when she was dissuaded by an Anglican bishop. But Astell's ideas were strongly influential on the pamphlet and fiction writing in favor of women's education throughout the eighteenth century (in works by writers like Judith Drake, Mary Lady Chudleigh, and Sarah Scott). On the influences of Astell's *Serious Proposal*, see Perry, esp. 103–5, and chap. 8.

41. See Augustine, *On Christian Doctrine* 4:164–68.

42. Sutherland briefly discusses Astell's use of conversation as a model for writing in "Mary Astell" 111. Perry offers a useful summary of the influence of Antoine Arnauld's *L'Art de Penser*, the Port Royal logic, in her biography, *The Celebrated Mary Astell* (84–87), but she overemphasizes Arnauld's influence. Although Astell borrows Arnauld's definition of ideas as linked to thought, not to real things, she does not borrow the Aristotelian apparatus of propositions and syllogism that Arnauld develops; and while Astell offers a method, it is neither Arnauld's "Method of Geometry," nor his "Method of Sciences" (Arnauld 410, 450–51). Although Astell mentions Bernard Lamy's *Art of Speaking*, the Port Royal rhetoric sometimes still attributed to Arnauld, she is influenced even less by it than by the logic. She leaves out Lamy's modern treatment of the physiology of speech, as well as his classical treatment of invention, memory, and pronunciation or delivery. She may have been influenced by Arnauld's short section in the *Logic* on examples of "bad reasoning in civil conversation and common discourse" (337), but Lamy's rhetoric mainly concerns the public art, unlike Astell's. She does seem to be influenced in her discussion of the ends of style (Lamy 25–41; Astell 119). But the major difference between the two rhetorics is Astell's emphasis on the equality between speaker and listener, compared to Lamy's emphasis on the power of the artful speaker: "the whole end of commerce and conversation is to persuade those with whom we deal, and reduce them to our sentiments" (Lamy 93). For further analysis of the influence of Augustine on Astell and her connections to Port Royal philosophy, see Sutherland, "Outside the Rhetorical Tradition."

43. On George Campbell's *Philosophy of Rhetoric* and other empiricist rhetorics as manipulative, see Sebberson, "Practical Reasoning," 95–111; and "Investigations."

44. Again Astell is adapting Augustine; see *On Christian Doctrine* 137: "Sometimes, when the truth is demonstrated in speaking, an action which pertains to the function of teaching, eloquence is neither brought into play nor is any attention paid to whether the matter or the discourse is pleasing, yet the matter itself is pleasing when it is revealed simply because it is true." This demonstrates another difference between Astell and the Port Royal school: a premise of Arnauld's logic is that humans by nature resist reason, while Astell has faith that humans by nature are attracted to the truth.

45. On power as the purpose of rhetoric in the Renaissance, see Rebhorn. The ideal woman of the Renaissance was "chaste, silent, and obedient," and early modern conservatives feared education for women because they assumed a connection between lack of control over a woman's tongue and lack of control over her sexuality; see Gibson 10–20; Jardine; Stallybrass, esp. 126–27; and Margaret Ferguson 113–16.

46. Linda Coleman read this chapter in an early draft and gave invaluable help in asking questions about the nature of categories. I also thank Sue Lanser for her insight into the pragmatics of this theory. Margaret Ferguson, in "A Room Not Their Own," asked a question that was extremely important to the conception of this chapter: "Could not writing be construed in opposition to public speech rather than in conjunction with it?" (101).

2. Conduct Book Rhetoric: Constructing a Theory of Feminine Discourse

1. Following Karlyn Kohrs Campbell's now-classic study of nineteenth-century U.S. women's speech-making, *Man Cannot Speak for Her,* feminists have begun "to look in places not previously studied for work by women that would not have been tradition-ally considered rhetoric" (Bizzell, "Opportunities" 51). Catherine Hobbes, Janet Carey Eldred and Peter Mortensen (in a series of articles), Annette Kolodny, Shirley Logan (in both an anthology and an analytic study), Carla Peterson, Joy Rouse, and Jackie Royster have studied women's rhetoric and the ways that women were taught writing. In a wide-ranging study, Anne Ruggles Gere describes the context of women's clubs and women's self-help and educational reading societies that encouraged women's literacy and writing practice as well as activism. See also Lindal Buchanan, "Forging and Fir-ing Thunderbolts," on nineteenth-century women's rhetoric constructing a "feminine" ethos; and Susan Miller, *Assuming the Positions,* on commonplace writing as part of the history of early nineteenth-century American education: this is one way in which women would have been schooled in rhetoric and composition.

2. On the requirements of chastity, silence, and obedience from women in conduct books for women by men, see Hull; Stallybrass; Margaret Ferguson; and Belsey. Mary Wollstonecraft's *Thoughts on the Education of Daughters* (1787) falls in this tradition.

3. On the range of women's advice for women on writing, see Kilcup.

4. In accounts of their oratory, even radical women are represented as bound by their domestic roles: Nan Johnson analyzes domestic imagery in the rhetoric of Frances Willard, Susan B. Anthony, and Elizabeth Cady Stanton, finding that they represent their oratory as housekeeping for the nation, the good mother overseeing the development of her children.

5. Eldred and Mortensen suggest that Hannah Foster connects illiteracy to seduc-tion, that Judith Murray celebrates the need for education of republican mothers, that Mrs. A. J. Graves's champions a belletristic rhetoric for Protestant democratic ladies, that Louisa Caroline Tuthill opposes women's liberatory rhetoric with a new Christian belletristic rhetoric, that Almira Hart Lincoln Phelps adapts the virtue of self-reliance for women, and that Charlotte Forten attempts to reconcile the belletristic rhetoric of the Lyceum with the passionate declamation of the abolitionists.

6. Broaddus treats William Ellery Channing, Ralph Waldo Emerson, James Russell Lowell, Oliver Wendell Holmes, and Thomas Wentworth Higginson; she mistakenly claims that, while women might be "literary," they could not be considered rhetorical (4); she thus misses the chance to discuss Bostonians Eliza Farrar and her conduct rhetoric for women, or Elizabeth Peabody and Margaret Fuller in the context of educa-tion reform or transcendentalism and rhetoric.

7. Beaufort synthesizes a number of scholars' studies to arrive at her definition of "discourse community"—"the social entity within which a set of distinctive writ-ing practices occur and beyond whose borders different writing practices occur" (57). She discerns "three features critical to any discourse community"—"communication channels," "norms for genres," and "writers' roles . . . and tasks" (33). These features of a discourse community, she argues, depend mainly on the "goals and values for the community," the "physical conditions" for writing, and individuals' "previous experi-ence . . . and skills" (34). If we apply Beaufort's definition of discourse community to the theories of communication within conduct books written by women, we can further see the importance, during the eighteenth and nineteenth centuries, of the markedly different spheres of gender activities in writing: women's communication channels,

genres, physical conditions for writing, and previous experience—all differ significantly from men's genres and conditions of writing.

8. On More's life, see Hopkins; M. G. Jones; Demers; and Ford. On More's rhetorical theory, see also Krueger.

9. On silence as "feminine" in Enlightenment men's rhetorical theory, see Brody 36 esp. On the role of listening in contemporary rhetoric, see Ratcliffe, esp. on the slighting of listening in classical rhetorical theories (20), on the gendering and racing of listening (21), and on rhetorical listening as a basis of rhetorical negotiation (27).

10. Almira Phelps cites More's "Bas-Bleu" when she discusses the learned woman, and bluestockings in particular, as spectacle; see Eldred and Mortensen, *Imagining Rhetoric* 168.

11. More's defense of the New Testament as a model of style (1:224–25) recalls not only Augustine's defense of the simple but effective plain style of the Bible in *De Doctrina Christiana*, but also the limitations of earlier generations on women's reading matter.

12. More elaborates that politeness, or appropriate feminine rhetorical behavior, "is not that artificial quality which is taken up by many when they go into society, in order to charm those whom it is not their particular business to please; and is laid down when they return home to those to whom to appear amiable is a real duty" (2:96), but rather politeness is "True good nature," which perseveres in ordinary domestic interactions (2:97–98).

13. The sophistries of communication were originally catalogued by Aristotle, in *On Sophistical Refutations*, so More is here adapting a tradition to the specific circumstances of women's conversation. Like Aristotle, for example, she discusses ambiguity and equivocation as faults (2:88).

14. Maria Edgeworth's "Essay on the Noble Science of Self-Justification" (1795), on the other hand, uses traditional eighteenth-century satire to question the morality and purpose of such a system of gendered and hierarchical rhetoric; see Donawerth, "Poaching."

15. On Sigourney's life, see Haight; Scherman; and Baym.

16. On Margaret Fuller and her conversations, see Annette Kolodny, "Inventing a Feminine Discourse"; and Joy P. Rouse, "Margaret Fuller." On reading societies for girls, see Eliza Farrar, *The Young Ladies' Friend*, 258–60.

17. The concept of the agreeable in conversation extends back to Madeleine de Scudéry's writings on salon conversation; see Donawerth, "'As Becomes a Rational Woman.'" Sigourney qualifies the goal of pleasure in conversation by emphasizing moral purpose (*Ladies* 191). The feminine role of listening is explored by Hannah More; see Donawerth, "Hannah More" 156.

18. On silence as rhetoric, see Glenn, *Unspoken*.

19. On Maria Edgeworth's rhetoric and the family's textbooks, see Marilyn Butler; and Donawerth, "Poaching" 245.

20. See Warren 28, 85–114. On Margaret Fuller, see Kolodny; and Rouse. On reading societies for girls, see also Farrar, *Young Ladies' Friend* 258–60.

21. On Farrar's biography, see Farrar, *Recollections of Seventy Years*; Huh 7:737–38; and Donawerth, *Rhetorical Theory* 157–58.

22. See a similar passage on politeness to the washerwoman in Farrar, *Young Ladies' Friend* 36. See also Ratcliffe's contemporary theory of rhetorical listening, esp. on listening to the stories of others (39).

23. Farrar advises that educated women must be careful to dress neatly, refuting the argument that educated girls are sloppy dressers; cultivated ladies must demonstrate attention to domestic affairs and neatness, in *Young Ladies' Friend* 139.

24. On the letter as conveying family feelings, see also Farrar, *Youth's Letter-Writer* 67, 117, and 150.

25. See also Farrar, *Youth's Letter-Writer* 8, 31, 37 (on "the easy, natural" style of conversation in letter writing), 64, 150 (on imagined conversation with family as inventional tool), and 158.

26. See Bizzell, *Academic Discourse* 234, on conflict between discourse communities.

27. For a very different reading of Hartley, see Nan Johnson, *Gender* 68–69, 91–93. My heartfelt thanks to Nan for giving me a copy of Hartley's *Ladies' Book* when I could not find it in local libraries, and for our many years' discussion of gender and nineteenth-century rhetoric.

28. See Farrar, *Friend* 244; for other examples of borrowings from Farrar, see Hartley on affectation (19), on politeness as the basis of family love (144), and on sarcasm (150).

29. On Willing's biography, see Lender; and Joanne Carlson Brown.

30. From sixteenth-century Europe to mid-twentieth-century America, young women of lower class and less wealthy middle class frequently worked a few years to save money before marriage; these women expected not to work after marriage. On sixteenth-century girls working in London, see Amussen; and on this pattern among nineteenth- and early twentieth-century teachers, see Solomon ch. 8. My own grandmother and mother followed this pattern, my grandmother teaching school for three years until she married, my mother working as a secretary for six years before she married a soldier returning from World War II. My mother, however, went back to work when her children were old enough for school.

31. See Spring for a case study of composition at one mid-nineteenth-century academy. Spring takes the "letter form" of composition practiced at Mount Holyoke as "evidence of a gendered antebellum epistolary culture" (633) and a "female" composition practice emphasizing "negotiated discourse" and collaboration (653).

3. Defenses of Women's Preaching: Dissenting Rhetoric and the Language of Women's Rights

1. In *Gendered Pulpit*, Mountford traces the view of the preacher as "a paragon of masculinity" (59) through centuries of preaching manuals and analyzes the very different styles of contemporary women preachers, who abandon the pulpit and focus on regenerating community through "creating intimacy and affirming the divinity in everyday spaces" (149). However, see also Brekus, who argues that the Great Awakening brought a more emotional style of preaching to the fore, a style that led preachers of both sexes to desert the pulpit and preach directly to the people in the pews (37).

2. See, for example, Plato's *Gorgias* (Steph. 502), where Socrates explains that Gorgias's kind of rhetoric is flattery because it is addressed to the crowd—which includes women, children, and slaves, and so cannot be rational. See, also, Cicero, *De Oratore* 1:167; 1.54.231, where Antonius sets forth the standard of "manliness" for oratory; Quintilian adapts this standard also: see *Institutio Oratoria* 1:251–52; 2.5.9–23.

3. I have treated only representative nineteenth-century defenses of women's preaching. For other defenses, see Bizzell, "Frances Willard, Phoebe Palmer"; and Zimmerelli.

4. On the Reformation, see esp. Dickens, *Reformation and Society*, and *English Reformation*.

5. On Grumbach's biography, see Matheson's introduction to Grumbach 4–23, 56–71.

6. Following the lead of this sixteenth-century commentator, Grumbach's translator, Peter Matheson, decries Grumbach's organization as arguments that "tumble on top of

each other" (64), and judges that her epistle is "not the work of a professional rhetorician" (69). It is true that a member of the nobility would never be a professional rhetorician, but I disagree with Matheson's disparagements; I think Grumbach shows a remarkable knowledge of humanist debate invective, albeit translated into German, not in Latin.

7. See also Dentière 276–78, for an early reformist pre-Calvinist Genevan woman's defense of women's preaching privately and in print (but not publicly in the pulpit). Dentière argues (by way of the Parable of the Talents) that women should not hide their talents, that women must support other women so that they may hear and read the Bible, and that men, not women, are the ones who developed and preached false doctrine (a reformist allusion to corrupt Roman Catholic clergy). Dentière also lists biblical women who preached: Sarah, Rebecca, Deborah, Ruth, the Queen of Sheba, Mary, Elizabeth, the Samaritan woman, and Mary Magdalene. On Dentière and Rachel Speght in *Mortalities Memorandum* (1621) as early defenses of women's preaching, see Thysell.

8. See MacKinnon, *Towards a Feminist Theory* 227: "Abstract equality necessarily reinforces the inequalities of the status quo to the extent that it evenly reflects an unequal social arrangement."

9. Fell's pamphlet is anthologized in Moira Ferguson 114–27; Bizzell and Herzberg, 748–60; Ritchie and Ronald 66–70; and Donawerth, *Rhetorical Theory* 59–70.

10. On Fell's biography, see Ross; and Kunze.

11. All quotations of Fell's *Women's Speaking Justified* are from Donawerth, *Rhetorical Theory*, 60–70. For other seventeenth-century Quaker pamphlets defending women's preaching, by Elizabeth Bathurst, Priscilla Cotton and Mary Cole, and Richard Farnsworth, see Hobby, *Virtue*.

12. On Quaker style and rhetoric, see Cope, who explains the style as based on the merging of metaphorical and literal meanings, the importance of Christ as Word, the use of biblical words to construct a plain but allusive style, incantatory reiteration, ecstatic abandonment of grammar, imitation of scripture, lack of personal detail, and the presentation of scripture as key to its own meaning. On Quaker style, see also Wilcox x: "Their style is frequently rambling, sometimes incoherent, and invariably packed with quotations from and allusions to the Scriptures." In "Hidden Things," Nigel Smith concludes, "for the Quakers," faith meant "a complete transformation of the 'language' one owned into *scriptura rediviva*" (68).

13. On Margaret Fell's rhetoric and style, see the two influential essays by Gardiner, who finds Fell's rhetoric to be "familial, affective rhetoric for public purposes," a "rhetoric of attentive care," but not distinctively a feminine voice ("Re-Gendering Individualism" 212–14); characterized by "appropriation and refiguration of biblical imagery and rhetoric," superimposing "several historical periods and their divine purposes upon one another and [weaving] Biblical quotations seamlessly into her own, using Biblical genres like prophecy and epistle, . . . and Biblical modes of address, including the promising and admonitory second person and the authoritative first person of . . . prophets" ("Margaret Fell Fox" 48–49). Fell is quoting the Bible from memory and so her quotations, while generally true to the King James or Authorized Version of the Bible, are often inaccurate in small details; on Fell's literacy, see Donawerth, "Women's Reading Practices."

14. On such misogyny, see, e.g., Belsey 178; Hobby 6; Constance Jordan 25, 63, 129; and Susanne Woods, introduction to *Poems of Aemilia Lanyer* xxxvi–xxxvii.

15. Fell is so careful to distinguish between appropriate and inappropriate speaking by women perhaps because the London Quaker meetings during 1655 to 1657 had been

disrupted by Martha Simmonds, Hannah Stranger, and other women using "Ranter" tactics in favor of James Naylor against George Fox (whom Fell supported); see Ross 101–14; and Mack 197–206. For other interpretations of Fell's arguments against a literalist reading of Paul, see Thickstun 272; and Luecke 84–88.

16. For this observation on the shift among sectarians to meetings in private houses, I am grateful to Gary Hamilton's unpublished paper, "*Paradise Regained* and the Private House."

17. See Cavendish, *The Worlds Olio*, sig. D2ʳ; and Astell, *Serious Proposal* 20.

18. I am indebted to an unpublished paper on "Margaret Fell" by Will Stofega, who points out that the inclusion of the "blind priests" "gives her text a 'villain' of sorts who is responsible for silencing women," and allows her to attack those who misinterpret the Bible, rather than the Bible itself.

19. Compare Mack's very different reading in *Visionary Women* 174: "the liberation that allowed Quaker women to assume authority as political prophets had little to do with their conception of the rights of women," and "the Quaker female prophet was more aggressive than the visionaries of the 1640s because her disengagement from her own social identity or 'outward being' was more radical."

20. But see Hogan and Solomon 34, 38–40, who argue that Lucretia Coffin Mott was influenced by Margaret Fell.

21. In 1770 in London, Miss R. Roberts published *Sermons Written by a Lady*, which was republished as *Seven Rational Sermons* in Philadelphia in 1777. While this volume does not share these characteristics of the defense of women's preaching with Grumbach and Fell, it might be viewed as a formulary sermon rhetoric by a woman, and Roberts does defend women's education in the final sermon of her collection. On British Methodist encouragement, then later, debate about women's preaching, see Valenze 71 and 149 on Mary Taft's and Ann Mason's arguments in defense of women's preaching. Valenze hypothesizes that the Wesleyan appeal to cottage religion sparked the Methodist movement's sympathy to female preaching, especially in the working classes. On Mary Bosanquet's epistolary exchange with John Wesley defending women's preaching, which was circulated in manuscript, see Vicki Tolar Burton 164–66; this book on the literacy practices of Wesley and Methodism is a storehouse of information on early Methodism and women's preaching.

22. Nothing is recorded about Lee after her 1849 edition of the biography. On Jarena Lee's biography, see, of course, her autobiography, and also William Andrews, introduction to *Sisters of the Spirit* 4–7. Lee's spiritual narrative follows a pattern of spiritual narratives and is especially similar to Towle's 1832 *Vicissitudes Illustrated*. Brekus's *Strangers and Pilgrims* on United States women preachers in the eighteenth and nineteenth centuries is an invaluable background for this study of defenses of women's preaching.

23. On the style of women's conversion narratives as compared to men's, see Brekus 39–42: women more often use the passive voice and a language of pollution and defilement, and women more often represent conversion as a force that strips them of individuality. For an analysis of Foote's 1879 *Brand Plucked from the Fire* as a hybrid of spiritual autobiography, letter, sermon, and hymn, see Zimmerelli 109–54. Elizabeth Stuart Phelps (Ward) (1844–1911), daughter of the writer Elizabeth Stuart Phelps (1815–52) and antivivisectionist and advocate for mill girls, adapts the short story as a defense of women's preaching in "A Woman's Pulpit," in which a young woman is called to an isolated country pastorate in "New Vealshire," and gradually wins over her flock.

24. Zilpha Elaw's 1846 *Memoirs* is also an instance of a conversion narrative as an argument in defense of women's preaching. As a sinner in a conversion narrative is called but at first resists, then falls into despair and anguish until s/he accepts salvation, so Zilpha Elaw records that she was called to preach, resisted, followed the call but was discouraged, felt anguish, and recovered when she accepted her mandate from God. She preached in Philadelphia, Baltimore, Washington, even in Alexandria in Mrs. Lee's chapel, in Annapolis, New York, New Haven, Hartford, Boston, Salem, Portland, Augusta, Bangor, Providence, and, in England, in London, Leeds, Liverpool, Manchester, and Newcastle. On Elaw, see Brekus 180. A similar conversion narrative-defense of women's preaching is Julia Foote's 1879 *Brand Plucked from the Fire*. An instance of conversion narrative as a method of argumentation, this autobiography, conversion narrative, and spiritual memoir records the conversion, sanctification, and career of Foote, who preached all over the Northeast and Midwest—Philadelphia, Binghamton, Ithaca, Geneva, Rochester, Troy, New York, Cincinnati, Albany, Poughkeepsie, Princeton, Trenton, Newark, Columbus, Chillicothe, Cleveland, and even Canada. She was excommunicated from the AME church for demanding to preach and argued that men and women are equal before Christ (and so women should also preach) and lists women in the Bible who preached (208–9). She cites harassment in preaching because of race as well as gender: her house routinely searched for run-away slaves, an invitation to preach by white Methodists who dictated that no Blacks might be in the congregation. Foote ends with an exhortation "To My Christian Sisters," urging them "not [to] let what man may say or do, keep you from doing the will of the Lord or using the gifts you have for the good of others" (227–29). Here she also employs the language of rights, urging her sisters not to let themselves "be kept in bondage" (227). On the AME organization of black women preachers, see Brekus 296.

25. My thanks to Lisa Zimmerelli for this reference.

26. On Mott's biography, see the introduction by Dana Greene to *Lucretia Mott: Her Complete Speeches and Sermons*, esp. 4–12.

27. See also Hogan and Solomon 34–38 and 44; they place Mott's "Discourse on Woman" in the context of the Quaker tradition and the development of the Women's Rights Movement, and suggest that Mott may have been directly influenced by Margaret Fell's *Women's Speaking Justified*.

28. The original text reads "profile exercise," which must be a mistake.

29. Woman "is deprived of almost every right in civil society, and is a cypher in the nation, except in the right of presenting a petition" (Mott 154). The primary public political tool of the great nineteenth-century women's movements supporting abolition, temperance, and women's rights was the collective petition. That the petition is the first women's right is clear from the history of women's ability to use the individual petition to courts and monarchs throughout Europe and England in the late Middle Ages and Renaissance, and throughout the history of the United States. See Sadlack, who documents a portion of this history of the first women's right.

30. I have found no biographical entries on Stewart, and so the biographical information as well as the theory come from her autobiography; see esp. 5–7, 11, 13, 16, 58, 71, 125.

31. An excellent explanation of the difference between exhortation and preaching may be found in Brekus 48–49; in general, exhortation was spoken from the pew by a congregation member, while preaching took place from the pulpit by a recognized or licensed preacher.

32. This passage is an allusion to Matthew 5:13, AV: "Ye are the salt of the earth: but if the salt have lost his savour, wherewith shall it be salted? It is thenceforth good for nothing, but to be cast out, and to be trodden under foot of men."

33. On this argument for an educated republican motherhood, see Eldred and Mortensen, *Imagining Rhetoric*, esp. 13–14, 51.

34. Quoting Margaret Fuller, Stewart links women's rights to abolition and the rights of African Americans (141).

35. See Brekus 125: the wealthiest and most established churches were the least likely to allow women's preaching.

36. Brekus argues that women's preaching was rooted in a view of religion as emotional and anti-intellectual (145).

37. See Pamela J. Walker, "Booth, Catherine," and "A Chaste and Fervid Eloquence." Palmer wrote two defenses of women's preaching: *Promise of the Father* (1859) and a shorter version, *Tongue of Fire* (1859); on Palmer and Willard, see Bizzell, "Frances Willard, Phoebe Palmer."

38. A similar argument is deployed by Hunter in her 1905 treatise, *Women Preachers*: Hunter structures her treatise around the list of women preaching, devoting chapters to Old Testament female prophets, New Testament female preachers, a refutation of Paul's strictures that becomes a list of women ministers praised by Paul, and a series of spiritual autobiographies of contemporary women preachers.

39. See Mary Bosanquet (later Fletcher), June 1771, to John Wesley on Women's Preaching, in Chilcote 299–304: Bosanquet wrote to Wesley to ask for his "advice and direction" on the question whether or not it was appropriate for women to preach. She interprets Paul's injunction that "a woman ought not to teach, nor take authority over a man" to mean a woman should not take authority over her husband or direct church affairs, but a woman may still "entreat sinners to come to Jesus." Her letter refutes the assumptions that preaching violates the modesty required of a Christian woman, and that women are more easily deceived than men. In "Preaching from the Pulpit Steps," Burton argues that Bosanquet's letter requires scholars to redefine women's participation as "a continuum of public discourse." It is interesting that the first three defenses of women's preaching (by Argula Van Grumbach, Margaret Fell, and Mary Bosanquet) are initially "private" letters (insomuch as any letter was private before the twentieth century) that are then printed.

40. On Willard's life and achievements, see Bordin.

41. On Willard's *Woman in the Pulpit*, see also Donawerth, "Poaching 252–55, and *Rhetorical Theory*, 241–54; on Willard's rhetoric, see also Dow 298–307; Willard, "*Do Everything Reform*; Nan Johnson, *Gender* 124–28; Mattingly, *Well-Tempered Women*; Watson; and Zimmerelli 155–210.

42. In "Empowered Foremothers," Stanley argues that the Wesleyan doctrine of holiness, emphasizing the authority of the Holy Spirit, empowered many women to speak out; she examines in particular Phoebe Palmer, Frances Willard, and Jennie Willing.

43. Thomas De Witt Talmage (1832–1902) was an American Presbyterian clergyman, an author, an editor of several religious journals, and a famous preacher who built the Tabernacle in Brooklyn to accommodate his crowds. Joseph Cook, Flavius Josephus Cook (1838–1901), was a preacher and lecturer, famous for twenty years for his Boston Monday lectures on religion, science, and morality. I have been unable to locate biographical information on Dr. Joseph Parker.

44. But see Brekus 224, who argues that only a small number of female preachers invoked the discourse of women's rights; my findings dispute this conclusion. On the causal relationship between women's preaching and woman suffrage in Britain, see deVries 319: "At its height between 1903 and 1914, the suffrage movement aimed to open opportunities for women to exercise their moral and spiritual influence in public."

45. See Ede and Lunsford 133:

> This dialogic mode is loosely structured and the roles enacted within it are fluid: one person may occupy multiple and shifting roles as a project progresses. In this mode, the process of articulating goals is often as important as the goals themselves and sometimes even more important. Furthermore, those participating in dialogic collaboration generally value the creative tension inherent in multivoiced and multivalent ventures. What those involved in hierarchical collaboration see as a problem to be solved, these individuals view as a strength to capitalize on and to emphasize. In dialogic collaboration, this group effort is seen as an essential part of the production—rather than the recovery—of knowledge and as a means of individual satisfaction within the group. This mode of collaboration can in some circumstances be deeply subversive.

4. Elocution: Sentimental Culture and Performing Femininity

1. For selections from the works of Morgan, Stebbins, and Hallie Quinn Brown, see Donawerth, *Rhetorical Theory* 172–212, 255–66.

2. Most useful is Buchanan's definition of *delivery* as "socially situated public performance" (*Regendering Delivery* 4).

3. On the development of the art of elocution in the eighteenth century, see Mahon; and Spoel.

4. The history of elocution remains to be written; Susan Miller, *Trust in Texts* 129–38, provides some directions such a history might take. For a good, brief survey of elocution, see Brenda Gabioud Brown. In their study, Bahn and Bahn summarize the development from classical delivery to later elocution but offer little analysis. On Delsarte, see Shawn; in her two monographs, Ruyter briefly sketches the influence of Delsarte on American culture and the history of modern dance. Several of the essays in Karl Wallace focus on elocution.

5. Hallie Quinn Brown's diaries give an overview of the various cultural sites where elocution flourished—lecture halls, chautauquas, public schools, parlor entertainments. The effect of this emphasis on elocution lasted well into the twentieth century: I had to memorize a poem and recite it in sixth grade; my grandmother expected every grandchild who could not play an instrument to "speak a piece" at her Christmas celebration; and my mother went over and over dramatic expression when I was asked to recite a poem at a Memorial Day Service in my small hometown in Ohio. See also Edwards; and Tapia 94–96.

6. In McCorkle's 2005 essay "Harbingers of the Printed Page," for example, there are no women elocution theorists cited.

7. On women in the elocution movement, see the essays in Wallace, esp. Haberman; Hochmuth and Murphy; Robb; and Shaver.

8. Among other texts, Shoemaker published *Little People's Speaker* (1886), *Delsartean Pantomimes* (1891), and *Advanced Elocution* (1896). For further information on Shoemaker, see *Who Was Who in America*, vol. 1: 1896–1942, 1121.

9. See esp. Blood and Riley's very technical series of handbooks for elocution concepts and exercises, *Psychological Development of Expression*, published by their school, the Columbia School of Oratory in Chicago, in four editions: vol. 1, 1894; vol. 2, 1893; vol. 3, 1894; and vol. 4, 1899; the authors represented include Emerson, Shakespeare, Dickens, Ruskin, Whittier, Wordsworth, Milton, Webster, Browning, Shelley, Cicero, and Lincoln, but also Mary Livermore, George Eliot, Elizabeth Barrett Browning, and Katharine Stevenson.

10. See also Bishop 30: Bishop describes her classes as composed of "twenty or thirty earnest young women." Stebbins, *Delsarte System* xxi, describes Delsarte's audience as "ladies." In *Regendering Delivery*, Buchanan argues that women's training in elocution became so successful that there was a backlash, and sections on elocution were restricted in textbooks aimed at women (160). This is not the case in women's elocution handbooks.

11. Following Karen Halttunen, I use the phrase *sentimental culture* for the Anglo-American emphasis in literature, art, psychology, and moral philosophy on sentiment, sensibility, sympathy, or emotion. On the sources of American sentimental culture, see also Todd, who surveys British sentimental culture; Stern, esp. 2–3, 12–13, who suggests that the postrevolutionary American novels filled with gothic emotional excess and gendered feminine (told mainly through the epistolary voice of a woman) are not simply maudlin imitations of British fiction, but rather political explorations (relying on the political philosophies of Jean-Jacques Rousseau, Adam Smith, Mary Wollstonecraft, and Edmund Burke) of national "collective mourning" over the effects of the Revolution; and Ellison, esp. 19, who stresses the sources in "masculine tenderness" and "parliamentary manhood" for the construction of the gentleman in Enlightenment British culture.

12. See Wendy Dasler Johnson, who links women and sentimental culture to rhetoric: "Cut from the cloth of empiricism, sentimental rhetoric sought to reproduce sensory impressions in verbal discourse that would get response from everybody in an audience.... [and] strong impressions counted for experience or empirical evidence" (206). Although Johnson does not cite him directly, George Campbell, whose *Philosophy of Rhetoric* was one of the most popular rhetorics in England and the United States from the late eighteenth century through the nineteenth century, would be one such rhetor who emphasized the emotional force of sensory experience as a means to persuasion.

13. On eighteenth-century sentimental culture, see Todd. On nineteenth-century women's sentimental poetry, see the introduction to Bennett's anthology. On the sentimental novel, see Tompkins 122–46 (on *Uncle Tom's Cabin*); Hendler, *Public Sentiments*; and the essays collected in Samuels. On the association of women and sentiment or sympathy, and its political function, even in very early fiction, see Kahn. Bennett explains that "sentimentality was unquestionably a primary rhetorical mode for many nineteenth-century writers" (xxxvi).

14. Bennett argues that "sentimentality celebrates . . . the affectional bonds that hold society . . . together" (xxxviii); and Barnes proposes that "evoking and circulating feeling" in American fiction was seen as the means of arousing the sympathetic identification that held the republican state together (x, 95). For further discussion of the emphasis on emotion in sentimental culture, see also Dobson 267: "The principal theme of the sentimental text is the desire for bonding, and it is affiliation on the plane of emotion, sympathy, nurturance, or similar moral or spiritual inclination for which sentimental writers and readers yearn. Violation, actual or threatened, of the affectional

bond generates the primary tension in the sentimental text and leads to . . . anguished . . . representations of human loss, as well as to idealized portrayals of human connection or divine consolation." In addition, see Barnes, who points out that the work of the sentimental novel is "to educate the heart" (39), and the function of nineteenth-century sentimental art is to arouse emotion (40).

15. On sentimental rhetoric used for social reform in antebellum America, see Steel.

16. Compare Susan Miller's description of emotion in connection with the history of rhetoric: "a cultural scene of interaction in which specific groups are bonded and thus found mutually acceptable or not against a standard that is enforced in recurring lessons and remembrance of them" (x).

17. Wendy Dasler Johnson connects sentimental rhetoric to the disciplining of young girls (215–17). Barnes suggests self-possession is a suitably capitalist goal aimed at in conduct book education of women's feelings (89). Sánchez-Eppler argues that in sentimental fiction the body is a reliable sign, through emotional display, of who one is (100), and that "reliance on the body as the privileged structure of communicating meaning" is central to such fiction (103). See also Halttunen on the "self-conscious and theatrical forms of bourgeois etiquette," the performance of true feelings (93). On the ancient sophists' interest in rhetoric as a "bodily art," see Hawhee, esp. 144.

18. For those who argue that sentimental culture appeared in America in middle-class poetry and fiction (especially that by women) mainly from about 1820 to 1850 or 1860, disappearing after that, see Halttunen, who traces the movement to origins in eighteenth-century British literature focusing on sympathy; Dobson; and Hendler, *Public* esp. 3–7. Hendler cites the psychology of Adam Smith as one point of origin of the shift to sentiment as a basis of moral persuasion, and he traces sentimentality through to its political effects in mid-nineteenth-century America. Dobson, e.g., defines *sentimentalism* as "that body of mid-nineteenth-century American literature, usually but not always written by women, that takes as its highest values sympathy, affection, and relation (and indeed builds these values into its very language and literary form)" (283); and Barnes argues that sentimentality earlier in the century transmutes to the emotional transcendence of domestic fiction by midcentury (11–13). See also Hartnett, who suggests that sentimentality is a rhetorical response to the political crisis of the *onset* of modernism and the impersonality of capitalism and its aim is to overwhelm the audience with emotion when rationality is no longer a sufficient response (1–18).

19. For further information on the life of Anna Morgan, see Sozen.

20. Similarly, in a treatise I do not analyze in depth in this chapter, Shoemaker maintains that "Our principal vocal school is conversation" (*Advanced Elocution* 19).

21. In *Art of Speech,* Morgan gives a brief rehearsal of the advice on conversation (28–30) as developed in conduct book rhetoric, which we examined in ch. 2.

22. Even in the very technical *Advanced Elocution* by Rachel Shoemaker, a treatise that I do not treat in depth in this chapter, elocution is linked to emotion: "A perfectly cultivated voice responds instantly to the demands of thought and emotion" (20–21), Shoemaker somewhat paradoxically explains. "There is nothing in speech which has greater power to interpret, to give variety, and to suggest the light and shade of sentiment than the proper use of *Inflections* or *Slides.* . . . the tones of the voice which . . . are the natural language of man" (35).

23. Barnes argues that sentimental fiction also works by arousing in readers feelings that are represented as universal (97).

24. On conduct book rhetoric by women, see Nan Johnson, *Gender*; and Donawerth, "Nineteenth-Century."

25. On dress as similarly both a means of disciplining women and a site of resistance, see Mattingly, *Appropriate[ing] Dress* 7.

26. On the rhetoric of women's dress, see Mattingly, *Appropriate[ing] Dress*.

27. Compare Hallie Quinn Brown, in *Elocution and Physical Culture*, who scolds her students, "The neck, chest and abdomen should be free from anything that tends to constrict them in the form of corsets or tight belts" (*Elocution* 39).

28. For further information on the life of Genevieve Stebbins, see Stebbins, *New York School*; Ruyter, *Reformers and Visionaries; Cultivation of Body and Mind*; and "Genevieve Stebbins"; and Kendall, esp. 24–25, 29–30. I thank Anne Warren for pointing out to me the importance of Stebbins and elocution in the origins of modern dance.

29. In the *Delsarte System*, Stebbins publishes a transcript of a lecture Delsarte gave during a United States tour and quotes from an interview and from writings by l'Abbé Delaumosne, the biographer of Delsarte. Besides the technical vocabulary and charts of gestures and body positions, from Delsarte Stebbins takes the ideas of art as nurturer of the soul, the Platonic view of art as the wings of the soul, the purpose of art as elevation of the mind and soul, and a position against the contemporary philosophy of art for art's sake.

30. But sentimental rhetoric does not preclude self-conscious criticism of itself; see Jacobson, esp. 123: "By mocking the artificial sentimentality of genteel social life through the persona of an authentically sentimental yet humorously uninformed Yankee, Stephens expresses her serious hesitations about the value of parlor melodrama—as well as the role ascribed to women writers as narrators of parlor life—without the risk of alienating herself from the literary culture."

31. See also Blood and Riley 1:11, on higher emotions; and 4:10, on the link between emotions and moral persuasion.

32. See "Emily Montague Bishop" in *Who Was Who* 1:97. On women, elocution, and the "health movements" of the late nineteenth century, see Rieser 228–34.

33. I am grateful to the Hallie Quinn Brown Library of Central State University in Ohio for use of the Brown materials, both the manuscript and rare print texts. For further information on the life of Brown, see the anonymous "Sketch of the Life" (for this citation I thank Shirley Logan); McFarlin; Donawerth, "Textbooks for New Audiences"; Kates, "Embodied Rhetoric," and *Activist Rhetorics* 53–74; and Strom. Elocution seems to have been an accepted part of college study for late nineteenth-century African American women: Ida B. Wells at LeMoyne-Owen College and Fisk University and Selena Sloan Butler at the Emerson School of Oratory also studied elocution, and Butler taught elocution in the Atlanta public schools; see Royster 158, 194; and Logan, *Liberating Language* 44, 109.

34. Brown generally self-published her books by having them printed and then serving as her own distributor. She had them put into preprinted paper covers, with their own dates, and so the dates for her works may only be guessed at.

35. While Delsarte is the immediate source of the emphasis on emotion, classical rhetoric also taught that action or delivery was a natural, universal language of the emotions that appealed especially to the vulgar: see Cicero, *De Oratore* 3.57.216 and 3.59.221; Quintilian, *Institutio Oratoria*, 2.3.2–14, 3.3.61–62; and *Rhetorica ad Herennium* 3.15.27. For an overview of this idea, see Donawerth, *Shakespeare* 75–76, 84–85.

36. This sort of sentimental theory of the relationship between speaker and audience moves into public speaking in Mary Augusta Jordan's *Correct Writing and Speaking* (1904). In a section on public speaking, Jordan suggests that "the individual in his public spirit must somehow or other draw upon the reserve of sympathy and common living which influences him more rather than less than it does the silent members of his audience. . . . he does not give them his tongue, but finds their tongues for them" (66). In a further comment, she urges that "The successful speaker . . . will use all his art to enable him to discern the signs of the spiritual forces coming into action in his presence. His aim will be to conserve them, to let as little as possible real energy go to waste" (69).

37. On gesture and delivery as a language of the passions, see, e.g., Sheridan x.

38. One elocutionist I did not treat in detail in this chapter, Mrs. J. W. (Rachel) Shoemaker, also directed her theory toward public speaking. *Advanced Elocution* (1896) is a purely technical manual, scientific rather than philosophical in approach (compared to the theorists discussed in this chapter). There is so much emphasis on articulation that the handbook seems especially adapted to the goal of training in the codes of class status. The manual is explicitly addressed to men (in contrast to the other women discussed in this chapter, who address female or mixed audiences), but Shoemaker includes illustrations of women in pantomime poses; this contradiction further suggests training in codes of class status, through purveying masculine knowledge to women.

39. See also Washington 176, 189.

40. See also Hallie Quinn Brown, Untitled speech 159.

41. See also Hallie Quinn Brown, Untitled speech 156, 159–61.

42. Tompkins's 1985 *Sensational Designs* was a groundbreaking defense of nineteenth-century sentimental fiction; see esp. her chapter on *Uncle Tom's Cabin*, 122–46.

43. My understanding of the effect of elocution here is also influenced by theories of gender as performance, esp. Riviere and Judith Butler, *Gender Trouble*.

44. With regard to the sentimental novel, Hendler, in "Limits of Sympathy," argues that nineteenth-century women who attempted to build a feminist politics on sympathy failed because this strategy meant accepting female selflessness as an ideal. I do not see how altruism, which requires putting someone before oneself temporarily, necessarily implies selflessness, and in any case, elocution might perhaps involve the performance or ritual representation of selflessness without its damaging effects on the identity.

45. On the female vs. male models of delivery for women speakers, see Buchanan, *Regendering Delivery*, esp. 8, 77–83, 91.

Conclusion: Composition Textbooks by Women and the Decline of a Women's Tradition

1. In *Archives of Instruction*, an extraordinary survey of nineteenth-century rhetoric and composition textbooks, Carr, Carr, and Schultz classify textbooks differently from the categories I have chosen: they distinguish more theoretical rhetorics in the early part of the century, readers throughout, and more practical composition textbooks after the Civil War (17–18). I do not treat readers because they do not often theorize communication, but I have found that textbooks that include composition exercises often also provide theory, if often in short passages. I divided the general field of textbooks that concentrate on writing into rhetorical grammars, belles lettres textbooks, empiricist, and classical-influenced rhetorics. As Carr, Carr, and Schultz admit, textbooks are often "hybrid," merging rhetoric and composition (24), and so I have not attempted

to distinguish these as separate fields. Finally, I disagree with their dismissal of belles lettres rhetoric as a useful category for nineteenth-century rhetoric (28–29), for I have often found an attention to taste and literary analysis as basic in these textbooks.

2. On the changeover from oral persuasion to written composition as resulting from women's admission to colleges, see Connors, "Women's Reclamation." For critiques of Connors's argument that rhetoric was "feminized," moving from masculine agonistic to feminine expressive, from challenging to nurturing teaching styles, see Buchanan, *Regendering Delivery* 42–44. While I agree with Connors on the changes in rhetoric, I do not agree that they were caused mainly by male professors' protection of female students in co-educational institutions.

3. Brandt explains, "texts take their natures from the ways that they are serving the acts of writing and reading" (*Literacy as Involvement* 13). For an overview of contemporary work on literacy, see Cushman et al. On the debate over definitions of literacy, see Keller-Cohen 7–11. I find helpful Flower's definition of *literacy*: literacy is an action, but a literate action operates within a discourse practice, and becoming literate depends on knowledge of social conventions and abilities in problem-solving because discourse practices are tools of a discourse community (20–23).

4. See Brandt, "Sponsors of Literacy" 182–83.

5. See Solomon, 32–33; Enoch; and Connors, "Women's Reclamation" 275, who sets the figure as 90 percent of English teachers as female by 1900. See also Carr, Carr, and Schultz on the change during the course of the nineteenth century from rhetorics to composition (32, 67); college composition textbooks were not published until nearly the end of the century.

6. Even in all-women colleges, rhetoric was reconceived for women who were expected to speak publicly and participate in written public discourse; see, for example, Gold, whose study of the curriculum of Texas Woman's University shows that students were "encouraged to participate in public discourse as rhetors" (9); see also 87–112.

7. Thus, for Flower, while composition is a social act, it is also performed by an agent: writers' "interpretations and the knowledge they construct is their own, but it is built out of and in response to other voices, prior texts, social expectations, and ideological alternatives" (31).

8. Current-traditional rhetoric is seen as uniformly faulty in most accounts of the history of rhetoric and composition. On the function of composition as gatekeeper to elite colleges, see Berlin, *Writing Instruction* 72; on the class mobility in the late nineteenth-century United States that occasioned a concomitant emphasis on "grammatical purity," see Boyd 447. But the grammar-based rhetorics of the nineteenth-century United States, as Connors pointed out in "Erasure of the Sentence" 97–98, encompass multiple uses and different levels of insistence on correctness. Indeed, some of these grammar-rhetorics may be seen to teach sentence generation rather than grammatical correctness; see Carr, Carr, and Schultz 32. For a discussion of these issues in contemporary composition studies, see Micciche.

9. See the entry on Elizabeth Oram in Grace and Wallace 478.

10. Carr, Carr, and Schultz point out that not every student had a textbook and all students did not necessarily have the same textbook except in private academies; they argue that the pedagogical practices of memorizing and copying result from the scarcity of textbooks (61–63).

11. On the influence of Johann Heinrich Pestalozzi (1746–1827) and object teaching on nineteenth-century composition teaching, see Schultz, *Young Composers* ch. 3, esp. 57, 63–84.

12. Mary Hyde (1888–1903) was the most industrious publisher among women compositionists and also the most conservative, repeating through nearly a dozen books admonitions to correctness. Needless to say, she does not appropriate conversation as a model for discourse. See *Intermediate Grammar, Practical Lessons,* and *Two-Book Course in English.*

13. On the association of ideas and nineteenth-century psychology, especially that of Alexander Bain, see William F. Woods, esp. 25.

14. I owe finding Mary Augusta Jordan to Susan Joseph, a graduate student at the University of Maryland. In my graduate course, "Readings in the History of Rhetorical Theory," we had read Gertrude Buck, who taught at Vassar. In response to my assignment to "find the first woman rhetorical theorist," Susan Joseph, an alumna of Smith, longed to find a Smith equivalent—and did, with help from the archivists at Smith's library, for which we are both grateful. For biographical information, I am indebted to Susan's unpublished paper, "Mary August Jordan, 1855–1921," submitted as a course requirement. I regret that Susan felt unable to write further on Mary Augusta Jordan, and I appreciate very much her supplying me with a copy of Jordan's text.

15. On Jordan's biography and her pedagogy, see Kates, *Activist Rhetorics* 29–52.

16. The white women's colleges of the end of the century had engaged in a debate about their mission: was it to educate women, to adapt curricula to women's experience, or to dispense knowledge—up to that time, male knowledge—to women? See Jordan's thoughts on this issue from "The College for Women" (1892) in Kates, *Activist Rhetorics* 31: "The college for women must solve the problem of education first hand. To that end, it must cut loose from the traditions of men, not because they are men's nor indeed because they are traditions, but because the best men have no saving faith in them." See also Wagner 197–99 esp., on Jordan.

17. See Warnick on the eighteenth-century development of a rhetoric based on audience reception rather than speaking skills.

18. For an analysis of the importance of class to the nineteenth-century concept of "correctness," see Berlin, *Writing Instruction* ch. 6.

19. Writing of the period 1914–45, Cohen explains that "Almost all the authors of this period, including women authors, made almost exclusive use of the masculine third person pronoun. If one did not know the usage of the time, one could assume from these publications that all students and all readers were male" (xii). Jordan and Buck, then, were exceptional in developing strategies that resisted the universality of the masculine pronoun. Hallie Quinn Brown also used such strategies. In her lecture on elocution, "*Man* manifests the three states of *his* being through voice, muscle and speech" (Untitled speech 159), but, on the next page, a baby develops: "*she* begins to think. . . . *She* separates herself from the objects that surround *her*" (160). Brown represents universal experience by both pronouns. She was a committed feminist, who applied her politics to her theory: "Thanks to elocution," she writes, "the sickly, young lady with her puny form and wasp waist, is being supplanted by the strong, vigorous woman, who is to preside in the home and to move to and fro over the land as a queen among men" (163). Brown's use of the alternation of pronouns, then, seems a means of including women in the same quest for cultivation of power that she offers her male students.

20. Male theorists later used conversation as a model for public discourse: see Cohen 25–26, on William Mathews's *The Great Conversers* and George Hervey's *The Rhetoric of Conversation*; Cohen 94, on conversation not distinctly separate from public

speaking in J. A. Winans's *Public Speaking* (1915); Cohen 103, on conversation as an art in Everett L. Hunt's 1917 essay on "Academic Public Speaking" in the *Quarterly Journal of Public Speaking*; Cohen 110–12, on conversation as a model for speaking style in E. D. Shurter's *The Rhetoric of Oratory* (1911); and Cohen 275, on group discussion and reaching consensus in A. D. Sheffield's *Joining in Public Discussion* (1922).

21. Contrast Thomas De Quincey in his 1847–60 essay on conversation, for example, who sees the art of conversation as a basis for individual performance and display, even though he cautions against the vices of indulgence or vanity of individual speakers (264–88).

22. The titles of Farrar's conduct books are *The Young Lady's Friend* (1836) and *The Youth's Letter-Writer* (1840)—both of which went through multiple editions.

23. I am thinking of these women in the context described in Carroll Smith-Rosenberg's "The Female World of Love and Ritual: Relations between Women in Nineteenth-Century America," in *Disorderly Conduct* 53–76. See also the Sisters of St. Joseph, *Language Manual*, published in South St. Louis in 1889, which, through exercises and sample composition topics, tries to establish students as a discourse community of idealized Catholic republican citizens held together by letters and conversation.

24. Lockwood married Dr. William E. Lockwood in 1887, but continued to teach—extremely rare for a woman in the nineteenth century. Besides *Lessons in English*, Lockwood also published a revised version of *The Essentials of English Grammar by Prof. W. D. Whitney of Yale* (1891), and a revision of her own textbook with M. Alice Emerson, *Composition and Rhetoric* (1901).

25. See also Knox, *Elementary Lessons* pt. 1, xiv–xvi, and xxi, where teachers are urged to use questions more often than lecture to instruct.

26. Keeler was an early feminist, the first woman to orate at the Oberlin College graduation ceremony, against the school tradition of women reading rather than speaking their speeches. See Buchanan, *Regendering Delivery* 62 (quoting Hosford 102): "Women ABs continued to have their graduation essays read by proxy [at Oberlin graduation] until 1858 when officials ruled that women might read (but *not* orate) their own compositions. This revised tradition remained intact until Harriet Louise Keeler's graduation in 1874:

> Demurely [Keeler] tripped upon the stage, holding conventional pages like the other sweet girl graduates. Demurely she read the first sentence, eyes modestly fixed upon her manuscript—and then the paper was discarded, the brave eyes swept the rows of startled faces, and the sweet girl graduate addressed the audience!

27. As well as the rhetoric that she published with Emma Davis, Keeler coauthored *High School English* with Mary E. Adams in 1906, and further published seven books on trees and flowers. She was an abolitionist and was active in the woman suffrage movement.

28. For further information on Keeler, see Donawerth, *Rhetorical Theory* 267–68.

29. The title page of *The Problem of Elementary Composition* tells us that Spalding was a teacher of English at Pratt Institute, and her examples in this treatise suggest that she had been an abolitionist (23). Besides her treatise on composition pedagogy, Spalding also co-wrote with Frank R. Moon *The Language-Speller* (1900–1901), and later published *The Principles of Rhetoric: With Constructive and Critical Work in Composition* (1905). See the entry on Elizabeth Hill Spalding in *Who Was Who* 4:887. Spalding approvingly cites "Mrs. Lockwood" for her exercise translating nursery rhymes into Latinate diction (33), suggesting that she sees herself in a tradition of American female schoolteachers.

30. When Spalding discusses the hypothetical teachers who will use her book, she designates them by the feminine pronoun "she" (111), and when she gives instructions for letter writing, she advises that addressing the envelopes is within the reach of "even the very young members" of the class, further suggesting that her book is addressed to that very large class of one-room schoolhouse teachers. Both my grandmother, Rhoda Smith Kendrick, and my mother-in-law, Marjorie Hall Scally, were one-room schoolhouse teachers, my grandmother in Ohio at the beginning of the twentieth century, my mother-in-law in Maine during the 1950s.

31. See Allen, "Gertrude Buck" and "Gertrude Buck's Rhetoric"; Berlin, *Writing Instruction*; Bordelon, "Gertrude Buck's Participation"; Rebecca Burke, "Gertrude Buck's Rhetorical Theory"; JoAnn Campbell, *Toward a Feminist Rhetoric*; and Gerald Mulderig, "Gertrude Buck's Rhetorical Theory and Modern Composition Teaching."

32. See Bordelon, *Feminist Legacy*, ch. 2, on Buck's use of progressive educational theory. Buck's co-authored treatise *A Course in Narrative Writing* is so late (1906) that I am not including it in this discussion.

33. Mary Yost, who later also received her Ph.D. from Michigan and taught at Vassar, developed the earliest sociological analysis of the speech situation, arguing for harmony as the goal of communication in an essay in the *Quarterly Journal of Public Speaking*; see Cohen 67–72.

34. On woman's paradoxical situation of maintaining gendered spheres through relegation to the private and domestic, while also participating in national, political, and religious movements, see Ryan.

Works Cited

Alcott, Louisa May. *Eight Cousins; or, The Aunt Hill*. Boston: Roberts Brothers, 1875.

Allen, Virginia. "Gertrude Buck and the Emergence of Composition in the United States." *Vitae Scholasticae: The Bulletin of Educational Biography* 5 (Spring/Fall 1986): 141–59.

——— . "Gertrude Buck's Rhetoric for the New Psychology." Unpublished paper. Conference on College Composition and Communication. Chicago, 1989.

Amussen, Susan Dwyer. *An Ordered Society: Gender and Class in Early Modern England*. New York: Blackwell, 1988.

Andrews, William L., ed. *Sisters of the Spirit: Three Black Women's Autobiographies of the Nineteenth Century*. Bloomington: Indiana UP, 1986.

Aragona, Tullia d'. *Dialogue on the Infinity of Love*. Ed. and trans. Rinaldina Russell and Bruce Merry. Chicago: U of Chicago P, 1997.

Aristotle. *On Sophistical Refutations*. Trans. E. S. Forster. London: William Heinemann, 1955.

——— . *Rhetoric*. Trans. W. Rhys Roberts. *Aristotle: Rhetoric, Poetics*. New York: Random House Modern Library, 1954. 1–218.

Arnauld, Antoine. *Logic; or The Art of Thinking*. London, 1693.

Aronson, Nicole. *Mademoiselle de Scudéry*. Trans. Stuart Aronson. Boston: G. K. Hall and Co., 1978.

Askew, Anne. *The Examinations of Anne Askew*. Ed. Elaine Beilin. New York: Oxford UP, 1996.

Astell, Mary. *A Serious Proposal to the Ladies, Parts I and II*. 1697. 4th ed., 1701. Reprint, New York: Source Book, 1970.

Augustine. *On Christian Doctrine*. Trans. D. W. Robertson Jr. Indianapolis: Bobbs-Merrill, 1958.

——— . "The Teacher" [*De Magistro*]. *The Teacher, The Free Choice of the Will, Grace and Free Will*. Vol. 59 of *The Fathers of the Church*. Trans. Robert P. Russell. Washington, D.C.: The Catholic U of America P, 1968. 1–61.

Austen, Jane. *Lady Susan*. *Lady Susan, The Watsons, Sanditon*. Ed. Margaret Drabble. 1974. Reprint, London: Penguin, 2003. 41–103.

Bacon, Jacqueline. *The Humblest May Stand Forth: Rhetoric, Empowerment, and Abolition*. Columbia: U of South Carolina P, 2002.

Bahn, Eugene, and Margaret Bahn. *A History of Oral Interpretation.* Minneapolis: Burgess, 1970.

Baker, Houston A., Jr. *Modernism and the Harlem Renaissance.* Chicago: U of Chicago P, 1987.

Barnes, Elizabeth. *States of Sympathy: Seduction and Democracy in the American Novel.* New York: Columbia UP, 1997.

Bartholomae, David. "Inventing the University." *The St. Martin's Guide to Teaching Writing.* Ed. Cheryl Glenn, Melissa A. Goldthwaite, and Robert Connors. 5th ed. New York: Bedford/St. Martin's, 2003. 403–17.

Battigelli, Anna. *Margaret Cavendish and the Exiles of the Mind.* Lexington: UP of Kentucky, 1998.

Baym, Nina. "Lydia Sigourney." *American National Biography.* Ed. John A. Garraty and Mark C. Carnes. Vol. 19. New York: Oxford UP, 1999. 926–28.

Beasley, Faith E. *Revising Memory: Women's Fiction and Memoirs in Seventeenth-Century France.* New Brunswick, N.J.: Rutgers UP, 1990.

Beauchamp, Virginia Walcott, Elizabeth H. Hageman, and Margaret Mikesell, eds. *The Instruction of a Christen Woman,* by Juan Luis Vives. Urbana: U of Illinois P, 2002.

Beaufort, Anne. *Writing in the Real World.* New York: Teachers College of Columbia U, 1999.

Beck, Evelyn Torton, and Susan Sniader Lanser. "[Why] Are There No Great Women Critics? And What Difference Does It Make?" *The Prism of Sex: Essays in the Sociology of Knowledge.* Madison: U of Wisconsin P, 1977. 79–91.

Belenky, Mary Field, Blythe McVicker Clinchy, Nancy Rule Goldberger, and Jill Mattuck Tarule, eds. *Women's Ways of Knowing: The Development of Self, Voice, and Mind.* New York: Basic Books, 1986.

Belsey, Catherine. *The Subject of Tragedy.* London: Methuen, 1985.

Bennett, Paula Bernat, ed. *Nineteenth-Century American Women Poets: An Anthology.* Malden, Mass.: Blackwell, 1998.

Berlin, James. "Revisionary Histories of Rhetoric: Politics, Power, and Plurality." *Writing Histories of Rhetoric.* Ed. Victor J. Vitanza. Carbondale: Southern Illinois UP, 1994. 112–27.

———. "Revisionary History: The Dialectical Method." *Rethinking the History of Rhetoric.* Ed. Takis Poulakos. Boulder, Colo.: Westview, 1993. 135–51.

———. *Writing Instruction in Nineteenth-Century American Colleges.* Carbondale: Southern Illinois UP, 1984.

Biesecker, Barbara. "Coming to Terms with Recent Attempts to Write Women into the History of Rhetoric." *Philosophy and Rhetoric* 25. 2 (1992): 140–61.

Bishop, Emily M. *Self-Expression and Health: Americanized Delsarte Culture.* 5th ed. Chautauqua, N.Y.: Published by the Author, 1895.

Bizzell, Patricia. *Academic Discourse and Critical Consciousness.* Pittsburgh, Pa.: U of Pittsburgh P, 1992.

———. "Frances Willard, Phoebe Palmer, and the Ethos of the Methodist Woman Preacher." *Rhetoric Society Quarterly* 30.4 (Fall 2006): 377–98.

———. "Opportunities for Feminist Research in the History of Rhetoric." *Rhetoric Review* 11.1 (Fall 1992): 50–58.

Bizzell, Patricia, and Bruce Herzberg, eds. *The Rhetorical Tradition: Readings from Classical Times to Present.* 2nd ed. Boston: Bedford, 1990.

Blair, Carole. "Contested Histories of Rhetoric: The Politics of Preservation, Progress, and Change." *Quarterly Journal of Speech* 78 (1992): 403–28.

Blair, Hugh. *Lectures on Rhetoric and Belles Lettres.* 3 vols. London, 1785.

Blood, Mary A., and Ida Morley Riley. *The Psychological Development of Expression.* 4 vols. Chicago: Columbia School of Oratory, 1893–99.

Booth, Catherine Mumford. *Female Ministry: or, Woman's Right to Preach the Gospel.* 1859. Reprint, London: G. J. Stevenson, 1860. Victorian Women Writers, Indiana U Libraries, http://www.Indiana.edu.

Bordelon, Suzanne. *A Feminist Legacy: The Rhetoric and Pedagogy of Gertrude Buck.* Carbondale: Southern Illinois UP, 2007.

———. "Gertrude Buck's Participation in a Pedagogy of Democratic Ideas and Social Ethics." Unpublished paper. Conference on College Composition and Communication. Washington, D.C., 1995.

Bordin, Ruth. *Frances Willard: A Biography.* Chapel Hill: U of North Carolina P, 1986.

Borkowski, David. "Class(ifying) Language: The War of the Word." *Rhetoric Review* 21.4 (2002): 357–83.

Bosanquet, Mary. Letter (June 1771) to John Wesley on Women's Preaching. *John Wesley and the Women Preachers of Early Methodism,* by Paul Wesley Chilcote. Metuchen, N.J.: Scarecrow, 1991. 299–304.

Boutcher, Warren. "Vernacular Humanism in the Sixteenth Century." *The Cambridge Companion to Renaissance Humanism.* Ed. Jill Kraye. Cambridge: Cambridge UP, 1996. 189–202.

Boyd, Richard. "Mechanical Correctness and Ritual in the Late-Nineteenth-Century Composition Classroom." *Rhetoric Review* 11.2 (Spring 1993): 436–55.

Brandt, Deborah. *Literacy as Involvement: The Acts of Writers, Readers, and Texts.* Carbondale: Southern Illinois UP, 1990.

———. "Sponsors of Literacy." *College Composition and Communication* 49.2 (May 1998): 165–85.

Brekus, Catherine A. *Strangers and Pilgrims: Female Preaching in America, 1740–1845.* Chapel Hill: U of North Carolina P, 1998.

Brereton, John C., ed. *The Origins of Composition Studies in the American College, 1875–1925.* Pittsburgh, Pa.: U of Pittsburgh P, 1995.

Bricker-Jenkins, Mary, and Nancy Hooyman. "Feminist Pedagogy in Education for Social Change." *Feminist Teacher* 2.2 (1987): 36–42.

Broaddus, Dorothy C. *Genteel Rhetoric: Writing High Culture in Nineteenth-Century Boston.* Columbia: U of South Carolina P, 1999.

Brody, Miriam. *Manly Writing: Gender, Rhetoric, and the Rise of Composition.* Carbondale: Southern Illinois UP, 1993.

Brown, Brenda Gabioud. "Elocution." *Encyclopedia of Rhetoric and Composition: Communication from Ancient Times to the Information Age.* Ed. Theresa Enos. New York: Garland, 1996. 211–14.

Brown, Hallie Quinn. Diaries of elocutionary tours, 1881–85. Manuscripts housed at Hallie Quinn Brown Library at Central State U, Wilberforce, Ohio.

———. *Elocution and Physical Culture, Training for Students, Teachers, Readers, Public Speakers.* Wilberforce, Ohio: Homewood Cottage, 1908?.

———. Untitled speech on Elocution, n.d. (1920s?). Typescript. Hallie Quinn Brown Library at Central State U, Wilberforce, Ohio. Copy in Appendix D, "Sample

Manuscript of Text." Annjennette S. McFarlin. "Hallie Quinn Brown—Black Woman Elocutionist: 1845(?)–1949." Diss., Washington State U, 1975.

Brown, Hallie Quinn, ed. *Bits and Odds: A Choice Selection of Recitations, for School, Lyceum and Parlor Entertainments Rendered by Miss Hallie Q. Brown.* Introduction and sketches by Faustin S. Delaney. c. 1880. Xenia, Ohio: Chew, c. 1910.

Brown, Joanne Carlson. "Jennie Fowler Willing." *American National Biography.* Ed. John A. Garraty and Mark C. Carnes. Vol. 23. New York: Oxford UP, 1999. 529–30.

Buchanan, Lindal. "'Forging and Firing Thunderbolts': Collaboration and Women's Rhetoric." *Rhetoric Society Quarterly* 33.4 (Fall 2003): 43–63.

———. *Regendering Delivery: The Fifth Canon and Antebellum Women Rhetors.* Carbondale: Southern Illinois UP, 2005.

Buck, Gertrude. *A Course in Argumentative Writing.* New York: Henry Holt, 1899.

———. "Make-Believe Grammar." *School Review* 17 (January 1909): 21–33.

———. "The Metaphor—A Study in the Psychology of Rhetoric." *Contributions to Rhetorical Theory,* no. 5. Ed. Fred Newton Scott. Ann Arbor, Mich.: Inland, 1899.

———. "Recent Tendencies in the Teaching of English Composition." *Educational Review* 22 (November 1901): 371–82.

Buck, Gertrude, and Elisabeth Woodbridge Morris. *A Course in Narrative Writing.* New York: Henry Holt and Company, 1906.

Burke, Kenneth. *A Rhetoric of Motives.* Berkeley: U of California P, 1969.

Burke, Peter. *The Art of Conversation.* Ithaca, N.Y.: Cornell UP, 1993.

Burke, Rebecca. "Gertrude Buck's Rhetorical Theory." *Occasional Papers in the History and Theory of Composition,* no. 1. Ed. Donald C. Stewart. Manhattan: Kansas State U, 1978. 1–26.

Burton, Vicki Tolar. "Preaching from the Pulpit Steps: Mary Bosanquet Fletcher's Defense of Women's Preaching." Paper presented to Conference on College Composition and Communication. San Francisco, March 2005.

———. *Spiritual Literacy in John Wesley's Methodism: Reading, Writing, and Speaking to Believe.* Waco, Tex.: Baylor UP, 2008.

Butler, Judith. *Excitable Speech: A Politics of the Performative.* New York: Routledge, 1997.

———. *Gender Trouble: Feminism and the Subversion of Identity.* New York: Routledge, 1990.

Butler, Marilyn. *Maria Edgeworth: A Literary Biography.* Oxford: Clarendon, 1972.

Campbell, George. *The Philosophy of Rhetoric.* 1776. Reprint, ed. Lloyd Bitzer. Carbondale: Southern Illinois UP, 1963.

Campbell, JoAnn, ed. Introduction to *Toward a Feminist Rhetoric: The Writing of Gertrude Buck.* Pittsburgh, Pa.: U of Pittsburgh P, 1996. ix–xliii.

Campbell, Karlyn Kohrs. "Gender and Genre: Loci of Invention and Contradiction in the Earliest Speeches by U.S. Women." *Quarterly Journal of Speech* 81.4 (November 1995): 479–95.

———. *Man Cannot Speak for Her.* Vol. 1 *A Critical Study of Early Feminist Rhetoric.* Vol. 2 *Key Texts of the Early Feminists.* New York: Greenwood, 1989.

Carr, Jean Ferguson, Stephen L. Carr, and Lucille M. Schultz. *Archives of Instruction: Nineteenth-Century Rhetorics, Readers, and Composition Books in the United States.* Carbondale: Southern Illinois UP, 2005.

Castiglione, Baldassare. *The Book of the Courtier.* Trans. Sir Thomas Hoby. London: J. M. Dent & Sons, 1928.

Cavendish, Margaret, Duchess of Newcastle. *The Blazing World and Other Writings.* Ed. Kate Lilley. London: Penguin Books, 1992.

———. "The Female Academy." *Plays*. London, 1662. 653–79.

———. *The Life of . . . William Cavendish*. London, 1667.

———. *Orations of Divers Sorts, Accommodated to Divers Places*. London, 1662.

———. *Sociable Letters*. Ed. James Fitzmaurice. New York: Garland, 1997.

———. *The Worlds Olio*. London, 1655.

Certeau, Michel de. "Reading as Poaching." *The Practice of Everyday Life*. Trans. Steven F. Randall. Berkeley: U of California P, 1984. 165–76.

Chilcote, Paul Wesley. *John Wesley and the Women Preachers of Early Methodism*. Metuchen, N.J.: Scarecrow Press, 1991.

Chittenden, Miss L[ucy] A. *The Elements of English Composition: A Preparation for Rhetoric*. Chicago: S. C. Griggs, 1886.

Christine de Pizan. *The Book of the Body Politic*. Ed. and trans. Kate Langdon Forhan. New York: Cambridge UP, 1994.

Cicero, Marcus Tullius. *De Officiis*. Trans. Walter Miller. 1913. Reprint, London: William Heinemann, 1928.

———. *De Oratore*. 2 vols. Trans. E. W. Sutton and H. Rackham. London: William Heinemann, 1948.

Clark, Gregory. *Dialogue, Dialectic, and Conversation: A Social Perspective on the Function of Writing*. Carbondale: Southern Illinois UP, 1990.

Clark, Suzanne, and Lisa Ede. *Instructor's Notes: The Academic Writer, Lisa Ede*. Boston: Bedford/St. Martin's, 2009.

Cohen, Herman. *The History of Speech Communication: The Emergence of a Discipline, 1914–1945*. Annandale, Va.: Speech Communication Association, 1994.

Collins, Patricia Hill. "Moving Beyond Gender: Intersectionality and Scientific Knowledge." *Revisioning Gender*. Ed. Myra Marx Ferree et al. Thousand Oaks, Calif.: Sage Publications, 1999. 261–84.

Connors, Robert J. "The Erasure of the Sentence." *College Composition and Communication* 52 (2000): 96–128.

———. "Women's Reclamation of Rhetoric in Nineteenth-Century America." *Selected Essays of Robert J. Connors*. Ed. Lisa Ede and Andrea A. Lunsford. Boston: Bedford/St. Martin's, 2003. 259–78.

Cope, Jackson I. "Seventeenth-Century Quaker Style." *PMLA* 71 (1956): 725–54.

Crowley, Sharon. "Let Me Get This Straight." *Writing Histories of Rhetoric*. Ed. Victor J. Vitanza. Carbondale: Southern Illinois UP, 1994. 1–19.

———. *The Methodical Memory: Invention in Current-Traditional Rhetoric*. Carbondale: Southern Illinois UP, 1990.

Cushman, Ellen, Eugene R. Kintgen, Barry M. Kroll, and Mike Rose, eds. *Literacy: A Critical Sourcebook*. New York: Bedford/St. Martin's, 2001.

Dean, David. "Wentworth, Peter (1524–1597)." *Oxford Dictionary of National Biography*. Oxford: Oxford UP, September 2004. Online edition, http://www.oxforddnb.com/view/article/29051. Accessed 1 Oct. 2008.

Demers, Patricia. *The World of Hannah More*. Lexington: UP of Kentucky, 1996.

Dentière, Marie. *Epistre très utile* (Geneva, 1539). Trans. Thomas Head as *A Most Beneficial Letter, Prepared and Written Down by a Christian Woman of Tournai, and Sent to the Queen of Navarre, Sister of the King of France, against the Turks, the Jews, the Infidels, the False Christians, the Anabaptists and the Lutherans* (1539). Selections in *Women Writers of the Renaissance and Reformation*. Ed. Katharina M. Wilson. Athens: U of Georgia P, 1989. 275–81.

De Quincey, Thomas. *Selected Essays on Rhetoric*. Carbondale: Southern Illinois UP, 1967.

deVries, Jacqueline R. "Transforming the Pulpit: Preaching and Prophecy in the British Women's Suffrage Movement." *Women Preachers and Prophets through Two Millennia of Christianity*. Ed. Beverly Mayne Kienzle and Pamela J. Walker. Berkeley: U of California P, 1998. 318–33.

Dickens, A. G. *The English Reformation*. New York: Schocken Books, 1964.

——— . *Reformation and Society in Sixteenth-Century Europe*. New York: Harcourt, Brace, & World, 1966.

Dobson, Joanne. "Reclaiming Sentimental Literature." *American Literature* 69 (1997): 263–88.

Donawerth, Jane. "'As Becomes a Rational Woman to Speak': Madeleine de Scudéry's Rhetoric of Conversation." *Listening to Their Voices: Essays on the Rhetorical Activities of Historical Women*. Ed. Molly Wertheimer. Columbia: U of South Carolina P, 1997. 305–19.

——— . "Bibliography of Women and the History of Rhetorical Theory to 1900." *Rhetoric Society Quarterly* 20.4 (1990): 403–14.

——— . "Changing Our Originary Stories: Renaissance Women on Education, and Conversation as a Model for Our Classrooms." *Attending to Early Modern Women*. Ed. Susan Amussen and Adele Seeff. Newark: U of Delaware P, 1998. 263–77.

——— . "Conversation and the Boundaries of Public Discourse in Rhetorical Theory by Renaissance Women." *Rhetorica* 16.2 (Spring 1998): 181–99.

——— . "Hannah More, Lydia Sigourney, and the Creation of a Women's Tradition of Rhetoric." *Rhetoric, the Polis, and the Global Village: Selected Papers from the 1998 Thirtieth Anniversary Rhetoric Society of America Conference*. Ed. C. Jan Swearingen. Mahwah, N.J.: Lawrence Erlbaum, 1999. 155–62.

——— . "Nineteenth-Century United States Conduct Book Rhetoric by Women." *Rhetoric Review* 21.1 (2002): 5–21.

——— . "Oratory and Rhetoric." *Renaissance Women Online*. Brown Women Writers Project, http://www.wwp.brown.edu/rwo/home.html. 1998.

——— . "Poaching on Men's Philosophies of Rhetoric: Eighteenth- and Nineteenth-Century Rhetorical Theory by Women." *Philosophy and Rhetoric* 33.3 (2000): 243–58.

——— . "The Politics of Rhetorical Theory by Women." *The Rhetoric of Politics and Renaissance Women*. Ed. Carole Levin and Patricia Sullivan. Albany: State U of New York P, 1995. 256–72.

——— . *Shakespeare and the Sixteenth-Century Study of Language*. Urbana: U of Illinois P, 1984.

——— . "Textbooks for New Audiences: Women's Revisions of Rhetorical Theory at the Turn of the Century." *Listening to Their Voices: The Rhetorical Activities of Historical Women*. Columbia: U of South Carolina P, 1997. 337–56.

——— . "Transforming the History of Rhetorical Theory." *Feminist Teacher* 7.1 (1992): 35–39.

——— . "Women's Reading Practices in Seventeenth-Century England: Margaret Fell's *Women's Speaking Justified*." *Sixteenth Century Journal* 37.4 (2006): 985–1005.

Donawerth, Jane, ed. *Rhetorical Theory by Women before 1900: An Anthology*. Lanham, Md.: Rowman & Littlefield, 2002.

Donawerth, Jane, and Julie Strongson. Introduction to *Selected Letters, Orations, and Rhetorical Dialogues*, by Madeleine de Scudéry. Ed. and trans. Donawerth and Strongson. Chicago: U of Chicago P, 2004. 1–38.

Dow, Bonnie J. "The 'Womanhood' Rationale in the Woman Suffrage Rhetoric of Frances E. Willard." *Southern Communication Journal* 56.4 (Summer 1991): 298–307.

DuPlessis, Rachel Blau. *Writing Beyond the Ending: Narrative Strategies of Twentieth-Century Women Writers*. Bloomington: Indiana UP, 1985.

Ede, Lisa, and Andrea Lunsford. *Singular Texts/Plural Authors: Perspectives on Collaborative Writing*. Carbondale: Southern Illinois UP, 1990.

Edgeworth, Maria. *Letters for Literary Ladies, to Which Is Added, an Essay on the Noble Science of Self-Justification*. London, 1795.

Edwards, Paul C. "Elocution and Shakespeare: An Episode in the History of Literary Taste." *Shakespeare Quarterly* 35.3 (Autumn 1984): 305–14.

Elaw, Zilpha. *Memoirs of the Life, Religious Experience, Ministerial Travels and Labours of Mrs. Zilpha Elaw, An American Female of Colour; Together with Some Account of the Great Religious Revivals in America*. London: privately printed, 1846. Reprinted in *Sisters of the Spirit: Three Black Women's Autobiographies of the Nineteenth Century*. Ed. William L. Andrews. Bloomington: Indiana UP, 1986. 49–159.

Eldred, Janet Carey, and Peter Mortensen. "Gender and Writing Instruction in Early America: Lessons from Didactic Fiction." *Rhetoric Review* 12.1 (Fall 1993): 25–53.

———. *Imagining Rhetoric: Composing Women of the Early United States*. Pittsburgh, Pa.: U of Pittsburgh P, 2002.

———. "Monitoring Columbia's Daughters: Writing as Gendered Conduct." *Rhetoric Society Quarterly* 23.3/4 (Summer/Fall 1993): 44–69.

———. "'Persuasion Dwelt on Her Tongue': Female Civic Rhetoric in Early America." *College English* 60.2 (February 1998): 173–88.

Ellison, Julie. *Cato's Tears and the Making of Anglo-American Emotion*. Chicago: U of Chicago P, 1999.

Enoch, Jessica. "A Woman's Place Is in the School: Rhetorics of Gendered Space in Nineteenth-Century America." *College English* 70.3 (2008): 275–95.

Erasmus, Desiderius. *The Praise of Folly and Other Writings*. Trans. Robert M. Adams. New York: Norton, 1989.

Farrar, Eliza. *Recollections of Seventy Years*. Boston: Ticknor & Fields, 1866.

———. *The Young Lady's Friend*. Boston: American Stationers' Company, 1836. Reprint, New York: Arno, 1974.

———. *The Youth's Letter-Writer; or, The Epistolary Art Made Plain and Easy to Beginners through the Example of Henry Moreton*. New York: H. & S. Raynor, 1840.

Fedele, Cassandra. *Letters and Orations*. Ed. and trans. Diana Robin. Chicago: U of Chicago P, 2000.

Fell, Margaret. "Women's Speaking Justified." 1666. *Rhetorical Theory by Women before 1900: An Anthology*. Ed. Jane Donawerth. Lanham, Md.: Rowman and Littlefield, 2002. 59–72.

Ferguson, Margaret. "A Room Not Their Own: Renaissance Women as Readers and Writers." *The Comparative Perspective on Literature*. Ed. Clayton Koelb and Susan Noakes. Ithaca, N.Y.: Cornell UP, 1988. 93–116.

Ferguson, Moira, ed. *First Feminists: British Women Writers, 1578–1799*. Bloomington: Indiana UP, 1985.

Fitzgerald, Kathryn. "A Rediscovered Tradition: European Pedagogy and Composition in Nineteenth-Century Midwestern Normal School." *College Composition and Communication* 53.2 (December 2001): 224–50.

Fleming, Marie. "Women and the 'Public Use of Reason.'" *Feminists Read Habermas: Gendering the Subject of Discourse.* Ed. Johanna Meehan. New York: Routledge, 1995. 117–37.

Flower, Linda. *The Construction of Negotiated Meaning: A Social Cognitive Theory of Writing.* Carbondale: Southern Illinois UP, 1994.

Foote, Julia A. J. *A Brand Plucked from the Fire: An Autobiographical Sketch.* Cleveland, Ohio: privately printed, 1879. Reprinted in *Sisters of the Spirit: Three Black Women's Autobiographies of the Nineteenth Century.* Ed. William L. Andrews. Bloomington: Indiana UP, 1986. 161–234.

Ford, Charles Howard. *Hannah More: A Critical Biography.* New York: Peter Lang, 1996.

Fraser, Nancy. "Rethinking the Public Sphere: A Contribution to the Critique of Actually Existing Democracy." *Social Text* 25/26 (1990): 56–80.

———. "What's Critical about Critical Theory? The Case of Habermas and Gender." *Feminist Interpretations and Political Theory.* Ed. Mary Lyndon Shanley and Carole Pateman. University Park: Pennsylvania State UP, 1991. 253–76.

Gardiner, Judith Kegan. "Margaret Fell Fox and Feminist Literary History: A 'Mother in Israel' Calls to the Jews." *Prose Studies* 17.3 (December 1994): 42–56.

———. "Re-Gendering Individualism: Margaret Fell Fox and Quaker Rhetoric." *Privileging Gender in Early Modern England.* Ed. Jean Brink. Sixteenth Century Journal Publications, no. 23. Kirksville, Mo.: Sixteenth Century Journal Publishers, 1993. 205–24.

Gere, Anne Ruggles. *Intimate Practices: Literacy and Cultural Work in U.S. Women's Clubs, 1880–1920.* Urbana: U of Illinois P, 1997.

Gibson, Joan. "Educating for Silence: Renaissance Women and the Language Arts." *Hypatia* 4 (Spring 1989): 9–27.

Giroux, Henry A., and Peter L. McLaren. Introduction to *Critical Pedagogy, the State, and Cultural Struggle.* Ed. Giroux and McLaren. Albany: State U of New York P, 1989. xi–xxxv.

Glenn, Cheryl. "Locating Aspasia on the Rhetorical Map." *Listening to Their Voices: Essays on the Rhetorical Activities of Historical Women.* Ed. Molly Meijer Wertheimer. Columbia: U of South Carolina P, 1997. 19–41.

———. "Regendering the Rhetorical Tradition." "Octalog II: The (Continuing) Politics of Historiography" (Forum). *Rhetoric Review* 16.1 (Fall 1997): 22–44.

———. "Rereading Aspasia: The Palimpsest of Her Thoughts." *Rhetoric, Cultural Studies, and Literacy: Selected Papers from the 1994 Conference of the Rhetoric Society of America.* Ed. Fred Reynolds. Hillside, N.J.: Lawrence Erlbaum, 1995. 35–44.

———. *Rhetoric Retold: Regendering the Tradition from Antiquity through the Renaissance.* Carbondale: Southern Illinois UP, 1997.

———. "sex, lies, and manuscript: Refiguring Aspasia in the History of Rhetoric." *College Composition and Communication* 45 (May 1994): 180–99.

———. *Unspoken: A Rhetoric of Silence.* Carbondale: Southern Illinois UP, 2004.

Gold, David. *Rhetoric at the Margins: Revising the History of Writing Instruction in American Colleges, 1873–1947.* Carbondale: Southern Illinois UP, 2008.

Goldsmith, Elizabeth. *Exclusive Conversation: The Art of Interaction in Seventeenth-Century France.* Philadelphia: U of Pennsylvania P, 1988.

Goodman, Dena. *The Republic of Letters: A Cultural History of the French Enlightenment.* Ithaca, N.Y.: Cornell UP, 1994.

Grace, George C., and David H. Wallace. *The New-York Historical Society's Dictionary of Artists in America, 1564–1860*. New Haven: Yale UP, 1957.

Grafton, Anthony, and Lisa Jardine. *From Humanism to the Humanities: Education and the Liberal Arts in Fifteenth- and Sixteenth-Century Europe*. London: Duckworth, 1986.

Grayson, Sandra M. "Tuthill, Louisa Caroline Huggins." *American National Biography*. Ed. John A. Garraty and Mark C. Carnes. New York: Oxford UP, 1999. 22:43–44.

Grumbach, Argula von. *Argula Von Grumbach: A Woman's Voice in the Reformation*. Ed. Peter Matheson. Edinburgh: T. & T. Clark, 1995.

Guthrie, Warren. "The Development of Rhetorical Theory in America, 1635–1850." *Speech Monographs* 15.1 (1948): 61–71.

Haberman, Frederick W. "English Sources of American Elocution." *History of Speech Education in America: Background Studies*. Ed. Karl R. Wallace. New York: Appleton-Century-Crofts, 1954. 105–26.

Habermas, Jürgen. *The Structural Transformation of the Public Sphere: An Inquiry into a Category of Bourgeois Society* (1962). Trans. Thomas Burger with Frederick Lawrence. Cambridge, Mass.: MIT P, 1994.

Haight, Gordon S. *Mrs. Sigourney: The Sweet Singer of Hartford*. New York: Yale UP, 1930.

Hall, Kim. "Culinary Spaces, Colonial Spaces: The Gendering of Sugar in the Seventeenth Century." *Feminist Readings of Early Modern Culture: Emerging Subjects*. Ed. Valerie Traub, M. Lindsay Kaplan, and Dympna Callaghan. Cambridge: Cambridge UP, 1996. 168–90.

Halloran, Michael. "Hugh Blair's Use of Quintilian and the Transformation of Rhetoric in the 18th Century." *Rhetoric and Pedagogy: Its History, Philosophy, and Practice; Essays in Honor of James J. Murphy*. Ed. Winifred Bryan Horner and Michael Leff. Mahwah, N.J.: Lawrence Erlbaum, 1995. 183–95.

Halttunen, Karen. *"Confidence Men and Painted Women": A Study of Middle-Class Culture in America, 1830–1870*. New Haven: Yale UP, 1982.

Hannay, Margaret P., ed. *Silent but for the Word: Tudor Women as Patrons, Translators, and Writers of Religious Works*. Kent, Ohio: Kent State UP, 1985.

Harth, Erica. "The Salon Woman Goes Public . . . or Does She?" *Going Public: Publishing in Early Modern France*. Ed. Elizabeth Goldsmith and Dena Goodman. Ithaca, N.Y.: Cornell UP. 179–93.

Hartnett, Stephen. "Fanny Fern's 1855 *Ruth Hall*, the Cheerful Brutality of Capitalism, and the Irony of Sentimental Rhetoric." *Quarterly Journal of Speech* 88 (2002): 1–18.

Hawhee, Debra. "Bodily Pedagogies: Rhetoric, Athletics, and the Sophist's Three Rs." *College English* 65.2 (November 2002): 142–62.

Henderson, Katherine Usher, and Barbara F. McManus, eds. *Half Humankind: Contexts and Texts of the Controversy about Women*. Urbana: U of Illinois P, 1985.

Hendler, Glenn. "The Limits of Sympathy: Louisa May Alcott and the Sentimental Novel." *American Literary History* 3.4 (1992): 685–706.

———. *Public Sentiments: Structures of Feeling in Nineteenth-Century American Literature*. Chapel Hill: U of North Carolina P, 2001.

Hobbs, Catherine, ed. *Nineteenth-Century Women Learn to Write*. Charlottesville: UP of Virginia, 1995.

Hobby, Elaine. "Handmaids of the Lord and Mothers in Israel: Early Vindications of Quaker Women's Prophecy." *Prose Studies* 17.3 (December 1994): 88–98.

——. *Virtue of Necessity: English Women's Writing, 1649–1688*. London: Virago, 1988.

Hochmuth, Marie, and Richard Murphy. "Rhetorical and Elocutionary Training in Nineteenth-Century Colleges."*History of Speech Education in America: Background Studies*. Ed. Karl R. Wallace. New York: Appleton-Century-Crofts, 1954. 153–77.

Hogan, Lucy, and Martha Solomon. "Extending the Conversation: Sharing the Inner Light." *Rhetoric Society Quarterly* 25 (1995): 32–46.

Hopkins, Mary Alden. *Hannah More and Her Circle*. New York: Longmans, Green, & Co., 1947.

Hosford, Frances. *Father Shipherd's Magna Charta: A Century of Coeducation in Oberlin College*. Boston: Jones, 1937.

Howell, Wilbur Samuel. *Eighteenth-Century British Logic and Rhetoric*. Princeton, N.J.: Princeton UP, 1971.

——. *Logic and Rhetoric in England, 1500–1700*. 1954. Reprint, New York: Russell & Russell, 1961.

Huh, Joonok. "Elizabeth Ware Rotch Farrar." *American National Biography*. Ed. John A. Garraty and Mark C. Carnes. New York: Oxford UP, 1999. 7:737–38.

Hull, Suzanne W. *Chaste, Silent and Obedient: English Books for Women, 1475–1646*. San Marino, Calif.: Huntington Publications, 1982, 1988.

Hunter, Fannie McDowell. *Women Preachers*. Dallas: Berachah Printing, 1905.

Hyde, Mary Frances. *Intermediate Grammar: Practical Lessons in the Use of English*. Indianapolis: Indiana School Book Co., 1893.

——. *Practical Lessons in the Use of English for Grammar Schools*. Boston: D. C. Heath & Co., 1888.

——. *Two-Book Course in English*. Vol. 2, *Practical English Grammar with Exercises in Composition*. Boston: D. C. Heath & Co., 1901.

Isocrates. *Isocrates*. Trans. George Norlin. 2 vols. Loeb Classical Library. London: W. Heinemann, 1928, 1945.

Jacobson, Beatrice. "Literary Cross-Dressing in Old New York: Ann Sophia Stephens as Jonathan Slick." *Her Own Voice: Nineteenth-Century American Women Essayists*. Ed. Sherry Lee Linkon. New York: Garland, 1997. 113–25.

Jardine, Lisa. "Shrewd or Shrewish? When the Disorderly Woman Has Her Head." *Still Harping on Daughters: Women and Drama in the Age of Shakespeare*. Totowa, N.J: Barnes & Noble Books, 1983. 103–40.

Jarratt, Susan C. *Rereading the Sophists: Classical Rhetoric Refigured*. Carbondale: Southern Illinois UP, 1991.

——. "Speaking to the Past: Feminist Historiography in Rhetoric." *Pre/Text* 11.3/4 (1990): 190–208.

Jensen, Katherine A. "Male Models of Feminine Epistolarity; or How to Write Like a Woman in Seventeenth-Century France." *Writing the Female Voice: Essays on Epistolary Literature*. Ed. Elizabeth C. Goldsmith. Boston: Northeastern UP, 1989. 25–45.

Johnson, Nan. *Gender and Rhetorical Space in American Life, 1866–1910*. Carbondale: Southern Illinois UP, 2002.

——. *Nineteenth-Century Rhetoric in North America*. Carbondale: Southern Illinois UP, 1991.

——. "The Popularization of Nineteenth-Century Rhetoric: Elocution and the Private Learner." *Oratorical Culture in Nineteenth-Century America: Transformations in the Theory and Practice of Rhetoric*. Ed. Gregory Clark and S. Michael Halloran. Carbondale: Southern Illinois UP, 1993. 139–57.

———. "Rhetoric and the Performance of Gender." Paper presented at the Penn State Rhetoric Conference, State College, Pa., July 1999.

Johnson, Wendy Dasler. "Cultural Rhetorics of Women's Corsets." *Rhetoric Review* 20 (2001): 203–33.

Jones, Kathleen. *A Glorious Fame: The Life of Margaret Cavendish, Duchess of Newcastle, 1623–1673.* London: Bloomsbury, 1988.

Jones, M[ary]. G. *Hannah More.* Cambridge: Cambridge UP, 1952.

Jordan, Constance. *Renaissance Feminism: Literary Texts and Political Models.* Ithaca, N.Y.: Cornell UP, 1990.

Jordan, Mary Augusta. *Correct Writing and Speaking.* The Woman's Home Library. Vol. 6. New York: A. S. Barnes & Co., 1904.

Kahn, Victoria. "Reinventing Romance, or the Surprising Effects of Sympathy." *Renaissance Quarterly* 55 (2002): 625–61.

Kates, Susan. *Activist Rhetorics and American Higher Education, 1885–1937.* Carbondale: Southern Illinois UP, 2001.

———. "The Embodied Rhetoric of Hallie Quinn Brown." *College English* 59 (1997): 59–71.

Keeler, Harriet L., and Mary E. Adams. *High School English: A Manual of Composition and Literature.* Boston: Allyn and Bacon, 1906.

Keeler, Harriet L., and Emma C. Davis. *Studies in English Composition with Lessons in Language and Rhetoric.* Boston: Allyn and Bacon, 1892.

Keller-Cohen, Deborah, ed. *Literacy: Interdisciplinary Conversations.* Cresskill, N.J.: Hampton, 1994.

Kelly, Ann Cline. "Swift's *Polite Conversation*: An Eschatological Vision." *Studies in Philology* 73 (April 1976); 204–24.

Kelly, Joan. "Early Feminist Theory and the *Querelle des Femmes*, 1400–1789." *Women, History, and Theory.* Chicago: U of Chicago P, 1984. 65–108.

Kendall, Elizabeth. *Where She Danced.* New York: Alfred A. Knopf, 1979.

Kennedy, George. *The Art of Persuasion in Greece.* Princeton, N.J.: Princeton UP, 1963.

———. *The Art of Rhetoric in the Roman World.* Princeton, N.J.: Princeton UP, 1972.

———. *Greek Rhetoric under Christian Emperors.* Princeton, N.J.: Princeton UP, 1983.

Kilcup, Karen L. "'Essays of Invention': Transformations of Advice in Nineteenth-Century American Women's Writing." *Nineteenth-Century American Women Writers: A Critical Reader.* Malde, Mass.: Blackwell, 1998. 184–205.

King, Margaret L., and Albert Rabil Jr. "The Other Voice in Early Modern Europe: Introduction to the Series." Madeleine de Scudéry, *Selected Letters, Orations, and Rhetorical Dialogues.* Ed and trans. Jane Donawerth and Julie Strongson. Chicago: U of Chicago P, 2004. xi–xxxi.

Kitzhaber, Albert. "Rhetoric in American Colleges, 1850–1900." Diss., U of Washington, 1953.

Knox, Nelly Lloyd. *Elementary Lessons in English for Home and School Use.* Part 1: *How to Speak and Write Correctly.* Teacher's Edition. Boston: Ginn, Heath, & Co., 1885.

Knox-Heath, Nelly Lloyd. *Elementary Lessons in English.* Part 2: *The Parts of Speech and How to Use Them.* Boston: Ginn & Co., 1886.

Kolodny, Annette. "Inventing a Feminist Discourse: Rhetoric and Resistance in Margaret Fuller's *Woman in the Nineteenth Century*." *Reclaiming Rhetorica: Women in the Rhetorical Tradition.* Ed. Andrea A. Lunsford. Pittsburgh, Pa.: U of Pittsburgh P, 1995. 137–66.

Kristeller, Paul Oskar. *Renaissance Thought: The Classic, Scholastic, and Humanist Strains.* 1951. Reprint, New York: Harper, 1961.

Krueger, Christine. *The Reader's Repentance: Women Writers, and Nineteenth-Century Social Discourse.* Chicago: U of Chicago P, 1992.

Kunze, Bonnelyn Young. *Margaret Fell and the Rise of Quakerism.* Stanford, Calif.: Stanford UP, 1994.

Lamy, Bernard. *The Art of Speaking.* London, 1676.

Landes, Joan B. "The Public and the Private Sphere: A Feminist Reconsideration." *Feminists Read Habermas: Gendering the Subject of Discourse.* Ed. Johanna Meehan. New York: Routledge, 1995. 91–116.

Lazard, Madeleine. *Les avenues de Fémynie: les femmes et la Renaissance.* Paris: Fayard, 2001.

Lee, Jarena. *The Life and Religious Experience of Jarena Lee.* Philadelphia: privately printed, 1836. Reprinted in *Sisters of the Spirit: Three Black Women's Autobiographies of the Nineteenth Century.* Ed. William L. Andrews. Bloomington: Indiana UP, 1986. 27–48.

Lender, Mark Edward. "Jennie Fowler Willing." *Dictionary of American Temperance Biography.* Westport, Conn.: Greenwood, 1984. 519–20.

Levin, Carole, and Patricia A. Sullivan, eds. *Political Rhetoric, Power, and Renaissance Women.* Albany: State U of New York P, 1995.

Lewis, Frances W. *Inductive Lessons in Rhetoric.* Boston: D. C. Heath & Co., 1900.

Lockwood, Sara Elizabeth. *Lessons in English, Adapted to the Study of American Classics. A Text-Book for High Schools and Academies.* Boston: Ginn & Co., 1888.

Logan, Shirley Wilson. "Black Women on the Speaker's Platform (1832–1899)." *Listening to Their Voices: The Rhetorical Activities of Historical Women.* Ed. Molly Meijer Wertheimer. Columbia: U of South Carolina P, 1997. 150–73.

———. *Liberating Language: Sites of Rhetorical Education in Nineteenth-Century Black America.* Carbondale: Southern Illinois UP, 2008.

———. "Literacy as a Tool for Social Action among Nineteenth-Century African-American Women." *Nineteenth-Century Women Learn to Write: Past Cultures and Practices of Literacy.* Ed. Catherine Peaden Hobbs. Charlottesville: UP of Virginia, 1994.

———. "Rhetorical Strategies in Ida B. Wells's 'Southern Horrors: Lynch Law in All Its Phases.'" *Sage* 8.1 (Summer 1991). 3–9.

———. *"We Are Coming": The Persuasive Discourse of Nineteenth–Century Black Women.* Carbondale: Southern Illinois UP, 1999.

———. "'What's Rhetoric Got to Do with It?': Frances E. W. Harper in the Writing Class." *Composition Forum* 7.2 (Fall 1996): 95–110.

Logan, Shirley Wilson, ed. *With Pen and Voice: A Critical Anthology of Nineteenth-Century African American Women.* Carbondale: Southern Illinois UP, 1995.

Lougee, Carolyn. *Le Paradis des Femmes: Women, Salons, and Social Stratification in Seventeenth-Century France.* Princeton, N.J.: Princeton UP, 1976.

Luckyi, Christina. *"A Moving Rhetoricke": Gender and Silence in Early Modern England.* Manchester: Manchester UP, 2002.

Luecke, Marilyn. "'God hath made no difference such as men would': Margaret Fell and the Politics of Speech." *Bunyan Studies* 7 (1997): 73–93.

Lunsford, Andrea A., ed. *Reclaiming Rhetorica: Women in the Rhetorical Tradition.* Pittsburgh, Pa.: U of Pittsburgh P, 1995.

Mack, Phyllis. *Visionary Women: Ecstatic Prophecy in Seventeenth-Century England.* Berkeley: U of California P, 1992.

MacKinnon, Catharine A. "Feminism, Marxism, Method, and the State: An Agenda for Theory." *The Signs Reader.* Ed. Elizabeth Abel and Emily K. Abel. Chicago: U of Chicago P, 1982. 227–56.

———. *Towards a Feminist Theory of the State.* Cambridge, Mass.: Harvard UP, 1989.

Maclean, Ian. *Woman Triumphant: Feminism in French Literature, 1610–1652.* Oxford: Clarendon, 1977.

Mahon, M. Wade. "The Rhetorical Value of Reading Aloud in Thomas Sheridan's Theory of Elocution." *Rhetoric Society Quarterly* 31.4 (Fall 2001): 67–88.

Makin, Bathsua. *An Essay to Revive the Ancient Education of Gentlewomen* (1673). *Educational and Vocational Books.* Comp. Frances Teague. The Early Modern Englishwoman: A Facsimile Library of Essential Works, Series 2. Burlington, N.H.: Ashgate, 2001.

Malcolmson, Cristina, and Mihoko Suzuki, eds. *Debating Gender in Early Modern England, 1500–1700.* New York: Palgrave, 2002.

Marinella, Lucrezia. *The Nobility and Excellence of Women and the Defects and Vices of Men.* Ed. and trans. Anne Dunhill. Chicago: U of Chicago P, 1999.

Mattingly, Carol. *Appropriate[ing] Dress: Women's Rhetorical Style in Nineteenth-Century America.* Carbondale: Southern Illinois UP, 2002.

———. *Well-Tempered Women: Nineteenth-Century Temperance Rhetoric.* Carbondale: Southern Illinois UP, 1998.

McCorkle, Ben. "Harbingers of the Printed Page: Nineteenth-Century Theories of Delivery as Remediation." *Rhetoric Society Quarterly* 35.4 (Fall 2005): 25–50.

McDowell, Paula. *The Women of Grub Street: Press, Politics, and Gender in the London Literary Marketplace, 1678–1730.* Oxford: Clarendon, 1998.

McFarlin, Annjennette S. "Hallie Quinn Brown: Black Woman Elocutionist." *Southern Speech Communication Journal* 46 (1980): 72–82.

Micciche, Laura R. "Making a Case for Rhetorical Grammar." *College Composition and Communication* 55.4 (June 2004): 716–37.

Miller, Hildy, and Lillian Bridwell-Bowles, eds. *Rhetorical Women: Roles and Representations.* Tuscaloosa: U of Alabama P, 2005.

Miller, Susan. *Assuming the Positions: Cultural Pedagogy and the Politics of Commonplace Writing.* Pittsburgh, Pa.: U Pittsburgh P, 1998.

———. *Trust in Texts: A Different History of Rhetoric.* Carbondale: Southern Illinois UP, 2008.

Monfasani, John. "Humanism and Rhetoric." *Renaissance Humanism: Foundations, Forms, and Legacy.* Vol. 3: *Humanism and the Disciplines.* Ed. Albert Rabil Jr. Philadelphia: U of Pennsylvania P, 1988. 171–235.

More, Hannah. "The Bas Bleu, or, Conversation." Vol. 5 of *The Complete Works of Hannah More.* 1783–86. New York: Harper & Brothers, 1868. 359–71.

———. *Strictures on the Modern System of Female Education.* 2 vols. London, 1799.

———. "Thoughts on Conversation." *Essays on Various Subjects, Principally Designed for Young Ladies.* 1777. Vol. 2 of *The Complete Works of Hannah More.* New York: Harper & Brothers, 1868. 343–51.

Morgan, Anna. *The Art of Speech and Deportment.* Chicago: A. C. McClurg & Co., 1909.

———. *An Hour with Delsarte: A Study of Expression.* Boston: Lee and Shepard, 1890.

Mott, Lucretia. "Discourse on Woman." 1849. *Lucretia Mott: Her Complete Speeches and Sermons.* Ed. Dana Greene. New York: Edwin Mellen, 1980. 143–62.

Mountford, Roxanne. *The Gendered Pulpit: Preaching in American Protestant Spaces.* Carbondale: Southern Illinois UP, 2003.

Mulderig, Gerald. "Gertrude Buck's Rhetorical Theory and Modern Composition Teaching." *Rhetoric Society Quarterly* 14 (1984): 95–104.

Murphy, James J. *Rhetoric in the Middle Ages.* Berkeley: U of California P, 1974.

New Catholic Encyclopedia. 2nd ed. Detroit: Thomson/Gale and Catholic U of America, 2003.

Nicholson, Linda. "Interpreting Gender." *Signs* 20.1 (Autumn 1994): 79–105.

Norbrook, David. "Rhetoric, Ideology and the Elizabethan World Picture." *Renaissance Rhetoric.* Ed. Peter Mack. New York: St. Martin's, 1994. 140–64.

Oram, Elizabeth. *First Lessons in English Grammar and Composition with Exercises in the Elements of Pronunciation, Words for Dictation, and Subjects for Composition.* New York: Paine & Burgess, 1846.

Palmer, Phoebe. *The Promise of the Father.* Boston: Henry V. Degen, 1859.

——. *Tongue of Fire on the Daughters of the Lord.* 1859. *Phoebe Palmer: Selected Writings.* Ed. Thomas C. Oden. New York: Paulist, 1988. 3–56.

Perry, Ruth. *The Celebrated Mary Astell.* Chicago: U of Chicago P, 1986.

Peterson, Carla. *"Doers of the Word": African American Women Speakers and Writers in the North (1830–1880).* New York: Oxford UP, 1995.

Phelps, Elizabeth Stuart. "A Woman's Pulpit." *Atlantic Monthly* 26.1 (July 1870): 11–19. Reprinted in *The American Short Story Series*, vol. 85. New York: Garrett, 1969. 176–200.

Plato. *Gorgias.* Trans. W. C. Helmbold. New York: Liberal Arts, 1952.

——. *Phaedrus.* Trans. W. C. Helmbold and W. G. Rabinowitz. New York: Liberal Arts, 1956.

Portnoy, Alisse. *Their Right to Speak: Women's Activism in the Indian and Slave Debates.* Cambridge, Mass.: Harvard UP, 2005.

Poulakos, Takis. Introduction to *Rethinking the History of Rhetoric: Multidisciplinary Essays on the Rhetorical Tradition.* Ed. Poulakos. Boulder, Colo.: Westview, 1993. 1–10.

Quintilian. *Institutio Oratoria.* 4 vols. Trans. H. E. Butler. Cambridge, Mass.: Harvard UP, 1966.

Ratcliffe, Krista. *Rhetorical Listening: Identification, Gender, Whiteness.* Carbondale: Southern Illinois UP, 2005.

Rebhorn, Wayne. *The Emperor of Men's Minds: Literature and the Renaissance Discourse of Rhetoric.* Ithaca, N.Y.: Cornell UP, 1995.

Renshaw, Edyth. "Five Private Schools of Speech." *History of Speech Education in America: Background Studies.* Ed. Karl R. Wallace. New York: Appleton-Century-Crofts, 1954. 301–25.

Rhetorica ad Herennium. Ad C. herennium de ratione dicendi. Trans. Harry Caplan. Loeb Classical Library. Cambridge, Mass.: Harvard UP, 1964.

Rieser, Andrew C. *The Chautauqua Moment: Protestants, Progressives, and the Culture of Modern Liberalism.* New York: Columbia UP, 2003.

Ritchie, Joy, and Kate Ronald, eds. *Available Means: An Anthology of Women's Rhetoric(s).* Pittsburgh, Pa.: Pittsburgh UP, 2001.

Riviere, Joan. "Womanliness as a Masquerade." 1929. *Formations of Fantasy.* Ed. Victor Burgin, James Donald, and Cora Kaplan. New York: Methuen, 1986. 35–44.

Robb, Mary Margaret. "The Elocutionary Movement and Its Chief Figures." *History of Speech Education in America: Background Studies*. Ed. Karl R. Wallace. New York: Appleton-Century-Crofts, 1954. 178–201.

Roberts, Miss R. *Seven Rational Sermons, on the Following Subjects, Viz. I. Against Covetousness II. On the Vanity of this Life. III. Against Revenge. IV. Of Mirth and Grief. V. The Cruelty of Slandering innocent, and defenseless Women. VI. The Duty of Children. VII. The Advantages of Education*. 1770. Reprint, Philadelphia: Robert Bell, 1777.

Robins, Helen J., and Agnes F. Perkins. *An Introduction to the Study of Rhetoric: Lessons in Phraseology, Punctuation, and Sentence Structure*. New York: Macmillan Co., 1903.

Ross, Isabel. *Margaret Fell, Mother of Quakerism*. London: Longmans, Green, & Co., 1949.

Rouse, Joy P. "Margaret Fuller: A Rhetoric of Citizenship in Nineteenth-Century America." *Oratorical Culture in Nineteenth-Century America: Transformations in the Theory and Practice of Rhetoric*. Ed. Gregory Clark and S. Michael Halloran. Carbondale: Southern Illinois UP, 1993. 110–36.

Royster, Jacqueline. *Traces of a Stream: Literacy and Social Change among African American Women*. Pittsburgh, Pa.: U of Pittsburgh P, 2000.

Royster, Jacqueline Jones, and Jean C. Williams. "History in the Spaces Left: African American Presence and Narratives of Composition Studies." *College Composition and Communication* 50.4 (1999): 563–84.

Ruyter, Nancy Lee Chalfa. *The Cultivation of Body and Mind in Nineteenth-Century American Delsartism*. Westport, Conn.: Greenwood, 1999.

———. "Genevieve Stebbins." *American National Biography*. Ed. John A. Garraty and Mark C. Caines. New York: Oxford UP, 1999. 20:598–99.

———. *Reformers and Visionaries: The Americanization of the Art of Dance*. New York: Dance Horizons, 1979.

Ryan, Mary P. *Women in Public: Between Banners and Ballots, 1825–1880*. Baltimore: Johns Hopkins UP, 1990.

Sadlack, Erin A. "Petitioning Power: The Rhetorical Fashioning of Elizabethan Women's Letters." *New Ways of Looking at Old Texts*. Ed. Michael Denbo. Papers of the Renaissance English Text Society, 2002–6, no. 4. Tempe: Arizona Center for Medieval and Renaissance Studies and Renaissance English Text Society, 2008. 229–37.

Samuels, Shirley, ed. *The Culture of Sentiment: Race, Gender, and Sentimentality in Nineteenth-Century America*. New York: Oxford UP, 1992.

Sánchez-Eppler, Karen. 1992. "Bodily Bonds: The Intersecting Rhetorics of Feminism and Abolition." *The Culture of Sentiment*. Ed. Shirley Samuels. New York: Oxford UP, 1992. 92–114.

Scherman, Thomas H. "Lydia Huntley Sigourney." *The Oxford Companion to Women's Writing in the United States*. Ed. Cathy N. Davidson and Linda Wagner-Martin. New York: Oxford UP, 1995. 807.

Schilb, John. "Future Historiographies of Rhetoric and the Present Age of Anxiety." *Writing Histories of Rhetoric*. Ed. Victor Vitanza. Carbondale: Southern Illinois UP, 1994. 128–38.

———. "The History of Rhetoric and the Rhetoric of History." *Pre/Text* 7 (1986): 11–34.

Schultz, Lucille M. "Elaborating Our History: A Look at Mid-19th-Century First Books of Composition." *College Composition and Communication* 45 (1994): 10–30.

———. *The Young Composers: Composition's Beginnings in Nineteenth-Century Schools.* Carbondale: Southern Illinois UP, 1999.

Schurman, Anna Maria Van. *Whether a Christian Woman Should Be Educated and Other Writings from Her Intellectual Circle.* Ed. and trans. Joyce L. Irwin. Chicago: U of Chicago P, 1998.

Scudéry, Madeleine de. *Choix de Conversations de Mlle Scudéry.* Ed. Phillip J. Wolfe. Ravenna: Longo, 1977.

———. *Conversations sur divers sujets.* 2 vols. Paris, 1680.

———. *"De L'Air galant" et autres conversations.* Ed. Delphine Denis. Paris: Honoré Champion, 1998.

———. *Les Femmes illustres; ou, Les haranges heroiques, de Mr de Scudery.* 1642. Reprinted, Paris, 1665. Translated by James Innes as *Les Femmes Illustres; or, The Heroick Harangues of the Illustrious Women,* 2 vols. Edinburgh, 1681.

———. *Selected Letters, Orations, and Rhetorical Dialogues.* Ed. and trans. Jane Donawerth and Julie Strongson. Chicago: U of Chicago P, 2004.

Sebberson, David. "Investigations for a Critical Theory of Rhetoric: Issues in Practical Reasoning and Rhetorical Proof." Diss. U Maryland, 1988.

———. "Practical Reasoning and Wordsworth's 'Preface.'" *Spirits of Fire: English Romantic Writers and Contemporary Historical Methods.* Ed. G. A. Rosso and Danny Watkins. Rutherford, N.J.: Fairleigh Dickinson UP, 1990. 95–111.

Sharer, Wendy B. *Vote and Voice: Women's Organizations and Political Literacy, 1915–1930.* Carbondale: Southern Illinois UP, 2004.

Shaver, Claude L. "Steele MacKaye and the Delsartian Tradition." *History of Speech Education in America: Background Studies.* Ed. Karl R. Wallace. New York: Appleton-Century-Crofts, 1954. 202–18.

Shawn, Ted. *Every Little Movement: A Book about François Delsarte.* 2nd ed. New York: Dance Horizons, 1968.

Sheridan, Thomas. *A Course of Lectures on Elocution.* 1762. Reprint, New York: Benjamin Blom, 1968.

Shoemaker, Rachel (Mrs. J. W.). *Advanced Elocution: Designed as a Practical Treatise for Teachers and Students in Vocal Training, Articulation, Physical Culture and Gesture.* Philadelphia: Penn Publishing Co., 1896.

———. *Delsartean Pantomimes with Recital and Musical Accompaniment Designed for Home, School, and Church Entertainments.* Philadelphia: Penn Publishing Co., 1891.

———. *The Little People's Speaker.* Philadelphia: The National School of Elocution and Oratory, 1886.

Sigourney, Lydia. *Letters to My Pupils: with Narrative and Biographical Sketches.* 1837. Reprint, New York: Robert & Carter and Brothers, 1851.

———. *Letters to Young Ladies.* 1833. Reprint, New York: Harper & Brothers, 1852.

Sisters of Saint Joseph. *Language Manual; Intended to United the Catholic Child's Letter-Writer with the Language Work, Especially in the Lower Grades.* South St. Louis, Mo., 1889.

"A Sketch of the Life of Miss Hallie Quinn Brown." *AME Church Review* 6 (1889–90): 256–61.

Smarr, Janet Levarie. *Joining the Conversation: Dialogues by Renaissance Women.* Ann Arbor: U of Michigan P, 2005.

Smith, Hilda. *Reason's Disciples: Seventeenth-Century English Feminists.* Urbana: U of Illinois P, 1982.

Smith, Nigel. "Hidden Things Brought to Light: Enthusiasm and Quaker Discourse." *Prose Studies* 17.3 (December 1994): 57–69.

Smith-Rosenberg, Carroll. *Disorderly Conduct: Visions of Gender in Victorian America.* New York: Oxford UP, 1985.

Snyder, Jon R. *Writing the Scene of Speaking: Theories of Dialogue in the Late Italian Renaissance.* Stanford, Calif.: Stanford UP, 1989.

Solomon, Barbara Miller. *In the Company of Educated Women: A History of Women and Higher Education in America.* New Haven: Yale UP, 1985.

Sozen, Joyce. "Anna Morgan." *Notable American Women, 1607–1950.* Ed. Edward T. James. Cambridge, Mass.: Harvard UP, 1971. 2:577–79.

Spalding, Elizabeth Hill. *The Principles of Rhetoric, with Constructive and Critical Work in Composition.* Boston: D. C. Heath & Co., 1905.

———. *The Problem of Elementary Composition: Suggestions for Its Solution.* Boston: D. C. Heath & Co., 1896.

Spitzack, Carole, and Kathryn Carter. "Women in Communication Studies: A Typology for Revision." *Quarterly Journal of Speech* 73.4 (November 1987): 401–23.

Spoel, Philippa M. "Rereading the Elocutionists: The Rhetoric of Thomas Sheridan's *A Course of Lectures on Elocution* and John Walker's *Elements of Elocution.*" *Rhetorica* 19.1 (Winter 2001): 49–91.

Spring, Suzanne B. "'Seemingly Uncouth Forms': Letters at Mount Holyoke Female Seminary." *College Composition and Communication* 59.4 (June 2008): 633–75.

Stallybrass, Peter. "Patriarchal Territories: The Body Enclosed." *Rewriting the Renaissance: The Discourses of Sexual Difference in Early Modern Europe.* Ed. Margaret Ferguson, Maureen Quilligan, and Nancy J. Vickers. Chicago: U of Chicago P, 1986. 123–46.

Stanley, Susan. "Empowered Foremothers: Wesleyan/Holiness Women Speak to Today's Christian Feminists." *Wesley Center Online.* Ed. Michael Mattei for the Wesley Center for Applied Theology at Northwest Nazarene U, 2000, http://wesley.nnu.edu/WesleyanTheology.

Stanton, Domna. *The Aristocrat as Art: A Study of the Honnête Homme and the Dandy in Seventeenth- and Nineteenth-Century French Literature.* New York: Columbia UP, 1980.

Stebbins, Genevieve. *The Delsarte System of Expression,* 5th ed. New York: Edgar S. Werner, 1894.

———. *The Genevieve Stebbins System of Physical Training.* 1898. Rev. ed., New York: Edgar S. Werner & Co., 1912.

———. *The New York School of Expression.* New York: Edgar S. Werner, 1893.

Steel, Jeffrey. "Douglass and Sentimental Rhetoric." *Approaches to Teaching the Narrative Life of Frederick Douglass.* Ed. James C. Hall. New York: Modern Language Association of America, 1999. 66–72.

Stern, Julia. *The Plight of Feeling: Sympathy and Dissent in the Early American Novel.* Chicago: U of Chicago P, 1997.

Stewart, Ellen. *Life of Mrs. Ellen Stewart, Together with Biographical Sketches of Other Individuals.* Akron, Ohio: Beebe & Elkins, 1858.

Strom, Claire. "Hallie Quinn Brown." *American National Biography.* Ed. John A. Garraty and Mark C. Carnes. New York: Oxford UP, 1999. 3:676–77.

Sutherland, Christine Mason. "Aspiring to the Rhetorical Tradition: A Study of Margaret Cavendish." *Listening to Their Voices: The Rhetorical Activities of Historical Women.* Ed. Molly Meijer Wertheimer. Columbia: U of South Carolina P, 1997. 255–71.

———. "Mary Astell: Reclaiming Rhetorica in the Seventeenth Century." *Reclaiming Rhetorica: Women in the Rhetorical Tradition.* Ed. Andrea A. Lunsford. Pittsburgh, Pa.: U of Pittsburgh P, 1995. 93–116.

———. "Outside the Rhetorical Tradition: Mary Astell's Advice to Women in Seventeenth-Century England." *Rhetorica* 9.2 (Spring 1991): 147–63.

Sutherland, Christine Mason, and Rebecca Sutcliffe, eds. *The Changing Tradition: Women in the History of Rhetoric.* Calgary, Canada: U of Calgary P, 1999.

Tapia, John E. *Circuit Chautauqua: From Rural Education to Popular Entertainment in Early Twentieth Century America.* Jefferson, N.C.: McFarland & Co., 1997.

Teague, Frances. *Bathsua Makin, Woman of Learning.* Lewisburg, Pa.: Bucknell UP, 1998.

———. "The Identity of Bathsua Makin." *Biography* 16.1 (Winter 1993): 1–17.

Tebeaux, Elizabeth. "Technical Writing for Women in the English Renaissance: Technology, Literacy, and the Emergence of a Genre." *Written Communication* 10.2 (April 1993): 164–99.

Thickstun, Margaret Olofson. "Writing the Spirit: Margaret Fell's Feminist Critique of Pauline Theology." *American Academy of Religion Journal* 63 (1995): 269–79.

Thysell, Carol. "Unearthing the Treasure, Unknitting the Napkin: The Parable of the Talents as a Justification for Early Modern Women's Preaching and Prophesying." *Journal of Feminist Studies in Religion* 15.1 (September 1999): 7–20.

Todd, Janet. *Sensibility: An Introduction.* London: Methuen, 1986.

Tompkins, Jane. *Sensational Designs: The Cultural Work of American Fiction, 1790–1860.* New York: Oxford UP, 1985.

Towle, Nancy. *Vicissitudes Illustrated, in the Experience of Nancy Towle, in Europe and America.* Self-published. Charleston, 1832.

Turner, G. "Texts and Contexts." *British Cultural Studies: An Introduction.* Ed. David Thiorburn. Boston: Unwin Hyman, 1990. 87–130.

Turner, Mark. *The Literary Mind.* New York: Oxford UP, 1996.

Valenze, Deborah. M. *Prophetic Sons and Daughters: Female Preaching and Popular Religion in Industrial England.* Princeton, N.J.: Princeton UP, 1985.

Vitanza, Victor J. Editor's preface to *Writing Histories of Rhetoric.* Carbondale: Southern Illinois UP, 1994. vii–xii.

Waddy, Virginia. *Elements of Composition and Rhetoric, with Copious Exercises in Both Criticism and Construction.* Richmond, Va.: Everett Waddey, 1888.

Wagner, Joanne. "'Intelligent Members or Restless Disturbers': Women's Rhetorical Styles, 1880–1920." *Reclaiming Rhetorica: Women in the Rhetorical Tradition.* Ed. Andrea A. Lunsford. Pittsburgh, Pa.: U of Pittsburgh P, 1995. 185–202.

Walker, John. *Elements of Elocution.* London, 1781.

Walker, Pamela J. "Booth, Catherine (1829–1890)." *Oxford Dictionary of National Biography.* Oxford: Oxford UP, 2004. Online at http://www.oxforddnb.com/view/article/2874. Accessed 1 February 2005.

————. "A Chaste and Fervid Eloquence: Catherine Booth and the Ministry of Women in the Salvation Army." *Women Preachers and Prophets through Two Millennia of Christianity.* Ed. Beverly Mayne Kienzle and Pamela J. Walker. Berkeley: U of California P, 1998. 288–302.

Wallace, Karl R., ed. *History of Speech Education in America: Background Studies.* New York: Appleton-Century-Crofts, 1954.

Wallace, W. Stewart. *A Dictionary of North American Authors Deceased before 1950.* Toronto: Ryerson, 1951.

Warnick, Barbara. *The Sixth Canon: Belletristic Rhetorical Theory and Its French Antecedents.* Columbia: U of South Carolina P, 1993.

Warnicke, Retha M. *Women of the English Renaissance and Reformation.* Westport, Conn.: Greenwood, 1983.

Warren, James Penn. *Culture of Eloquence: Oratory and Reform in Antebellum America.* University Park: Pennsylvania State UP, 1999.

Washington, Booker T. *Up from Slavery: An Autobiography.* Garden City, N.Y.: Doubleday & Co., 1963.

Watson, Martha. *Lives of Their Own: Rhetorical Dimensions in Autobiographies of Women Activists.* Columbia: U of South Carolina P, 1999.

Wertheimer, Molly Meijer, ed. *Listening to Their Voices: The Rhetorical Activities of Historical Women.* Columbia: U of South Carolina P, 1997.

Whigham, Frank. *Ambition and Privilege: The Social Tropes of Elizabethan Courtesy Theory.* Berkeley: U of California P, 1984.

Who Was Who in America. Vol. 1: 1897–1942. Chicago: Marquis Publications, 1966.

Who Was Who in America. Chicago: Marquis Who's Who, 1968.

Wilcox, Catherine M. *Theology and Women's Ministry in Seventeenth-Century English Quakerism: Handmaids of the Lord.* Studies in Women and Religion, no. 35. Lewiston, N.Y.: Edwin Mellen, 1995.

Willard, Frances. *"Do Everything Reform": The Oratory of Frances E. Willard.* Ed. Richard W. Leeman. Westport, Conn.: Greenwood, 1992.

————. *Woman in the Pulpit.* 1889. Reprint, Washington, D.C.: Zenger, 1978.

Williams, Gweno. "'No *Silent Woman*': The Plays of Margaret Cavendish, Duchess of Newcastle." *Women and Dramatic Production, 1550–1700,* by Alison Findlay and Stephanie Hodgson Wright with Gweno Williams. Reading, Mass.: Longman of Pearson Education, 2000. 95–122.

Willing, Jennie. *The Potential Woman: A Book for Young Ladies.* 1881. Reprint, Boston: McDonald and Gill, 1887.

Witte, John, Jr. *The Reformation of Rights: Law, Religion, and Human Rights in Early Modern Calvinism.* Cambridge: Cambridge UP, 2007.

Wollstonecraft, Mary. *Thoughts on the Education of Daughters with Reflections on Female Conduct in the More Important Duties of Life.* 1787. Reprint, Clifton, N.J.: Augustus M. Kelley, 1972.

Woods, Susanne, ed. *The Poems of Aemilia Lanyer.* New York: Oxford UP, 1993.

Woods, William F. "Nineteenth-Century Psychology and the Teaching of Writing." *College Composition and Communication* 36.1 (February 1985): 20–41.

Zimmerelli, Lisa. "A Genre of Defense: Hybridity in Nineteenth-Century Women's Defenses of Women's Preaching." Ph.D. diss., U of Maryland, 2009.

Index

Jane Donawerth is a professor of English and an affiliate in women's studies at the University of Maryland, where she has directed the academic writing program. She is an award-winning teacher who has published prize-winning books and articles on pedagogy, Shakespeare, Renaissance women writers, science fiction by women, and the history of rhetorical theory, including *Rhetorical Theory by Women before 1900: An Anthology.*

Studies in Rhetorics and Feminisms

Studies in Rhetorics and Feminisms seeks to address the interdisciplinarity that rhetorics and feminisms represent. Rhetorical and feminist scholars want to connect rhetorical inquiry with contemporary academic and social concerns, exploring rhetoric's relevance to current issues of opportunity and diversity. This interdisciplinarity has already begun to transform the rhetorical tradition as we have known it (upper-class, agonistic, public, and male) into regendered, inclusionary rhetorics (democratic, dialogic, collaborative, cultural, and private). Our intellectual advancements depend on such ongoing transformation.

Rhetoric, whether ancient, contemporary, or futuristic, always inscribes the relation of language and power at a particular moment, indicating who may speak, who may listen, and what can be said. The only way we can displace the traditional rhetoric of masculine-only, public performance is to replace it with rhetorics that are recognized as being better suited to our present needs. We must understand more fully the rhetorics of the non-Western tradition, of women, of a variety of cultural and ethnic groups. Therefore, Studies in Rhetorics and Feminisms espouses a theoretical position of openness and expansion, a place for rhetorics to grow and thrive in a symbiotic relationship with all that feminisms have to offer, particularly when these two fields intersect with philosophical, sociological, religious, psychological, pedagogical, and literary issues.

The series seeks scholarly works that both examine and extend rhetoric, works that span the sexes, disciplines, cultures, ethnicities, and sociocultural practices as they intersect with the rhetorical tradition. After all, the recent resurgence of rhetorical studies has been not so much a discovery of new rhetorics as a recognition of existing rhetorical activities and practices, of our newfound ability and willingness to listen to previously untold stories.

The series editors seek both high-quality traditional and cutting-edge scholarly work that extends the significant relationship between rhetoric and feminism within various genres, cultural contexts, historical periods, methodologies, theoretical positions, and methods of delivery (e.g., film and hypertext to elocution and preaching).

Queries and submissions:
Professor Cheryl Glenn, Editor
   E-mail: cjg6@psu.edu
Professor Shirley Wilson Logan, Editor
   E-mail: Shirley_W_Logan@umail.umd.edu

Studies in Rhetorics and Feminisms
Department of English
142 South Burrowes Bldg.
Penn State University
University Park, PA 16802-6200

Other Books in the Studies in Rhetorics and Feminisms Series